I HEAR NO BUGLES

I HEAR NO BUGLES

ROBERT WINSTON MERCY

NAVIGATOR BOOKS

SAN DIEGO, CALIFORNIA

I HEAR NO BUGLES

Copyright © 2008, 2013 by Robert Winston Mercy

Navigator Books

www.navigator-books.com

ISBN-13: 978-1-940397-01-6

Printed in the United States of America

FOREWORD

We search for North Korea's national motives in challenging an already chaotic war weary America and world with threats of "merciless annihilation by nuclear incineration." A look into their long tempestuous history might suggest an answer. Korea's prevailing myth of origin maintains that "Danguo," a descendent of heaven established the Kingdom circa 2333 BC. Except for a few hundred years of relative peace in that distantly murky past Korea has been a cauldron of intrigues, revolutions, rebellions, wars and the draconian armed occupations that had followed their numerous humiliating defeats. I believe it is those eons of enforced subjugation that has trampled out any sense of genuine national pride based on accomplishments. In essence the Koreans have never won a war and the price for that on the collective unconscious is a smoldering need to revenge a perceived loss of "Face." Added to this matrix is the culture's ancient but juxtaposed belief that their nation is the geographical center of the universe, which renders them both uniquely superior as a people and most favored by the gods—a formulation that never bodes well.

The current conundrum over what are the true intentions of the Pyongyang government under the leadership of Kim Jong-un is whether 'Great Leader' would initiate a revengeful 'preemptive' strike on either Seoul or America in order to expunge some psychotically envisioned past shames or swallowed insults. This would unquestionably bring on the immediate obliteration of himself and his bankrupted & starving nation under the assured rain of retaliatory nuclear devices that now can deliver weapon yields thousands of times greater than those dropped on Hiroshima and Nagasaki.

In the chronicles of Korea's history there have always been just three social stations in Korea: A ruling class, a military and tax collector strata and a literal "slave" population. This tier structure, which is still evident in North Korea today, led to massive government corruption and repression. Also to be considered is the people's long standing psychological fallout from their knowledge that Korea has remained a vassal state since 108 BC when the Han dynasty invaded; and the aftermath of which drove the defeated and contentious Koreans into what became known as the first of The Three Kingdoms. Another Three Kingdom era would emerge a few centuries later. Then in 1231, about the same time the Sixth Christian crusade was being fought in the Middle East Genghis Khan led the first of the subsequent six Mongol invasions into Korea. In 1271 the bulk of his army were conscripted Koreans who perished in the typhoons that saved Japan from the two invasions the Khan attempted. The Koreans participation in both those failed conquest attempts had to have been a major motivating revenge factor behind Japan's first intrusion into Korea in 1592. It was carried out by the preeminent warlord Toyotomi Hideyoshi, who returned again in 1598 determined to eradicate the influence of the occupying Ming dynasty that extracted tributary payments from the Three Kingdoms and siphoned off the resources that expanding Japan needed. A hasty Chinese Korean alliance temporarily drove off the Japanese who'd inflicted much death and destruction to Korea's economy and culture. Then in 1687 the Mongol hoards armed with newly created western style cannons and a fresh alliance with the Manchurians again invaded Korea. Some three hundred years later, in the not too peaceful interim, there was an attempted coup d'état to unseat the King at the then capital of Pyongyang in hopes of establishing a pro Japanese government. The next two centuries were torn by armed rebellions between vying political factions and the peasantry's growing toxic hatred of the "Yangban," the aristocrats who mercilessly suppressed any threat of change to the status quo.

After the Industrial Revolution of the 18th Century, European nations began to colonize many of the globe's weaker nations under the voracious banners of international central banks, venture investment capital and avaricious Imperialism. In 1852-54 America's Asiatic Squadrons under the command of Admiral Matthew C. Perry forcibly opened a reluctant Japan to Western trade. Shortly thereafter and following the Meiji Restoration Japan transformed from a feudal to a modern society that recognized it had to westernize its military to ward off any further demeaning encroachments. Eventually Japan's emulation of western conquests devised its own imperial design into Korea and China. The competition was first unwelcomed by Caucasian European powers then feared after the destruction of the Russian fleet by admiral Togo in the Tsushima straits in 1904.

Korea's first violent encounter with Western power occurred in October of 1866 when the French government launched a strike against the Joseon Court in retaliation for the execution of three Catholic missionaries whose proselytizing efforts had garnered them some 17,000 converts, ten thousand of whom were martyred for their belief over the next century.

Korea's violent opposition to Western trade attempts was the direct result of their having witnessed the lasting consequences of those efforts that brought despair and ruin through two culturally destroying opium wars to China; and recognized, too, what part Christian religious zeal had played in the 1850 Taipei Rebellion that lasted fourteen years and claimed the lives of twenty million people. The rebellion was crushed with the help of British and French intervention. Equally unnerving was the leveling affect that Western encroachment had on the far more powerful Japanese. During the last quarter of that century not only had China, France and America come knocking on Korea's bolted door, but so also had England, Germany, Italy and Russia. Submission would spell doom.

Korea's first encounter with American interests was amicable in 1854 when the USS South America visited Pusan harbor for ten days as a preliminary to future treaty agreements. They also secured assurances of aid to shipwrecked seamen. Then in August of 1866 the paddle-wheeled steel plated General Sherman that was hired out by an English trading Company from a private American owner in Tenzin, China sailed into Pyongyang harbor with the intentions of initiating a trade treaty. Unfortunately the ship failed to heed the sent warning to stop at Keupsa Gate for official clearance and quickly drew battery fire when it proceeded on. The ship caught fire in the ensuing fight and some of its ten man China/Malay crew dove overboard only to be beaten to death by their enraged captors. In 1871 a flotilla of five American warships arrived at the harbor entrance to Seoul, ostensibly to gain a trade agreement and also to ascertain what actually happened five years earlier when the leased US merchant ship, the Gen. Sherman, came under fire. Ironically the five ship flotilla, like the Gen. Sherman was also greeted with salvos for their failure of not waiting for permission to proceed further. The US Admiral held his fire for ten days awaiting the demanded apology from the Joseon Dynastic Court, which never arrived. The admiral then launched a retaliatory expedition of some two hundred sailors and one hundred marines who stormed a series of fortified positions and left behind 243 Korean dead, with many wounded and ten captured. US losses, thanks to superior weapons, were only three dead.

An interesting footnote to the incident concerning the General Sherman was written in the late 1960s. Official historians in North Korea began to insist that the attack on the General Sherman was planned and led by a direct ancestor of the then North Korean dictator Kim Il-sung. Those claims, which had virtually no confirmation in historical records, were part of a campaign to promote the special role allegedly played by Kim Il-sung's family in Korean history, and thus facilitate the transfer of dictatorial power to son Kim Jong-il who is remembered for two stirring political speeches. In one he said: "Ask not what Korea can do for you, but what you can do for Korea." In the other he assured that "clean water will be given to all those who support the state and poison will be given to those who don't." Those statements are still repeated in North Korean publications, including school textbooks. North Korea issued a postage stamp in 2006 commemorating the sinking of the Gen. Sherman. Also mentioned in those text books is the pathetic tale of the USS Pueblo, a U.S. Navy intelligence ship that was captured in international waters off the North Korean coast in 1968; and the only U.S. warship still being held in captivity. It's currently moored at what is believed to be the very spot where the Gen. Sherman incident took place and both ships now serve as floating museums of 'American treachery' for the Korean public. Normally the firing upon and/or the seizure of any nation's service vessel, not to mention the killing of a crew member during its capture, the eleven month detainment and brutal torture of its officers and crew, would demand a declaration of war; but North Korea's two allies, Russia and China were both nuclear armed. Fortunately America had the foresight and fortitude not to initiate the conflagration of a third World War. Mao Tse-tung once sagely noted to President Richard Nixon that China could easily absorb the loss of thirty million or more people, and then questioned whether America could.

The Pueblo incident fostered in some parts of Asia the dangerously wishful illusion of America being "a paper tiger." Dangerous in that it could encourage a miscalculated step from which there would be no return. A little pseudo profiling on Kim Jong-un, who enjoys Johnnie Walker 'Red' scotch, drives a Mercedes Benz 600 sedan, enjoys vacationing in Switzerland and loves American films, removes him from the 'brooding fanatic' league who have private communications with God. Hopefully the young Kim Jong-un will live up to one of his newly anointed titles: "Brilliant Comrade."

Those accumulated centuries of subjugation, torture and death at the hands of foreign invaders and all too often their own governments, have weighed heavily on the soul of the Korean people and left deep scars that may never heal. The most searing of which was the Japanese annexation of Korea on 20 August 1910 and the harrowing brutality that followed.

Their next major trauma was the 1950 Korean War, which brought destruction to North Korea following 'Dear Leader" Kim IL-sung's unprovoked and devastating attack on South Korea on 27 June 1950, which had the approval and military support of Stalin. The Russians had penetrated the British Secret Intelligence Service [SIS] and knew America would not use the Atom bomb, thanks to "turned" agents "Kim" Philby and Guy Burgess. Current North Korean propaganda however distorts historical facts, listing South Korea as the aggressor who attacked at the behest of Wall Street war mongers that inflicted a highly distorted 'four million' civilian deaths on the country before they were beaten back by the heroic NK army. This is the same army that only five months after launching its offensive had been routed and was near total disintegration by November of 1950. No mention here either of the single alliance that saved them from an imminent defeat—The Chinese People's Liberation Army, who did suffer over a million casualties. North Korea is a gangster state that is heavily involved in the world's drug, weapons and slave trades, plus murders, kidnappings, assassinations, smuggling and the counterfeiting. Because the US dollar is the international monetary unit of exchange for the world markets it is a primary target of Pyongyang's counterfeiters. The U.S. Treasury and Federal Reserve will, as a precautionary measure, introduce a new $100.00 bill to be circulated in October of 2013. Noted one US official, "North Korea's high quality 'super-notes' have been of particular concern to us."

In the words off one United Nations human rights official, "North Korea's missile and nuclear weapons programs have diverted attention from human rights abuses that have no parallel anywhere in the world, even surpassing those of the Axis powers in WWII. They operate an elaborate network of political prisoner camps that hold more than 200,000 inmates. The camps not only punish people for peaceful activities, but also employ torture and other forms of cruel and inhumane treatment, summary executions, rape, slave labor and collective punishment that may amount to crimes against humanity." Food, medical supplies, electricity and running water are always in short supply and famine and malnutrition are pandemic, but not for high government officials and their families. The 1993-97 famine killed an estimated three million five hundred thousand people. A fourth of all North Korean children are stunted in growth and despite infusions of UN food aid some have been driven into cannibal practices; 24 million people struggle to find food from day to day. Over the years 100,000 North Koreans had been executed in purges, including some recent high ranking army staff officers who were "suspected of not being loyal enough." Kim-Jong-un's position has been made even more secure by the removal, either by execution or imprisonment, of two potential family rivals—uncle in law Jang Sung-taek and O kuk-ryol, the vice chairman of the National Defense Commission and two hundred of their protégés

Outside the prison camps the entire proletariat lives in abject fear of arousing any hint of suspicion that they may be harboring either displeasure or malice towards the regime. This fear is so compellingly hypnotic that when recently called upon to express their sorrow and grief for Kim Jong–il, the deceased father of the present leader, the entire nation [at least those who were around TV news cameras] broke out into inconsolable sobs, dirges and wailed laments. Their performances went beyond mass hysteria and reflected more the fear of appearing to the ever suspiciously watchful agents of the state's secret police and military intelligence that they had not genuinely held the revered Kim Jong-il in their hearts as the true Father of the nation; and were thus harboring malignant thoughts. Even their goose-stepping military carried out battalion sized 'cry-a-thons.' The inflexible demand for conformity filters down into the minutest function of day to day life and blankets every strata of society, which gives an inescapable credence to the relevancy of the Stockholm syndrome.

This syndrome is a psychological phenomenon in which hostages express empathy and sympathy and have positive feelings toward their captors, sometimes to the point of defending them. These feelings are generally considered irrational in light of the danger or risk endured by the victims, who essentially mistake a lack of abuse from their captors for an act of kindness. It's a form of traumatic bonding, which does not necessarily require a hostage scenario, but which describes "strong emotional ties that develop between two persons where one person intermittently harasses, beats, threatens, abuses, or intimidates the other; based on Freudian theory it also suggests that the bonding is the individual's response to trauma in becoming a victim. Identifying with the aggressor is one way that the ego defends itself. When a victim believes the same values as the aggressor, they no longer become a threat. These phenomena and other factors are what make the danger of North Korea so genuine. The syndrome is displayed in the dog-like devotion shown by the entrapped masses when they cry, scream and nearly faint at those staged events when young Kim Jung-un mingles with his people. Their narcissistic and megalomaniacal leader has come to believe the cultish hype promulgated by his state's propaganda agency, euphemistically known as The Korean Central News Agency, which promotes the belief that he is the nation's savior. Keep in mind that it's the government who supplies radios and TV sets to the public with the warning that they are not to be altered so as to pick up broadcasts from the south or abroad and with draconian prison punishments for those found in violation. This is the brainwashing of a population of twenty four million of which half are on active military duty and/or in standby reserve units. They will all unquestionably follow in whatever steps Kim Jong-un deems necessary to gain the universal prestige, honor and more significantly the fearful respect that the entire nation craves as recompense for their long history of subjugation and suffering. This makes the unthinkable possible.

History abounds with examples of tribes and nations who have been nearly obliterated, humbled and humiliated by punishing victors; and the defeated whose simmering and long held hatreds returned to them with a vengeance. One example is the rise of Fascism in Germany after the First World War, which was the direct result of the Treaty of Versailles and the mind boggling reparations that European bankers had demanded of Germany under the pretext of "crippling their future war potential." In actuality it was to annihilate any future competitive industrial threats that

Germany would or might have presented to the commercial interest of both Great Britain and France. Those enforced reparations destroyed Germany's economy and drove vast numbers into so severe a poverty cycle that they were made desperate for a savior of any stripe. North Korea's rage springs from a different origin, but which nevertheless manifests the same sort of bluster, military arrogance and the collective desire for revenge that we saw in Nazi Germany. Unfortunately we learn little from the aftermath of war because it is the victors who write the history books that sanctify the nation's cause.

We must also keep in mind that North Korea's modernized army, navy, air and nuclear strike forces are armed with 21st century weaponry, which were obtained at a price that relegated those outside the upper military tiers to near destitution. North Korea's tyrannical government has given the people two guiding lights that they must live by: "Uche [self-reliance]" and "Songun [The military first]." The Military First policy means the regime's legitimacy rests on the perception of strength, which makes it impossible for Kim to back-down. His demands for revocation of UN sanctions and, more importantly, universal recognition that North Korea is a nuclear power on a par with the United States are his non-negotiable demands. This Spartan state has led its people to believe that they are under imminent threat of annihilation from both South Korea and America. This has galvanized the masses to their corrupt and self-serving leadership. Weapons then are acquired on the conviction that they must and will be used—at the most opportune moment. If Kim's threats of carnage fail to extract the economic aid he so desperately needs from America and the IMF, as his father Kim Jung Il had succeeded in doing with President Clinton twenty some years ago then the stakes go up in his brinkmanship game of Showdown poker with the West.

Those manifest dangers when fused to the macrocosmic context of our planet's current moral and psychological instability give rise to a potential universal "meltdown," which elevates the omnipresent threat of annihilation. The root causes of which are: unsustainable population growth, climate change and pollution of our atmosphere and the oceans along with the rapid diminishment of wholesome food and water resources. Increasing inequalities both domestically and abroad coupled with rising levels of universal poverty and all forms of tribalism, violent nationalism and turbulent religious animosities add to the dilemma. Rampant and unwelcomed migration that has severely depreciated large swatches of Europe and harshly altered cultural norms and demographics has added more volatile unpredictability to an already explosive situation; a similar trend is occurring in America.

President Obama met on the 6th of May with visiting South Korean president Park Geun Hye in Washington and reassured her of America's continual military support. He also put Kim Jong-un on notice that blackmail and threats will no longer work as in the past because the rules of the game have now changed. Whether American and the west have to resolve to enforce this martial stance is the unnerving question. Nevertheless Kim Jong-un's next 'unpredictable move, 'which is bound to occur at some point in the veiled and not too distant future, will not end as tranquilly as it did in May of 2013.

I Hear No Bugles reveals some of the historic steps and cinematic stimuli that have led us to where we stand today.

CONTENTS

ACKNOWLEDGMENTS

The writing of this book has practically proven to be a lifetime effort, ever since my beloved Barbara first implanted the concept in my mind in the summer of 1979. Writing is an isolated task, but without the love and appreciated support given by a handful of people over the years this book never could have been written.

Special thanks as well to a fellow actor and heartfelt friend, the lovely Ms. Mary L. Snead of New York City, who now resides in her native Scepter'd Isle, England. I acknowledge, with inexpressible thanks, her months and years of generous tutoring, care and loving support. It's no exaggeration to say that without her influence, this story might not have been completed.

I also wish to express my appreciation to my editor Mr. Tom Houlihan, a former serving Marine whose dedication, honesty and commitment to mission has helped immeasurably in the creation of this book.

A very special thanks to Ms. Mary Simpson, whose love and Buddha-like nature have kept my body, soul and spirit together. My final note of appreciation goes to the Great Spirit who saw fit to put my twin brother and Richard E. Robertson in my life. Without them, there would be no story at all.

DEDICATION

"Shall I compare thee to a summer's day?
Thou art more lovely and more temperate...
...Nor shall Death brag thou wander'st in his shade,
when in eternal lines to time thou grow'st."

—William Shakespeare

This work is dedicated to the memory of Barbara Forst.

INTRODUCTION

The effects of propaganda films cannot be underestimated, particularly in this era of contending political and religious dogmas that relentlessly threaten to make this century even bloodier than the last. Indisputably, film is second to literature in the intellectual, philosophical and moral development of the human species. The defunct uniformed press gangs of history that 'Shanghaied' young men into military service have been supplanted by the more subtly hypnotic persuasion of TV and the "movies." Every image, symbol and mode of each delivered word is meticulously crafted to extract the desired emotional and moral support from its national audience. Those ships, planes, submarines, helicopters, tanks and the expended ammunitions of the armies of soldiers we see on the screen are freely given to the studios for that explicit purpose. *I Hear No Bugles* is a multifaceted tale of youthful idealism, psychology and war that shows how one such film—then many more—set a boy of four on an unalterable path that eventually led him into the Korean War and produced this single and only known firsthand account by a infantry rifleman who lived through eight campaigns in that first crucial year; and gives an insight into how astonishingly prophetic the first of those films proved to be.

Since early infancy my twin brother Richard and I had been fully mesmerized foster-children of the Hollywood film studios, and their cinematic lessons taught us about the world we'd soon inherit as they enthralled us with the glorified enormity of war. Who could fault the viewer's envy [or wish] as the camera panned upward while the peaceful eyes of the dying young hero gazed into the parting clouds that sang with the choral laced promise of God's eternal love? Die then, as we must— why not in combat, which made all other options seem meaningless and bland by comparison. That concept grew, with each youthful passing year

3

of movie viewing and my mind joyfully marched across the body-strewn trenches of World War I's *All Quiet on The Western Front* and flew with the *Dawn Patrol*. My imagination trooped across the scorching Moroccan Desert to Fort Zindernof, where the brutal Sergeant Markoff battled the Riff tribesmen in *Beau Geste*; over the rugged Khyber Pass with Her Majesty's disciplined troops, fought for God and King against the treacherous Islamic fanatics in *Drums* and *The Life of a Bengal Lancer*; on through the blistering Sudan against the savage Fuzzy Wuzzies of *The Four Feathers*; then beside Ronald Coleman in his blind valiant charge at Omdurman in *The Light That Failed*; and mournfully paced to the skirling of the regimental bagpipes in the India of the fallen *Gunga Din*. My deference to the sanctity of film kept me from cheering or hissing its heroes and villains in the glorious kaleidoscopic wash of silver-gray shadows that whisperingly promised a mirrored fate.

"The advent of DNA has given scientific confirmation as to each individual's biological uniqueness, which, in the case of infants, awaits the influencing hand of the prevailing culture to give it direction and meaning. It is those absorbed messages that will dictate what neural pathways will open and which interests will occupy the growing child's brain. Psychological clinical tests have proven that certain elements of a child's nature and outlook will not change as they grow into adulthood. Lived or fantasized events will forever remain imprinted, unchanged, in their memory and will form the ultimate background for all their adult life. This often sets into motion whole chains of associated thoughts, emotions and events."

Commentaries and dialogue written in italic print represents the speaker's stream of consciousness, or subtext thoughts.

CHAPTER 1

The Birth of Ideals

Tensions racked my four-year-old body as I sat next to my mother on the hard wooden fold-down seats of our Brooklyn neighborhood theatre, watching the Laurel and Hardy film *Babes in Toyland.* I sensed the terror of the children on screen being kidnapped by grunting hairy ape-like men that rampaged through their village. The film triggered a memory of being unable to cry out against the looming silhouette that darkened my bedroom doorway and caused me to faint in my crib. My activated internal emotions kept apace of those of the film's children, imposing themselves on the screen. The film flashed up a recent image of my enraged father, cursing, slapping and beating me to near unconsciousness over the hood of a car for having innocently taken his dime store pocket knife to play with in the street. I was suddenly heartened by the shifting scene on the screen showing a frightened young boy clutching his blanket while huddled behind a rock. His elation was mine when he was suddenly whisked up into the protective arms of one of the film's many life-sized wooden soldiers that were magically brought to life by Laurel & Hardy, to drive off the bogeymen with their rifles and bayonets. The vow I whispered then guided me through the next thirty years: *One day I'll be a soldier and have a real rifle with a bayonet!*

Happily, my father deserted our family the next year, around the time Richard and I saw Cecil B. De Mille's epic classic *The Crusades.* I eagerly absorbed one of the film's many important messages that went hand-in-glove with fealty, loyalty and bravery: a soldier must suffer pain stoically. The next day Richard's well-aimed broadsword swing during our reenacted battle put that theory to the test. I went home with a bleeding gash on my forehead that honored the cross-emblazoned bed sheet I wore for knightly armor. Nevertheless it wasn't the dueling scar I'd wished for, like George Sanders had in *Lancer Spy*. My mother screamed as I heroically marched through the door, and probably again, too, when Richard and I went back outside with our crayoned colored sign: "JOIN THE CRUSADES!"

Films became a refuge from reality for most of America during the depression era, but they were also educational by often touching on the not so latent cultural anxieties of the time. One specifically was "The Yellow Peril" a term attributed to Kaiser Wilhelm, who when meeting with Edward VII at Kiel during the Russo-Japanese War observed that the defeat of Russia by Japan would "bring the world face to face with the Yellow Peril."

In America more racial animosity emanated from the demeaning and ill-advised Chinese-Korean & Japanese Exclusionary Act, which was enacted by Congress in 1900 at the behest of labor unions to keep competitive workers from the market place. After the US annexation of Hawaii the west coast was flooded with thousands of Asian immigrants. Politicians knew that nothing would capture the attention of the American public quicker than a tabloid alerting them to a predatory sexual danger. A San Francisco Chronicle headline shouted: "Japanese a Menace to American Women;" and the William Randolph Hearst's Examiner warned that "Brown Asiatics Steal Brains of Whites." The city's mayor threw fuel on the fire by quarantining the city's Asian quarter on the false assertion of it being plague ridden. Magazines & dime novels featured adventure tales that dramatized the unfailingly treacherous, cruel and sinister characters that inhabit dangerously exotic Asia. As for example the authenticated story of Lieutenant Kawamoto Suemori who in 1931 acted on orders from the Imperial general staff to explode a bomb next to the Nippon owned railroad line in Manchuria. This created the illusion of attack by Chinese troops and became known as "The Mukden Incident," which justified the Japanese Kwantung army's invasion into China. Many xenophobic Americans viewed foreigners outside their own ethnic group as a threat, particularly Orientals who were thought to be satanically evil and capable of insidious tortures; and recorded atrocities from the Russo-China War, and later the Pacific in WWII, validated those impressions. As a child of five I saw it in the age-tinted pictures that were displayed in a neighborhood barbershop window. China's recent Manchu past was imprinted on the contorted face of a naked man who'd been skinned alive and left dangling from a pole between two expressionless guards; other pictures showed decapitated heads spitted on stakes. For sheer madness though, no one could hold a heated poker to Dr. Fu Manchu. His professed cinematic destiny breathed life into the encroachment of the Yellow Peril: "Destroy the accursed White race!" It may have been those unconsciously absorbed images and social currents that prompted me to innocently shout out a seemingly vacuous prophecy to Richard, over our 7th year birthday gifts. They were *Dick Tracy* toy machine guns that clattered and spewed out streams of sparks. "Someday we'll have real machine guns… and kill real Chinese."

As the years passed I encountered Eastern philosophy in the film that influenced me most, *The General Dies at Dawn*. It costarred the incomparable Akim Tamiroff who sympathetically played the dreaded Chinese warlord-bandit Yang who held three prisoners aboard his sampan: the film's hero, his beautiful soul mate and the drunkard who'd accidentally stabbed him while searching the boat's luggage for hidden cash. Yang's death took place beneath the spectral lantern on the fantail of his junk as it glided through the mystical fog-banked Yangtze River. Yang, surrounded by his dozen-man personal guard, shot his tipsy assassin before dooming Gary Cooper and his beautiful heroine Madeline Carroll to the same fate. Cooper, acculturated to the Asian ethos of facing death stoically coolly drawled, "If you kill us no one will be left to tell what really happened here. Your enemies will laugh in all the Sing-Song houses, saying that Yang was murdered by his own 'trusted' guard!" Yang gurgled out a protest, and then called out the name of each of his stoic soldiers. They lined up face-to-face, expressionless and with pistols drawn. "My men loyal… they die with me!" I was enthralled when Yang's raised arm dropped, and they unflinchingly fired into each other's chests. Smoke from their Mauser pistols swirled across Yang's face, which, brimmed with ancestral pride as he joyously sank into death.

It may have been the inexplicable and unconscious awareness that twins share, which allowed me to understand the guard's principled loyalty and willingness to self-sacrifice. It moved me deeply and launched my imagination then and forever more eastward into the mystical heart of fabled Asia: *How brave those soldiers were…maybe someday…I too could die like that.*

Hundreds of films later, I was ten years old, five foot-four inches tall and weighed a hundred and ten pounds. *Movie-Tone News* and *The March of Time* made me aware of war's inevitability in Asia and Europe. I thought I could lie my way into the Marine Corps, but took my mother's advice and first tried the Boy Scouts. Their Troop Master surprisingly rejected me, telling me that I looked like a German tank. It was a comment on my developing military posture, emblematic of my addiction to the war movies that I often returned to see a dozen times. It might have also been something in my face that showed a desire to escape the tenements, poverty and threatening hardships of New York's Hell's Kitchen. All was made psychologically worse perhaps by the unrecognized reality of the environment's inability to offer any images or goals worthy of emulation. Then, too, there was the "spare the rod, spoil the child" philosophy of the times. Nuns, teachers, cops, shopkeepers, bullies and even passing strangers often acted on that near Biblical mandate. I found that dark cloud's silver lining in nearby Columbus Circle where the impassioned global opinions of venting soapbox orators initiated me to political awareness. The Circle, like 'Red Square' down on 14th Street, seethed with voiceless social misfits and full-blown political psychopaths that were constantly either at each other's communist/fascist or religious/secular throats. The after school ten-cent shoeshine monies I earned there helped purchase movie tickets. Nights were spent listening to President Roosevelt's melodious fireside radio chats and Gabriel Heater's ominous "Ah, there's bad news tonight" war news. I believed that most of what I saw in the movies, which educated America on culture, etiquette and the pitfalls of crime, was absolutely true.

In the winter of 1941, church parishioners, like 11th century Crusaders, were assured that whoever died fighting in the approaching war would be a martyred soldier of Christ and awaken in the Kingdom of Heaven seated at the left hand of God. This appealed to my Catholic ear. Every Sunday morning I looked to see if God would signal His recognition of my devotion, perhaps on the rays of sunlight that streaked through the church's stained glass windows or in the shimmered reflections thrown from the bejeweled golden chalice held high by the priest. God remained elusive, until that morning I received communion and started back to my pew with the dry wafer lodged in my parched throat. Fretfully I plucked it out and it fell to the floor. A shrill scream echoed throughout the vast vault of Saint Paul's cathedral, as a frenzied Nun that perceived sacrilege shouted "Don't touch it! Don't touch it!" and she flew towards me with her black cowl and arms flaying out madly and her eyes ablaze with loathing and where she wrenched back my hand before I could retrieve the Host. "God jumped out of your mouth, you filthy little evil boy!"

My painful embarrassment was later vanquished by the compelling late afternoon shouts that filled the city's streets: "War! War! WAR!!" I ran home and told my mother and grandmother the startling news about the attack on Pearl Harbor. A week later, Germany declared war on The United States.

The destructive attack on Pearl Harbor mended most of the country's fractured ideologies and threw me like a storm-tossed stick into the tidal wave of zealous patriotism and a fear-laced hysteria that swept over America. Nevertheless the country was galvanized as never before and I suspect never will be again. Every newspaper, radio, pulpit and overheard adult conversation cried for retaliation and total war. Kids transformed cowboy and Indian games to Japs and Marines. Suddenly, imaginative and heart-stirring recruiting posters were everywhere. They showed the haunted eyes of battle-fatigued men with outstretched arms appealing for help against the advancing evil tide of victorious Nazis, treacherous Japanese and the questionably benign Italians. I wanted to join them, even in certain defeat. The near-mortal wounds the enemy had inflicted on our military brought a reality to the prospect of a vanquished America.

My mother, grandmother and countless others unrealistically expected the dreaded *Luftwaffe* to soon bomb New York. Nevertheless in our escape the following week we raced through the crowded corridors of Grand Central Station with our frayed, cord-tied suitcases and a three-day supply of paper bag lunches. Wedged into the packed coach train for three days we eventually arrived in orange blossom-scented Los Angeles.

Accompanying my mother in April on her job hunt in downtown LA, we were drawn into a crowd gathering beneath a loudspeaker that blared out, "Our Philippine outposts at Bataan and Corregidor have fallen!" America hadn't yet recovered from the loss of the entire beleaguered Marine garrison on Wake Island less than a month after Pearl Harbor. Prior to defeat they inflicted six thousand casualties on the invading Japanese. Their final non-coded message to Naval Headquarters in Hawaii was 'deciphered' for the American public: "Send us more Japs!" In actuality it read, "Get us the hell out of here!" The intervention of a ranking naval officer saved the marines from the mass execution the Japanese ground commander revengefully intended.

I gripped my mother's hand, hoping to relieve the deep concern etched across her face while we silently stood within a surging human sea that waved General MacArthur placards and roared the general's departing vow, "I shall return!" A momentary calm followed, broken by a panicked voice crying from the crowd, "Our army men can't seem to hold them back!"

The fearful people called the Japanese "savage" and "little monkeys." Some spoke of the captured English soldiers who, when Singapore fell in February, were stuffed into gunnysacks and used for bayonet practice, or the hospital patients in Hong Kong and Shanghai who were bayoneted on operating tables and in their beds. The German legation in China protested, as did the international press, to the burying alive of an entire hamlet.

9

Japanese General Nakajima's men raped, decapitated, flayed, dismembered and burned civilians alive in Nanking by the thousands. Someone cried, "They'll be invading L.A. next!" I visualized the invincible wooden soldiers of *Babes in Toyland,* hoping to be as brave as they with a bayonet against the approaching Fu Manchu army.

I saw slivers of hope radiating in the apprehensive eyes of people who waved and patted the backs of passing soldiers, sailors and Marines. They shouted, "God be with you! We love you! God bless America!" Longing to be the object of the pride seen in so many dewy eyes and recounting the heroic movie deaths of soldiers suddenly filled me with a willingness to die, like our troops in the Philippines. Emerging from that bubbling cauldron of faith, fear and hope, my heart instinctually knew that becoming a soldier was the only thing that would give life meaning.

Rumor-filled-months passed. Public fears of Fifth Columnists and secret Asian Dragon Societies grew. The film *Little Tokyo USA* warned of plots against southern California's war industry by treacherous Japanese. Their lurking assassins, saboteurs and spies had to be confined to save the country's destruction from within. A genuine Japanese spy networks did exist and extended up from Panama through Mexico, Baja California and up along the pacific west coast before it circled back to Hawaii.

Being too young to serve added to Richard's and my frustration. So we decided the next best thing would be to impersonate the least imposing official figure in wartime America—the Air Raid Warden. We painted our toy World War I type helmets with the triangular red and white-striped logo of the Civil Air Defense. That night, armed with flashlights and forced confidence, we brazenly stopped a car headed downtown on Main Street. My shout to the driver as I pointed skyward was a fairly good impression of what Clark Gable might have sounded like before his voice changed; and I mimicked his military posture, too, as remembered from the film *They Met in Bombay*: "Dim those damn lights, that could be a Jap plane up there!" The driver surprisingly obeyed. Wow! Fortunately uniformed baby-faced soldiers were not an uncommon sight.

School interest at Morningside Elementary gave way to the demands of war. Richard and I collected old hunting knives for our Marines, as well as used cooking fat to be converted into ammunition. We raided nearby groves and gave oranges to soldiers aboard the sweltering troop trains that periodically stopped at San Fernando's railroad junction.

We'd moved to Venice, where the night time coastline was off limits to civilians. Campfires could be used, it was thought, to guide in those rumored subs that carried saboteurs and/or infantry for the invasion of California. Studying how our soldiers guarded the beaches prompted me to ask Mom to lie again about my age so I could enlist, believing I could do a better job than they. "I've seen them, Mom, honest, sitting down, drinking canteen water, smoking, and not even watching the ocean!"

She was unmoved, but my lust for soldiering knew no bounds. That very night I attempted to try and sneak up on one of the bored chain-smoking sentries along the beachfront; and imagined him a Jap soldier. I had second thoughts during my snaky fifteen-minute crawl: *What if he turns around and shoots me?* Luckily he continued his zombie-like walk and I went undetected.

Richard and I admired the soldier's new styled helmets and especially their bayonet-fixed bolt-action rifles. That's how we had imagined the wooden sticks we carried while playing Marines taking a Jap island as we waded ashore one morning through the Santa Monica surf. It was God, or some other protective spirit that made us turn to see the three and, only a second away, twin-boomed P-38 fighters zooming in wing tip to wing tip. Their roaring engines swirled twin steel props across the tops of low crested waves. The whirling blades of one passed but a foot above our sand pressed bodies and drew us to our feet with wild screams of adulation that was lost in their thundering wake. "Hooray! Hooray!" The full-throttled fighters in a mock strafing run sliced between clusters of weathered beachfront houses then ripped up through a clear blue sky. They looped and barreled into the blinding sun. I prayed: *Please, God, don't let the war end before I can get in it*! The Army Air Corps didn't curtail the developing skills of their pilots, which they needed against superior-performing Japanese Zeroes that claimed more U.S. planes than could be publicly acknowledged. A California newspaper reported that the Air Corps' "ground support maneuvers have run up an awesome toll of decapitated rural farmers and cattle. Overzealous watchdogs nipping at their propellers, rows of cornfields and wash-lines had been shredded; coastal fishing boats capsized and cars caused to ditch on isolated roads."

Financial realities eventually forced us to move back into San Fernando to live with Aunt Elsie and her six-year-old daughter Tootsie. Uncle Mudge, a career Navy chief petty officer, was out with the Pacific fleet. Our 815 Lucas Street house was a few yards from the edge of the desert and a perfect spot for war games. Richard and I excluded sweet little cousin Tootsie from those games. "The boys get to do everything," she would cry.

We finally got our long promised Daisy Red Ryder BB guns and I immediately taped the wooden bayonet I'd carved onto mine. We used them against the rows of dried dying cactus we'd transformed into Jap infantry; and shot imaginary snipers out of stubby trees. The sand dunes became enemy bunkers to storm, as did the coiled barbed-wire perimeter of a small nearby army outpost.

Some of the friendlier soldiers there sometimes gave us their binoculars to spot and identify whatever type planes flew within visible range of their watchtower post, which, surprisingly they failed at; and adamantly refused to let me personally use their tower phone to call in my identifications to headquarters. One soldier rewarded me with a five-round clip of live .30-caliber ammo from his cartridge belt. I kept the treasure under my pillow. I soon learned their infantryman's code: "Your rifle is part of you." I applied this to my BB gun later that month when I fought with a gang of schoolyard kids who'd chased me home. I leapt from my bike, ran into the house and quickly reappeared with my hip-held pellet gun firing indiscriminatingly into their rapidly dispersed ranks. Had my spelling been better I would have written myself up for a Bronze star.

I accompanied Mom and Aunt Elsie to the Lockheed aircraft plant where they worked as riveters and were disappointed by coworkers who insisted they slow down so everyone could collect overtime. Mom and Aunt Elsie's concern was that planes were desperately needed on all fronts. The plant itself sat under a series of huge camouflage nets hung over paper-mâché hills dotted with machine gun nests and soldiers whose binoculars scanned the skies for Zeroes and Mitsubishi bombers that never arrived. I counted the number of guards, what weapons they carried along the barbed wired perimeter and carefully read the ubiquitous war posters: "Loose Lips Sink Ships—The Enemy Is Everywhere—Uncle Sam Needs You" and "Buy Bonds."

Those illustrative gems shone from every bus stop, luncheonette and recruiting station across America, as did the blue and gold star banners in the front windows of many proud and despairing mothers.

CHAPTER 2

The War Rages On

The price of movies skyrocketed from eleven to thirty-five cents, which meant either having to scavenge more deposit bottles for admission money, or hone my skills at jimmying open the fire exit doors at theaters. Some of Hollywood's early propaganda films were so overly filled with cloyed calls for self-sacrifice that even an eleven-year-old valor junkie like me found them unrealistic. Take the 1942 class B movie that starred Don 'Red' Barry as a pre-war expatriate working in a German munitions factory. At one point in the film, he jumps out of the German plane he'd commandeered hugging what appeared to be a singularly unimpressive ten-pound bomb, to make sure it hit the target. The exploding factory shot was a frame-lift from the 1938 film *Dawn Patrol.* The message was clear: A true American will jump at the chance to die for his country: *But if a Jap or Kraut does this they're Godless fanatics?*

I thought *Bataan, The Purple Heart* and *Manila Calling* were better films. Their implied lofty principles whetted my appetite for the promised heroic transformation that only war can bring. Old newsreel clips showed the Japanese in Manchuria catching sky-tossed babies on their bayonets and retaliatory actions by the avenging Chinese seemed equally frightening. To fight Asians then meant there was no option to surrender only "warring to the death." The admonishments of Admiral 'Bull' Halsey resonated in my mind: "Kill Japs and then kill more Japs."

I prepared and learned a few Japanese words from secondhand books, hoping to do as well as Gary Cooper did with his Cantonese in *The General Dies at Dawn.* Apace to my military addiction was the growing acceptance that death was a reasonable price to pay for the heady

13

experience of killing in war: *If I die the government will pay a ten thousand dollar insurance policy. That's enough to support Mom, Grandma and Richard for life!*

Films depicted those who survived war as morally and psychologically more evolved, respected and capable than others who'd never fought and killed. I secretly came to admire the German and Japanese civilians in those propaganda films for the greater loyalty and fanatical dedication they showed, compared to what I'd learned about the conduct of our own population from the nightly radio news.

Counterfeited ration coupons, black marketing, hoarding food and siphoned gas were a daily enterprise. There were bar girls, known as "allotment grabbing Gerties," who'd marry multiple G.I.s on the eve of their overseas deployment in hopes of collecting on their death insurance policies. Bureaucrats vied for priority status to separate themselves from the common herd. College-educated men got draft deferments because their intellects were classified as "strategic assets." Some men bribed doctors and officials to issue physical-unfitness 4-F deferments, while a few were shamed into suicide when given that same qualification.

For domestic political reasons one of America's enemies were treated quite differently in war films. Italy, the third major Axis power, was viewed more benignly. All the Italian soldiers in *Five Graves to Cairo,* for example, were against the war and not only were they 'pretty nice guys,' but great singers, too! This helped to create a more friendly reception for the Italian POWs who were allowed to visit New York City; and was deeply appreciated by the predominant Italian population whose traditional Democratic vote was counted on for Roosevelt's eventual postwar reelection. They walked freely about town dressed in their distinctive national uniforms, accompanied by attractive women. They munched on pepperoni pizza pies while their heavily-guarded Aryan allies dug for begrudged raw potatoes over in New Jersey, even as they maintained iron discipline among themselves. The few Japanese who were captured remained out on the Pacific Islands.

We moved back to New York City while battles raged between the Marines and banzai charging 'Nips' in 1943. I decorated my bedroom wall with two four-foot poster cutouts of Japanese soldiers in full battle gear. I wondered what it would be like to lead a platoon or a company of such tenacious warriors while at the same time wanting to cut them down with machine gun fire. Those thoughts were interlaced with images of General Yang and his men in *The General Dies at Dawn;* and grainy black-and-white newsreel clips of Japanese soldiers rampaging over the bullet-pocked walls of ancient China.

Combat reports on imaginative booby traps motivated my wiring up our family icebox with an alarm clock that went off inside as the door opened; my confidence grew. I placed a 'found' one-ounce packet of dynamite, used by the nearby railroad yard as a signaling device to locomotives, between the metal door hinges of Public School 45. The last exiting student slammed them shut at 1510 hours, whereupon they unhinged with mercifully no 'collateral damage.' When rounded up the next morning I gave the incredulous school principal my improbable alibi. "I felt like I was making a dry run against a Jap munitions plant, sir."

My brother Richard and a friend at a penny arcade, circa 1944, age 13.

Monies from my after school ushering job bought Richard and me a pair of .22 caliber semiautomatic Mossberg rifles that looked similar to the British army's Enfield, which we carried across our backs in makeshift rifle cases. With our newly-made friend, the 'Rabbit,' we hitched rides on the back of any truck headed towards Idlewild. The swampy Long Island topography [later transformed into the JFK airport] of tulles and sand dunes was perfect for our "advanced" war games. Crayon-colored cardboard targets of Emperor Hirohito and General Tojo were set up on mounds, as though seen through a bunker's firing port. We practiced semi-automatic covering fire, bayonet disarming and ambush techniques. I

15

always played the knife wielding Jap who screamed, "*Banzai*."

Robert standing in front of armory in Jamaica, Long Island, New York, prior to departing for Camp Smith. 1944, age 13.

Incredibly and most unexpectedly the shooting pulled in a uniformed cop from seemingly out of nowhere and turned the day into a combat endurance test when he shouted for us to "halt, in the name of the law!" Even though his long strides shrank the distance between us his second 'warning' shot went high. "What should we do?" yelled Rabbit and Richard. "Never surrender," I rasped. After grabbing their rifles I sprinted a quarter mile to bury the weapons and myself behind a dune. When Richard and Rabbit arrived they grumbled, "That goddamn cop wanted to steal our guns!"

Days later when Richard and I exited from a theater showing *All Quiet on the Western Front* we hastily hurried across the lobby to the New York State National Guard recruiting station and weapons display. The sergeant handed me a lustrously shined Thompson submachine gun and in my hands it took but a single whiff of this historic weapon's pungently scented metallic finish to transform the moment to one of love at first sight. My fate was sealed.

Mom, though seriously ill, gave her reluctant blessings to our enlisting on our thirteenth birthdays. We'd deftly altered our baptismal certificates to sidestep the official age requirement of seventeen then joined the 104th Field Artillery Battalion of the 42nd Rainbow Division in Jamaica, Long Island.

My earliest photo from those days. I am in the first row, seated sixth from the left. You can see the kid on my right leaning on me. Note the leggings and hat. Battery E, 149th Field Artillery Battalion, Camp Smith, Peekskill, New York. 1943-44, age 13.

Its understrength and marginally disciplined ranks were filled with overaged World War I holdovers, some current 4-Fs and other underage recruits who all hoped the war might 'go badly' so we'd be federalized and thrown into action. My proficiency with machine guns, the rifle and bayonet and grenades grew. Training manuals, brought home, were read more diligently than any school textbook. My well-tailored uniform and buffed combat boots were worn at every opportunity. I imagined myself as a full-fledged soldier.

Two years later in July of '45 while away on a two week summer training tour in upstate New York's Camp Smith our mother died of a heart attack at age thirty-three. In August atomic bombs destroyed the Japanese cities of Hiroshima and Nagasaki. Most Americans tried to imagine "The Bomb" in terms of the gigantic one-thousand pound "Block-busters" that obliterated Germany. Everyone knew no plane existed that could carry a bomb large enough to destroy an entire city. For days the story was considered pure propaganda.

I was joylessly swept up into the hysterical VJ Day crowds that flooded Broadway for two days and nights when the war ended. My mother's death added to the hollowness of spirit I felt over the failure of my martial fantasies, training and mental conditioning to have come to naught. Contrary to appearances there was little consolation in the lipstick smears that grateful war weary women left on my face, neck and uniform shirt.

Over seventy-five million people died in World War II, which ended on 15 August 1945. A year later Mao Tse-tung maneuvered his peasant communist army against inflexible Chiang Kai-shek's Nationalist forces and the final battle for China was on. I wondered why America with its atomic bomb and victorious standing army just didn't take over the world and enforce a universal order. Well, that totalitarian option seemed credible at the time.

The next summer's two-week training tour at Camp Smith nearly proved to be my Waterloo after I pinned a bogus lieutenant's bar to my helmet; and collected eight other like-minded troops to pose as the relief column for all the fixed guards posted around the camp. The forty minute exercise of what could be classified as 'espionage' succeeded and we disbursed. Inevitably I stood before the regimental commander who shouted in my face the next morning, "Were this wartime and the *regular* Army, Mercy, I'd have you shot for what you did!"

He objected strenuously to my reminder that our training lacked daring inventiveness and imagination. In addition he instantly approved my transfer to the 14th Infantry Regiment's armory in lower Manhattan and ordered me off the post forthwith.

The following summer Richard and I, with our new regiment, returned to the Camp Smith reservation, which was situated on a hundred foot rise above a roadway in Peekskill. Centered on its manicured parade field sat a 57mm pack howitzer beside a flagpole. The gun's axis was angled towards, and well within range, of the railroad tracks which literally skirted the expansive Hudson River by inches. On the morning of my Corporal of the Guard duty, I first loaded a 57mm blank shell into the gun's breach then, on an inexplicable impulse, dropped some 'unorthorized' rocks down the muzzel. Instantly after the gun's roar sounded Reveille, my eyes proudly followed the hoisted Colors up the pole. Looking back to the river seconds later, expecting to see stones harmlessly splashing into the river, I saw instead what fate had brought to within range by a thousand yards: the 5:30 A.M. northbound train out of New York! Vandalism and depraved indifference were far from my mind when I pulled the lanyard, but imagining myself as part of an English field battery at the Khyber Pass wasn't. The engine was pelted, complaints lodged, but not much else came of it, other than knowing I was going to love being a fulltime regular Army soldier.

After returning home, I experienced a vividly realistic dream, which would prove to have deep implications. It was pitch black yet I saw myself with two other G.I.s under a railroad boxcar. We were watching out over a field. Then, in a blinding flash an exploding Japanese grenade perferated my legs and blew my rifle away. I made a painful crawl over the train tracks with pistol in hand then awaited the inevitable *Banzai* attack. When awakening, the excruciating pain experienced in the dream lingered and was so real, that I called to my brother to bring my crutches. Annoyed, he told me that I didn't have any crutches and, strangely enough the pain felt in both legs remained for several days.

We dressed in our guard uniforms after school to go over to the USO Pepsi-Cola Canteen on Duffy Square in the city. We felt more at home among the decorated bomber pilots and wounded soldiers who cemented our bonding to the military. Without parents, life became something of a three-day pass, and the missed classes at delinquent-filled East New York Vocational High were inconsequential. The most produced items in their boring workshop classes were the lethal little zip guns that flooded the streets of Brooklyn and Manhattan. Given my military weapons qualifications, I saw them as mere toys, but did delve into making small experimental "grenade" capsules filled with a volital mix of phosphorus and potassium chlorate. I experienced their effectiveness while sitting in a theater munching a Mounds bar and watching Errol Flynn and Ann

Sheridan as Resistance fighters in *The Moon is Down*. One of the heat sensitive "grenades" suddenly exploded and blew off my shirt pocket; and although singed, it wasn't a discouraging wound.

CHAPTER 3

The Marines And Beyond

Communist burp gun fire on our Marine garrison's supply depot in Tientsin China in 1946 awoke my slumbering wartime fervor. I was sure the Marines would welcome me into their ranks as one of their "few good men," but a dark cloud hung over that promising new tomorrow. It would be the first lifetime separation from my twin who would remain home to care for grandma and continue at school.

It was an icy December morning when the Brooklyn subway carried me to Manhattan for my medical examination at the USMC recruiting station on Church Street. Afterwards the lieutenant in charge of my interview asked me to read a section from *The Articles of War*, which I found difficult. "You don't read too well, Kid," he said, "but everything else is okay, so you're in."

Gleefully I skimmed back outside over the sleet-streaked streets imagining myself in the Corps' distinctive dress blue uniform, and my grandmother's joy on receiving the forty-dollar monthly allotment checks the government would send. The glee disappeared two weeks later when the other 'boots' and I began exiting the train that took us to the Marine's training depot at Parris Island, South Carolina.

A pack of growling Drill Instructors (DIs) unceremoniously yanked us from the doorway by our ears, throats, and coat sleeves and kicked us into formation. A thirty-something gunnery sergeant bellowed, "At-teeen-shunnn!"

And not a single eyelash or pinkie twitched in the fear frozen half-hour pause before his next spittle-laced command. Non-coms, with slits for eyes, rewarded every unintended infraction of the rules with elevated degrees of corporal punishment during our march to the training company's barracks area.

USMC, Paris Island, South Carolina. 1946, age 16.

The chisel-faced draconian platoon sergeant, a veteran of hard times and a Japanese POW cage, vented his pent-up rage when I unthinkingly broke through ranks on his command to come "front and center." His right-cross punctured my eardrum and landed me in sickbay where a latent case of mononucleosis then surfaced. Richard, back in New York, was coincidentally hospitalized with it on the same day. After recovering weeks later I was first assigned to wax the hospital floors then a day later to load garbage trucks under the hot Carolina sun. The resurfaced syndrome confined me to bed for two more weeks where, in drifts of intermittent semi-consciousness, I heard voices, and even glimpsed a medical discharge form being waved in my face. I thought it a masochistic delirium before the officer beside my bed came into focus.

He offered me a chance to stay in the Corps by turning down the discharge forms. I gave an impassioned monologue refuting the theory that one had to be beaten into submission to become a loyal Marine. Second thoughts came to mind soon after he left, but they evaporated when during my fevered semi-consciousness I called for water. The ward's night medic arrived with his garrison belt tightly wound around his fist; and slapped its metal buckle into the turned up palm of his other hand.

"Now shut up, Boy, or I'll whoop yah real good with this!" A sergeant -patient two bunks down growled, "You better not try it." The medic disappeared and I was speechless over the first and only act of humanity I'd witnessed on Parris Island.

I returned home in a dress green uniform, a sixteen-year-old veteran, only to be entombed again in East New York's Vocational High School. The future did indeed seem gloomy. Illogically I let ego and wounded pride keep me from applying for the government's 'Fifty-two Twenty Club,' which paid veterans a $20.00 bonus for that many weeks. A tidy and helpful sum, which I felt I hadn't really earned or deserved.

It could also be of clinical interest that it wasn't long before the soothing balm of film re-convinced me that without military camaraderie, mission and war nothing was left but the slow meaningless grind of civilian life. Boys, however, live not by celluloid alone. I rejoined Richard in evening drills at the NYC 14th Infantry Regiment's armory. During summer training at Camp Smith the regimental commander suggested I use some "USMC techniques" on a platoon of resentful dead-end kids from lower Manhattan. That landed me in the guardhouse. It was time to leave the politics of the guard.

Our seventeenth birthday finally arrived and we enlisted for the U.S. 11th Airborne Division and occupational duty in Japan. I was newly determined to withstand whatever brutal training might lie ahead. Richard and I religiously prepared for the primary aspect of air borne duty by riding down the two hundred foot parachute jump in Coney Island, for as long as our money held out.

A week later we were at Fort Ord in Monterey California. The post was ringed by lush green rolling hills and a cobalt blue sea. The recruit reception process was light-years evolved from the Marines. Obvious prior training got me assigned as "senior recruit" in the new platoon. That and witnessing the mess sergeant's wife loading stolen food into the family car spelled trouble. I reported this to the company commander, but his 'investigation' unsurprisingly turned up nothing.

Robert (left), George Cronin (center), Demetrius Suttos (rear) and Richard (left front). Fort Ord, California, near the end of basic training in 1947. We were all 17. Demetrius was stationed at the 8th Army Stockade with me in Tokyo in 1949. George died in the run to Chinju.

Our first sergeant, Kowalski, was a stocky forty-year-old smiling veteran of the Italian campaigns; and the first authority figure to trust me with genuine responsibility. He assigned me to be a prison chaser, which was to escort soldiers from the stockade back to the battalion courtroom for trial. This duty was rarely if ever entrusted to a recruit. For a seventeen-year-old it's a heady sensation to be issued a clip of live ammo, and the clear understanding the prisoner must not escape.

Richard and I struck up an immediate friendship with George Cronin, a small bright-faced Irish kid from Chicago. He had a Midas touch in gambling, a perpetual grin and shared our conviction that the Army's lack of advanced tactics and first-class weapons training would prove costly in any future war; and how the pair of Ruger .22 caliber pistols Richard and I purchased in town would alter that, we weren't sure; but while most of the company was on a weekend pass in San Francisco we used them on the deserted rifle range then ran the obstacle and bayonet courses.

I filched .30-caliber ammo from the rifle range and wandered off alone into the rugged hills to practice long-distance sniping. I dug in after dark, and strung up a few training grenades, with trip cords, around my camouflaged foxhole. Had the all-knowing Sgt. Kowalski reported my clandestine soldiering, I would surely have gotten a Medical Section Eight discharge for psychological instability. We were told that "soldiers in the new peacetime Army were ambassadors of peace." They wanted to expunge wartime thinking from the ranks. The implication was clear—any soldiers who harbored latent martial impulses should bury them in his footlocker. When basic training ended in the spring both the mess sergeant and the company commander were charged with pilfering food. I was genuinely disillusioned on learning officers could be as corrupt as the least unprincipled civilian. George Cronin was sent to a 1st Cavalry unit stationed at Camp Drake, while Richard and I went to the 188th in Sendai. Our whole platoon went to San Francisco, for a weekend-long farewell party where we echoed the hallowed battle cry of World War II: "See ya in Tokyo!"

CHAPTER 4

Across The Wide Pacific

My head was still spinning from the previous night's carousing as we headed up the gangplank of the USS *General Brewster*. I momentarily froze upon recognizing the deck watch officer to be the same lieutenant I'd verbally brawled with in a bar the previous night. He glared then whispered behind a faint smile, "Forget about it." That was a good omen.

With our gear stowed, Richard and I made our way through steerage and struck up a quick friendship with a thin Philadelphian named Frank Korbell. His wiggly over-animated face, grimaces and random ticks, did little for my hangover, but he somehow reminded me of the actor Glenn Ford. There were other shipboard talents, including stand-up comics, wannabe crooners, card sharks, magicians and even a hypnotist.

The en-masse nausea, along with the allure of the encircling azure blue sea, ended on our third day out. Then wild rumors began to spread among the bored troops: leftover WWII mines were adrift off the bow... a hushed-up case of plague was aboard; and endless speculation, too, over which officer passengers were sleeping with which of the seventy in-transit wives who were quartered in the mid-ship cabins. We stood in our cramped starboard aft quarter quietly admiring the women's near-daily bathing suit appearances as we veered into warmer latitudes. And we were especially appreciative when they, like predatory cats in heat, would languidly recline on the upper deck's lounge chairs whilst their posted armed guards glared menacingly back at us. A week after leaving Hawaii, the *Brewster* lumbered into Guam Harbor and secured her mooring lines. The intercom repeatedly blared, "Now hear this! All troops are to remain on board. The waters are shark-infested. Only authorized personnel will be

26

allowed ashore."

The island's white sandy beach and emerald green hills invoked cinematic memory of wartime jungle fighting and commanded that we breach the ship's security and go ashore. Posing as disgruntled KP workers, Richard and I put Frank into an empty garbage can and carried him past the gangplank guards. Fortunately for us they weren't Marines, who'd have known the ship's slop had already been dumped before entering the harbor.

We knew the ship was to sail at dawn and planned to get back onboard by evening chow, using the same ploy that had gotten us ashore. Then, innocently enough, we 'borrowed' the two Jeeps we intended to return to the nearby unguarded motor pool. Richard and Frank rode in one and I drove the other alone. This way, if one vehicle broke down, we'd still have transportation out of the still-rumored-to-be-Jap-infested jungle. We had also picked up a case of beer from a native shop, which we split between us.

We unfortunately managed to get separated on the road and by that time both Richard and Frank were thoroughly zonked out. They got chased and apprehended by the local constabulary. Later I flipped my Jeep and landed in the hands of another pursuing PD posse. Unscathed we were brought back to the ship separately and isolated in the brig to await interrogation. I was angry over our collective lack of foresight that left us without a feasible alibi and the grim spectre of languishing forever in a naval dungeon under Marine guard. My only hope was that Richard would pick up on my telepathic message, as we'd been able to do in the past. I repeated my story over and over in my mind until the mantra: "A short young blondish sailor who was smoking a cigar had rented us the Jeeps for $20.00." The incantation was broken by a rattling of the guard's keys.

As I was brought to the interrogating lieutenant's desk, my brigand's brain was filled with genuine regret realizing that my labored for military career was in serious jeopardy; and silently vowed never to violate the law again—if I was freed.

In the half-hour of questioning I gave the officer a very unflattering description of the villain, using my absentee father as the model. "Well," he said, "your stories match. You boys are lucky. Don't worry, we'll get that bastard!"

The lieutenant didn't hear my audible sigh of relief.

"I sure hope so, sir. That nasty little son of a bitch deserves everything he gets!"

Richard told me later that he'd worked out that alibi with Frank in the Jeep, which left me unsure as to who'd actually received whose telepathic communication.

Stretched out that night on the forward hatchway, under a galaxy of pitching stars, I wondered if they'd even been seen above the flaring guns of the opposing fleets in the fiery battles of the Coral Sea, Leyte Gulf and fateful Midway; and how many of their rusting bone-filled hulks rested beneath the glittering wake of our passing ship. I thought, too, of China, Malaysia and the ten thousand slaughtered G.I.s in the Death March on Bataan. Then searched my conscience for which of the conflicting emotions I felt predominated: *the war is far from over....*

Days later, through an indigo dawn the dragon-back outline of defeated Japan loomed up off the port quarter. Once ashore in the former Imperial naval bastion of Yokosuka all the troops assigned to the 11th Airborne Division boarded the overnight train for the northern coastal city of Sendai.

A picture taken early in the occupation of curious, but cautious Japanese children.

Swatches of children shouted for gum at each station stop, while clusters of former Imperial soldiers stood stoically mute in the torn remnants of their once proudly worn uniforms. They were the first I had seen beyond a movie screen. Their inscrutable glances reignited within me some smoldering wartime embers which I thought had cooled but still burned in recalling their army's early arrogant victories. Equally irritating were the blank-faced G.I.s around me who indiscriminately showered them with smiles, sticks of gum and cigarettes. Those items would become the currency for barter after turning in our greenbacks for military scrip. American dollars netted a big profit on the flourishing black market and a court martial for those who were caught. I had no respect for profiteers nor anyone who dealt with our wartime enemy.

By dawn we'd reached our destination. Outside a stationmaster cried, *"Sendai, gozaimasu, Sendai, desu* [It is Sendai]!" Though fascinated by the early morning sights my mind grappled with the enigma of how things could seem both so foreign and heart-achingly familiar at the same time.

Richard (left), the 11th Airborne Division commander and me (right). This photo was taken in Sendai, Japan. 1948, age 18.

Kimono-clad men and women rhythmically glided to work on the musical clatter of their wooden shoes. Some considerately wore white surgical masks to protect others from possibly catching their colds. Farmers were dressed in bulky, sleeveless coats and hats of straw. Idling charcoal-fueled trucks belched smoke along the road. Throngs of rickshaws and school children patiently waited the authoritative wave from the pistol armed Japanese policemen directing traffic from a pedestal in the intersection.

There were also quaint relics of a recent *Samurai* past. Women still walked two steps to the left and three behind their men, so as to not impede the drawing of his sword—a weapon deemed forbidden by occupational decree.

I reluctantly acknowledged to myself that the serene Japanese seemed more polite, friendly and far less aggressive than Americans back in the States. Perhaps it was the perceived unexpected melting of my glacially locked convictions that allowed for the sudden and baffling sensation of feeling somewhat…at home.

CHAPTER 5

The Post

We boarded trucks for the dusty two-mile ride that passed clusters of wooden thatched-roofed shacks and rice paddies before reaching the main gate at Camp Schimmelpfenning. A sign read "Home of the 11th Airborne Infantry Regiment." Enclosed by a ten-foot barbed wire topped fence, the camp was formally used by the Japanese army, who built several wooden barracks on the flat one hundred acres. Japanese civilians maintained the water pump station, laundry plant, PX, NCO Club, enlisted men's beer hall, and motion picture theater. Quarters housing three American USO hostesses were flattered nightly with an armed guard. The division's Air Transport Command School, thirty miles to the north, trained troopers to jump from C-46s. The drop zone, Fryer Field, was a mile east of the post's rear gate.

Richard was assigned to the demolition platoon of the 2nd Battalion Headquarters Company. I drew a rifleman's slot in Easy Company. Our world revolved around highly polished jump boots, heavily starched uniforms and platoon formations endlessly double-timing around the post and countryside. Tight discipline punished failure to salute and violations of the dress code with fifty push-ups. We were there a month before we got our first off-post pass and a warning from the company commander.

"Don't eat the local food, drink beer or liquor and don't wash with native soap. Many of these items had been poisoned three years ago in expectation of our invasion."

With a tin of sardines in my pocket, and a canteen on my pistol belt I separated from the other G.I.s at the main gate. I was disillusioned again, that I hadn't been issued either a symbolic pistol, or bayonet, more as an

31

icon of victory rather than for self-defense. A 1945 GHQ decree by General Albert Wedemeyer, however, made any need for weapons unnecessary: "Any Japanese national who attacks a member of the Allied Forces will be lucky to reach the courtroom alive." Nevertheless officers, by virtue of their congressional "Officer and Gentleman" status were authorized to carry concealed weapons both in the States and abroad.

Camp Schimmelpfenning, Sendai, Japan, 1948.

In 1948 military strength was severely cut back and veterans of the war who remained were reminded again that they were 'ambassadors of peace.' Obligatory terminologies had redefined the War Department to the Department of Defense and downgraded "implacable enemy" to a less provocative "aggressors." The more draconian Articles of War were converted into a liberalized Uniform Code of Military Justice, thanks to General Jimmy Doolittle of the famed 1942 Tokyo bombing raid. I thought it only a matter of time before the Army would totally restrict the use of the word "war" itself. The politicians had deliberately de-glorified the Officer Corps' by replacing their distinctive wartime uniforms with one devoid of authority and glamour, as a defense perhaps against an unlikely military coup d'état.

A call from four ragged boys tagging behind me broke the reverie. "You, *soldier-san*," said one holding out the can of sardines that I had somehow dropped. I struggled inwardly: *Should I reward their honesty with the food, or, as a soldier be unmoved?* I simply bowed and walked away, wishing I'd been more generous and knowing such an act would never happen in New York under any circumstances.

I suspect it was our weightlifter frames that prompted the post provost marshal to ask Richard and me to join the MPs. Their white-laced jump boots, matching scarves and loaded .45 automatics were quite an inducement. Manning the front and rear gates to capture any soldiers or Japanese nationals attempting to enter or leave the post with contraband was also attractive. They also enforced the regimental dress code and anti-fraternization rules. These were totally ignored when involving officers or NCOs, but strictly applied to the lower ranks. Duty in the post beer hall on Friday and Saturday night became challenging when troops ignored the "twenty-minutes to closing" warning, when they'd order up cases of beer and defiantly start guzzling them down. This unfailingly started the much-anticipated beer hall riot. The entire MP detachment would turn down their promising weekend passes not to miss one.

I drew my pistol, ammo, nightstick and armband from supply. I shared second floor quarters with three other G.I.s. The isolated wooden building, at the far end of the post, served as MP headquarters. A nearby small detention shelter housed the prostitutes periodically pulled in for VD checks. Those uninfected were considered the "catch of the day" by certain testosterone-driven MPs. I was surprised to learn that many local women still operated on a 1945 decree issued by the hierarchy of Japan's Home Office.

Richard in his MP uniform.

Prior to the actual Occupation, they'd appealed to the 'lower social order' of womanhood to sexually sacrifice themselves to the barbarous Americans in order to save the nation's higher breeding stock from defilement. The mandate was often carried out with the will of *kamikaze* pilots. *Banzai*! Others took revenge on the victors with false claims of rape, but those who were proven guilty of the crime under the new Uniform Code received prison sentences, as opposed to the old stringent Articles of War that mandated death by hanging.

I was fortunate indeed to have met the exquisite nineteen year old Miss Junko Sugamoto one month after joining the MP Detachment. She worked at the PX as a portrait artist and used the opportunity to advance her skills. Her education, poise and linguistic abilities separated her from most other Japanese women.

Robert with his girlfriend Junko in Sendai.

After I'd engaged her to do a canvas from an old Look Magazine photo that depicted marines in combat on Tarawa I would stop off daily at her little studio to check her progress; and each day I became more mesmerized by her exotically inviting eyes and the softness of her voice. We spent marvelous hours at her house in the nearby little village of Tsutsujingaoka. Although my infatuation grew, I wouldn't (or couldn't) let my intensifying love and passion for her develop more—because WWII had been too deeply etched in my psyche, and my sense of duty came first. Still, conflicting ideology aside, we treasured our times together.

The nearby stockade was a rough place to serve a six-month special court martial sentence. Prisoners wore a foot-long, three-inch-wide strip of white tape across their backs. This made an easy target for the line company chasers, who guarded them on daily twenty-five mile runs. Rebellious prisoners dug ditches throughout the night and suffered corporal punishment. General court martial convictions went to the Eighth Army prison in Tokyo, or Fort Leavenworth, Kansas. These sentences ran from twenty years to death.

Each MP room was assigned a Japanese houseboy, a luxury not extended to line company troops. The two we had were both eager and friendly. They cleaned our living quarters, delivered and returned our uniforms from the post cleaners and shined jump boots and brass insignias for five dollars a month. I befriended the one who expressed an interest in our Old West, and baptized him the 'Sundance Kid.' I taught him how to 'quick-draw' a .45. He taught me Japanese as did the films shown in the nearby port city of Shiogama.

Watanabe and the 'Sundance Kid,' our room boys at the M.P. barracks in 1948-49.

Japanese film ethos differed greatly from ours and deified those who died for the best of all causes—a lost one, which also appealed to me. A small piece of wartime propaganda was dispelled when I once glanced back at an audience from a front row movie seat and saw them smile and moved to tears by human emotions. It was quite contrary to *our* wartime beliefs and *they* surely felt the same about us.

Shiogama, an entry point for smuggled contraband, proved educational on the night our detachment searched for black market ringleaders.

Handsome devil, aren't I?

I ordered half a dozen suspects to stand at attention in the middle of the dark and totally deserted street. It was an hour before I returned. They had not budged an inch. The Japanese have a collective iron-willed discipline. A crack might show, though, when MPs barged in on their *Geisha* house frivolities.

Robert (right) and Fontes (left), flanking a Japanese woman in Shiogama. She's trying hard not to laugh as she looks at the sketch of a bear I drew, which we went hunting for. I have my finger on the trigger in case she holds back information...

The city's police department reminded me of the "Thought Police" in the 1943 film *Blood on the Sun*. Both prided themselves on knowing everything. I stopped to urinate along a dark and desolate road an hour before I walked into their stationhouse and was greeted by desk sergeant Matsui Hiroshi. He gave me his best gold-capped tooth grin and adjusted his silver-framed glasses.

As with all Japanese I wondered what his wartime duties had been: *Probably with the Kempeitai, or maybe their special secret police, the*

Tukkotai. Had I parachuted in here two years ago, I probably would have blown his head off.

"Matsui-san," I said, "anything happening in town tonight?"

He paused. "No, is very, how you say…'quiet-o,' yes?"

I subtly sucked in air between my teeth. "*Hai, 'quiet-o' dadashi desu* [Yes, quiet is correct]."

He drawled and gave a small bobbed bow. "Oh, you very well Japanese speak. Is 'quiet-o' in Shiogama, but one more…hmmm…report-o I have. Jeep-ou stop on road, maybe one hour before and G.I. take, how you say, piss-ou *desu ka?*"

It was hard mirroring his poker-faced expression. "*Kamatana, hunto desu ka* [I'll be damned, is that true?]"

Mama-san and two girls at the local geisha house in Shiogama, which was usually my last stop on night patrol in the town.

I seriously wondered how they managed to lose the war on my stroll to a noodle shop for a snack of *Osoba* noodles. I checked the movie-house for what *Samurai* film would play next then went to see what new bashful giggling beauty was employed at Mama-san's *Geisha* house.

I enjoyed the ride back to the post in my open Jeep with the weight of the .45 on my hip. I felt grateful for having escaped Brooklyn, and becoming a soldier. Life was perfect and I hoped it would never change.

Two proud mothers with their babies in Shiogama. It was wonderful to have had a glimpse of old Japan.

Robert holding a cute Japanese girl while on highway patrol in Shiogama

CHAPTER 6

After Jump School

Our June introduction to the Yamoto jump school was a cadence-singing ten-mile run under a sweltering sun. The month long fifteen-hour training days conditioned us for the parachute-landing fall (PLF). This is equivalent to jumping off a two-story building, or from a truck doing 20 mph.

A sign at the Airborne Training Center.

It was cool and crisp on the morning of our first jump. Our exhilarated platoon ran down to the airstrip and struggled into T-4 chutes then jogged out to the two C-46s revving up next to the open hangar doors. Awash in the planes' icy prop-blast we climbed the ladder up into the fuselage of the first airplane any of us had ever been in. Flying was still a restricted luxury for the primarily rich or the military. Yet I had a sense of dé*jà vu* in its noisy interior, garnered perhaps from newsreels of the 101st Airborne jumping into Normandy, or Errol Flynn in *Objective Burma*. Soon there was a collective shout as the ship's wheels lifted from the blurred runway and hurtled it a thousand feet up into the clear blue sky. "AIRBORNE!"

Jumping over Sendai.

Richard and I sat next to the open doors we'd both lead our "sticks" through and were exchanging "thumbs up" salutes across the wind-gusted aisle just when the cabin's warning light flashed red. My heart raced on the jumpmaster's signal to "Stand up and hook up," then pivoting into the open door. My hands clutched its freezing aluminum exterior frame. Clamoring currents raced across my face, up my sleeves and under my helmet. When the ground DZ marker below slid beneath my extended foot I fantasized jumping back in time with the division onto Jap-held Corregidor; then catapulted down into a three second churning maelstrom. The chute jolted open, and I glided through spacious silence. Once on the ground, Richard and I ran towards each other shouting, "We made it," having found the closest thing to Heaven.

Robert waiting for the C-47 to taxi up.

The next week the officers and men of the 188th MP Detachment gave a "prop blast party" for the newly qualified jumpers. Each man had to stand atop the day room's bar and gulp down a near-lethal concoction of multiple alcohols while the assembly counted aloud, "One thousand, two thousand, three thousand," this being the time it took a chute to open. Only the drinker's tolerance determined whether he leapt or fell, to roll up to the presiding officer and salute shouting, "Private [Whoever] reporting for prop blast duty, sir!" The hope was that the honoree would miss some crucial step of the ritual then, after having to repeat the whole process again, pass out cold.

The stress of jumping honed my psychic senses. One morning I got halfway through the parachute issuing line and pitched back the chute a corporal threw into my outstretched arms.

"It won't open," I said.

The summoned sergeant mumbled, cursed and struggled to pry open the chute's cover. The twine that attaches the static cord to the apex was missing, and could never have opened. The sergeant's eyebrow arched, as if to ask "how did you know?" Then the "Great Spirit" spoke again the following month when I instantly pitched back a smaller reserve chute. Unseen beneath the cover flap was the seriously rusted release cord cable that stubbornly resisted the tandem pulling of two husky NCOs. Trusting the packing of our chutes to the parachute maintenance company proved hazardous.

Six months later as I left the Fryer Field DZ after a jump I didn't know whose chute it was that I'd watched streaming in to disappear behind the hangars at the edge of the field. I found out later in the mess hall when Richard ran in and told how he'd frantically tried to untangle the balled up canopy as he raced to the ground at 125 mph; then pulled the reserve handle only after seeing the stretching shadows thrown from the fast approaching blades of grass. With one second left the chute popped and he oscillated once before hitting ground. He said he knew the minute that rear-echelon clerk dropped the chute into his arms that it wouldn't work.

I soon learned that those whose job it was to enforce regulations were, for the most part, more undisciplined than the troops they policed. With no ranking NCOs living in quarters, except for the aptly named Corporal 'Roach,' heavy drinking and vast amounts of gun fire ripping through the barrack's paper thin wooden doors and walls was a near nightly occurrence. Surprisingly no one was either killed or maimed. I soon suffered from the same contagious pathology and one of my fired slugs harmlessly ricocheted back from a wall and bruised my chest. I wondered if that was a preview of some future event.

Equally mysterious was our Criminal Investigation Detachment (CID), led by a tall twenty-year-old, two-cases-of-Coke-a-day Texan, in charge of four other enlisted men of dubious training and distinction. Also assigned was a Japanese detective named 'Dick Tracy.' Their investigations, always "classified," never went to trial as far as I knew. Less confidential was their collaboration in the theft of mess hall food, which went to the black market and also supported their unauthorized off-base houses and girlfriends. Shakespeare was right: "thieves have authority for their robberies, when judges steal themselves." *Shades of Fort Ord*!

They nevertheless saw themselves as "secret agents of the *Gestapo*, functioning under *Führer* immunity," which allowed their beatings and mild torture of handcuffed Japanese nationals to go unchecked. Like the elfin truck driver who'd been stopped on the post and found with a four-inch cargo knife that he used to trim rope. He was handcuffed and suspended from the ceiling by a rope. As he hung there, 'Bear,' a 225-pound MP, used him as a punching bag for a few hours. The rationale was that his knife was 'intended for some G.I.'s back.' Interestingly, no Allied soldier had ever been attacked by a Japanese national since they first landed three years earlier. In truth the Second World War had not really ended for most of us, nor the small ultra-nationalists Japanese group of would-be guerrillas called The Gray Wolves, who also never actually attacked the occupying army. To do so would have dishonored the Emperor's edict. I suspected them, however, of having placed a tree log across a bend in the road I'd traveled down one night at high speeds, unwittingly disappointing them when I returned at a more rational pace.

One of the MPs who enforced the non-fraternization code in a draconian manner was a chain-smoking, overweight twenty-year-old Southern boy. This PFC was a borderline psychopath whose sexual crimes would have gotten him a Dishonorable Discharge and a long stretch of prison time at Ft. Leavenworth were it not for a momentary ill-placed sense of unit loyalty on my part, which was a gross error in moral discernment. He was also undergoing his nineteenth case of gonorrhea. The report of just one such occurrence would have removed him from duty on grounds of moral turpitude, but fortunately for him—and others, that a pair of medics named Frenchy and Rocky treated such cases off the record.

The questioning of this dualistic morality reduced my list of friends down to a six-foot-four southern Californian named Richard E. Robertson who, in movements reminiscent of a bolero dancer would whimsically uncoil his body in staccato bursts of movement whenever he drew his pistol, which was often. He was a combination of hedonism shrouded beneath an amiable reserve, with a quick wit and a near insatiable pathological drive for excitement. Like many of us, he too found a home in the Army, but more importantly he also wanted to lead Asian troops when war came with the communists.

45

On my first night's duty in the beer hall, a fight broke out between members of two rival line companies. An angered Mexican voice rang out over the flying tackles all around me. "Keel de fukin' white MP, man!" I braced against the forty-yard long stone-topped bar and flayed away at the rioters as Robertson's Jeep crashed through the bar's swinging front doors. His fired eight rounds up into the ceilings decoratively opened parachute failed to stop the tables, chairs and sloshing beer cans that rained down on and around me. A squad of MPs came in as I was picking myself up for the second time. Robertson water-skied towards me on the wet surface of the beer-soaked bar, with his flashlight bouncing off the heads of a few rioters; and then we fought side by side, until a flying wedge of MPs clobbered their way through to us. We arrested those that weren't able to stagger away.

The friction between Mexican *Pachuco* troops and MPs carried back to the Zoot-Suit riots in wartime L.A. six years earlier. Each member still wore their traditional tattooed cross with three sun rays on one or both hands. Some displayed it on their foreheads like an Ash Wednesday blessing. It was suspected that their known use of marijuana contributed to those fights, but there wasn't a single MP who could have identified its distinctive odor; and because it wasn't a native Japanese crop the assumption was that it had arrived via uncensored mail from home. All I knew about drugs came from the alarmist film *Reefer Madness*.

By July of 1948 the prospects of the two-year-old Cold War turning hot seemed promising when Russia's Chinese client Mao Tse-tung attacked the *Kuomintang* forces of Chang Kai-shek. Days later our regiment was sent north to blow up a deserted Japanese airstrip, which would deny the paranoid Russians a potential landing zone. In Tokyo the emotional appeal from condemned General Hideki Tajo's wife to General MacArthur to alter her husband's impending disgraceful mode of execution to one more honorable—death by firing squad, was denied. He was hanged at Sugamo prison for war crimes.

World events motivated us to spend all our free time practicing combat shooting and to stash cases of small arms ammo at strategic points beyond the post for the 'unforeseen emergency,' I deemed inevitable.

There was another riot in the beer hall that winter when the OD [Officer of the Day] whose Jeep I drove told me to go in alone and break it up. The visiting six-piece Japanese band was playing *Jingle Bells* as I walked through the door and reluctantly waded into the one-hundred-man melee. A riptide of punches blackened my eye three times over and as I attempted to arrest one of the ringleaders, a can of beer ricocheted off my helmet-liner. The escaping perpetrator ignored my two warning shots and

46

the next hip-fired round severed his left earlobe as he reached the door. I started towards him and was jumped from behind, but minutes later two MP squads arrived. I raced back outside and thankfully found no dead body, only the inebriated lieutenant snoring in the Jeep.

Mini-riots were not unknown to the MPs in our brother regiment, the 511th Airborne stationed up in northern Hokkaido. Rumor had it that one MP there allegedly killed four of a dozen knife-armed *Pachucos* in a beer hall brawl. Found guilty by a court martial he was fined one dollar for each life taken then transferred off post with four cartons of cigarettes, to offset his financial losses. That was the Standard Operating Procedure [SOP] for any soldier who'd killed another in the line of duty, which crossed my mind soon after I walked into the mess hall during the noonday feeding of the stockade's fifty prisoners.

A shower of profane threats came from the tables full of men that Robertson, Richard and I had helped put away, followed by their hurled cups and heavy metal trays. The startled guards flew at High Port into three corners of the room. I dashed into the nearby fourth under a flying barrage of utensils; creamed corn, broccoli and shouts of "kill the Mercy brothers!" The prisoners hurled whatever could be thrown while a few charged forward. My .45 crashed down on their heads, but it was the crunch of the chambered round that silenced the room and got them seated. The five wounded were taken to the hospital and guards prodded the others from the hall.

Called to Major Magadieu's office the following morning I'd expected his congratulations for putting down a prison mutiny. He told me instead that if I were convicted by the special court martial board that he was obliged to convene, he'd see to it that I'd serve my time up in northern Hokkaido. One thought burned through my disillusioned mind: *How can I smuggle a boot knife into that stockade?*

Months passed and then on the morning of 7 March I stood under guard in the very courtroom where I'd never seen a single acquittal. I felt fortunate that Captain Becker, the regimental prosecuting officer, defended my case in appreciation of past services. He decided to unseat Colonel Bottomley, the post commander who, at the last minute, had surprisingly appointed himself President of the Board. That drew silent blank stares and raised eyebrows from its seated junior officers. The unforgiving disciplinarian refused to step down on Becker's "cause" challenge and further astonished him—and everyone else—when the colonel shouted for him to "sit down and shut the hell up!" The courtroom was stunned to silence. The prosecutor, Captain John W. Simmons had no better luck with his legal challenge to the colonel's presence and the uncertainty of his motives formed beads of sweat across my brow.

I held my breath after the last turban-bandaged prisoner testified and the prosecution closed its case. The board rose to exit for deliberation. The colonel halted them in their tracks and without skipping a beat said, "Not guilty on all charges and specifications—dismissed!"

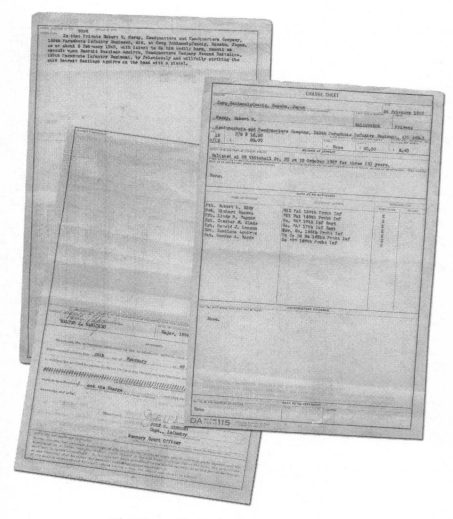

The Charge Sheets from my court martial.

I later learned that the officers convened for the trial had conspired to convict me because of the unintended discomforts I'd caused them on those nights they had to leave their cozy homes and come to the post to sign for the releases of their arrested men. Such accumulated 'incidents' on an officer's efficiency report often meant being passed over for promotion and was in essence a career killer. Though Colonel Bottomley sabotaged their plot when he took charge, my days as an MP were numbered.

The next month the bedraggled 17th Regiment of the 7th Division, rotated from occupational duty in Korea to Japan, slouched its way onto the post to relieve our regiment, scheduled to be shipped back to the States. I cringed at their total lack of airborne flair. Days later the Red Cross notified Richard and me of our grandmother's death from a heart attack. We left for New York filled with grief and remorse over the many thanks she'd never gotten for raising us and how many of her birthdays passed uncelebrated. The Army was now truly our only family and home.

CHAPTER 7

Emergency Furlough

Our emergency furlough papers winged us across the Pacific's island chains on an endless series of C-46 hops. The last plane, an Arkansas Air National Guard ship, landed on its weedy and deserted home field in Little Rock. We were in the middle of nowhere and without money. We'd failed to convert our military scrip to greenbacks and that left me with one unpleasant option.

I'd reluctantly removed the German Mauser machine pistol from my duffle bag and later startled a pawnshop owner when I pulled it from under my shirt. "Interested in buying an unusual gun," I asked the greatly relieved proprietor. The quick sale got us on the next train out to New York City. We felt like space aliens walking among the pressing crowds of glassy-eyed civilians and even the perfumed and shapely women. Their postwar indifference towards uniforms brought to mind the Rudyard Kipling's poem, *"it's Tommy this and Tommy that when the guns go boom, boom, boom, etc."*

After the brief funeral, we reported to Fort Hamilton and pulled MP patrol duties on the Brooklyn piers. The next week I was chosen to stand the initial Honor Guard watch over the first of the tens of thousands returning war dead from Europe. Their Liberty ship arrived on the morning tide and my jump boots and brass insignia were shined to a polished luster. My starched khaki uniform was void of a single crease. In measured steps I followed the carrying party's solitary flag-draped copper casket past the gangway and into a small airless room at the far end of the cavernous pier. When the bearer detail left, I came to Present Arms then assumed a solemn Parade Rest brace throughout my four-hour watch. Wordlessly, I spoke into the flag's blue galaxy of stars: *How did you die? How old are you? What was your rank?* I felt deeply honored by him, our flag and the uniform we wore. I wondered, too, if after my hoped-for war some soldier might one day be guarding an "unknown" me. The moment's solemnity and the reality of the shortness of life made me realize that a heroic death was infinitely more meaningful than any other. It should be welcomed and not feared.

We'd extended our enlistments for one year and were sent to San Francisco's Port of Embarkation to serve as MPs while awaiting shipment back to Japan. By some Olympian decree, I was again chosen to stand the initial guard over the first returned dead from the Pacific War. An uncanny chill rippled across my shoulders as I Presented Arms over the single casket in an eerily dusty and familiar room. The odds of this happening twice ruled out pure chance and seemed more of an omen. Again, I meditated on the flag draped over the coffin: *How did you die? Were we somehow...connected over time?* I heard nothing in the deathly silence but the drum beat of my heart. I ignored the chair provided for me, and remained braced at Parade Rest throughout my four-hour watch. The thought came again of how I might return from some yet unseen war I knew I was destined to fight.

Before shipping out the following week Richard and I invested our $85.00 monthly pay into a matching pair of long-barreled S&W .45 revolvers, over which I prophesized: "We'll soon be carrying these on the line."

CHAPTER 8

From The Monkey House To Sendai

Our MP MOS (Military Occupation Specialty) posted us within the dark drab Eighth Army's prison walls just outside Tokyo at Nakana-ku. The Japanese had aptly named it the "Monkey House." Winter oil heaters stained the Quonset huts, which also lacked fans against the stifling heat of summer. The mess hall food proved as grim as the atmosphere. The prison detachment's rank and file was completely devoid of spit and polish. They were justifiably bored with their mind-numbing four-hour shifts in the dozen watchtowers lines atop the quasi-penitentiary's thirty-foot high walls.

For some, the deadened predawn hours were sometimes enlivened by the 'ladies of the night,' who climbed up the prison's street-side ladders. An unofficial wink at the practice kept down requests for transfer away from an inmate population that reflected nearly every warped chromosomal pattern in the U.S. Far Eastern Command. Premier among these were the three rapists who murdered then cannibalized a young nurse on Guam. Despite ardent pleas from Mrs. Roosevelt they were hanged shortly after our arrival. So was nineteen-year-old 'Killer Kelly' who bound, gagged, and then cut the throat of a PX sergeant during a robbery.

In preparation for his fall through the gallows trap door he nightly jumped off the top of his cell's desk and, contrary to protocol, defiantly shined his shoes to "look sharp" in the requisite death photo of him still dangling from the gallows rope. On execution nights some ghoulish-natured guards would silently gather near the death chambers outside wall to hear the titillating spring of the trap door, which proved to some to be more entertaining than the dingy Japanese bar adjacent to the prison gate.

The less violent felons were guilty of every crime known to man and occasionally proved troublesome.

Our requests for transfer back to Camp Schimmelpfenning were routinely denied. One night Richard remained on post while I joined some friends and consumed a number of hot sakes, with cold beer chasers then, on a brainless challenge, agreed to run nonstop through some nearby plywood-paper houses. We sanctioned our ill-humored act on what "they" had done in World War II. Our suspicious captain summoned me to the Orderly room next morning when a group of Japanese arrived with their complaints. Richard agreed to go in my place. Then, after I'd walked in ten minutes later, the thoroughly confused witnesses retracted their positive identifications, which saved me from doing six months 'inside.' Magically our transfers to the 17th Regiment of the 7th Division were expedited.

Two days later we were back in Sendai sitting in the MP day room visiting Robertson before reporting in for duty with Able Company that night. Soldiering proved a welcomed relief after prison duties and was peaceful enough despite there being men in the barracks whom we'd previously jailed. Richard and I did little to dispel a circulated rumor that we were CID plants, which our periodic visits to the MP barracks seemed to validate. I did miss those undeniable MP perks of carrying a concealed weapon, noodle shop dinners and *Samurai* movies in Shiogama.

I quickly fell back into the regimen of guard and charge-of-quarter's duties, plus the company's periodic twenty-mile forced-marches to the coastline where we deployed against imaginary invasion forces. Surreally, there were no rifle or machine gun ranges, bayonet courses or advanced training of any kind on the post of a US infantry division, which left me with the impression that—next to the Dutch—ours was the most undertrained army in the world.

Nevertheless we continually improved our language skills in the hopes of commanding whatever Japanese would volunteer to serve in the war that we so ardently wished for. This would include those post security guards who, despite their obvious military bearing and training, would only admit to having fought against the Russians. This hint of 'partisan allegiance' got them cigarettes and pats on the back from approving G.I.s, but I sensed that beneath their mild veneer was an undercurrent of *Bushido* that hoped to reemerge in the dawning of a new warrior era for Japan. Robertson and I endlessly practiced *Kendo* with wooden swords and his Japanese metal shop owner friend in Shiogama converted two bayonets into a matching pair of razor-sharp brass-knuckled trench knives for us.

There was local communist agitation as well as events in Russia, China and nearby Korea that went unreported by *The Stars and Stripes* radio that instead gave endless sports coverage. I thought my psyche might prove the better prognosticator of potential political events when, near the close of May, it reproduced the very lucid dream I had three years earlier, showing me being wounded by a grenade. Then a week later I happened across a group of South Korean officers getting instruction on the operation of the .30 caliber water-cooled machine guns on the parade field. Both they and the heavy guns were a heretofore unseen novelty on the post and the implications sent a wave of goose bumps across my shoulders. This sensation reoccurred again when I answered the company phone at 2400 hours on the night of 27 June. "Able Company, Private Mercy, Charge of Quarters, speaking, sir."

I was sure the leveled voiced caller was a weekend drunk when he said, "Everyone's restricted to the post. War has broken out in Korea!" It turned out to be the regimental commander who'd cut short my scathing reply and had me repeat his explicit orders twice over.

The following night Richard, Frank Korbell and I discussed volunteering for Korea over cold Sapporo beers in a back alley joint in town. A nearby G.I. challenged me to a fight on overhearing me say that the regiment wasn't anywhere near being combat-ready. A lucky right cross sent him through the sliding door and into the alleyway. I'd called for another round of hot sake and beer chasers to celebrate the victory then my opponent suddenly reappeared...

Awakening fully dressed on my cot the next morning I noticed the dried blood on my hands then an order came for me to report to First Sergeant Campbell. He smirked when I entered the Orderly room. "The war is saving your ass from going to the stockade for beating up that Charlie Company soldier." Campbell neither quite forgave nor forgot the many times I'd sent his linemen to the stockade. He hoped to return the favor, but I was prepared to claim amnesia if he waved a charge sheet in my face and stuck to playing dumb.

"What war are you talking about Sarge?"

His eyes narrowed. "You, your brother and half the regiment will find out when we're in Korea next week. You're dis-fuckin'-missed!"

The 'morning after' dehydration found me at the PX for a badly needed milkshake and I noticed how un-movie-like the war-alerted post seemed without the obligatory excited soldiers and vehicles racing to and fro. That changed later when agitated sergeants bellowed for the troops to get aboard the trucks that careened into the battalion compound; then sped two miles north into the dependent's housing area.

The idyllic bliss of the regimental wives was shattered when the trucks screeched to a stop and an NCO shouted, "protect the women and children," and, "don't let hostages be taken!" Some nearby wives were transformed into mute pillars of salt, others stampeded with scooped up children to their homes. The troop's unfamiliar seriousness and aimless double-timing at High Port around the compound added to the alarm. When I snapped on my bayonet and wondered aloud why ammunition hadn't been issued I yelled to Sgt. Campbell. "Are we taking prisoners?"

He sneered at my glance towards a fleeing Japanese houseboy then spoke to the clustering troops in an unusually calm voice. "Alright men, now calm down, take off your jackets, sleep, play ball or abuse yourselves, but stop scaring the hell out of these here women folks!"

Soon the reassured and appreciative ladies brought out tea and graham crackers. The 'warlike' atmosphere had dispelled before we returned to the post in time to change into class A uniforms and stand Retreat formation. Each rifle-armed soldier double-timed out to the company's evening formation and the post's amplified bugle call and National Anthem swept in on the winds of impending war. Bayonet-fixed rifles saluted the Post's lowering Colors to the waves of rolling martial drums that washed over our braced phalanxes. I looked beyond the perimeter's barbed wire fence; the rice paddies reddened by the sinking sun knowing that the 'movie' I'd waited a lifetime for had just begun.

Two days later the many of us selected to be replacements marched in company formations beneath the morning's blazing sun then boarded the awaiting train. Beads of sweat trickled down the deeply furrowed cheeks of the graying stationmaster who fired off a succession of semaphore signals to the train's hissing black engine, as though back in time and on the bridge of some never-to-be-forgotten Imperial flagship. Our 'squadron' of eight rickety old cars creaked past the camp's chain link fence and the rows of waving *geishas*, children and old men. We streaked south past solitary huts, isolated villages, and endless rice fields, headed toward a still unknown destination.

The troops shifted painfully on the hard straight-backed benches that lined the aisle of the smoke-tinged compartments. Some played poker or slept beneath the M1 rifles that hung overhead from every hook and protrusion. Duffle bags stuffed with memorabilia and seasonal uniforms blocked the gangway. The overhead hemp baggage racks groaned with the weight of full field packs, helmets and assorted baseball gear.

I meditatively oiled my pistol, sharpened my bayonet and strangely recalled the words of my European grandmother spoken when I was seven. *"One day you'll fight Russians, but be kind to prisoners."* Then I thought of those flag-draped caskets from Europe and the Pacific and wondered how many of those around me would be coming back in a box: *They're soldiers, though. Not one has questioned where or why we were going.*

Sgt. Campbell's voice shattered my reverie, "Alright you men, I told you to take off those goddamned 7th Division shoulder patches, and so do it now! This here is a goddamned secret move! And pull down those window shades!" It was a laughable precaution against imagined communist spies sitting in the dark with abacuses tallying up our unit's strength as we rattled by through the night. Korbell entered the carriage to tell us he'd heard from a headquarters clerk that all we'll be doing in Korea is MP duty. As the car quieted down the soulful cry of the engine's whistle awakened the memory of our family's 1942 cross country trip and the inescapable fact of our always having lived in a state of continual war for as long as I could remember. I gave in to sleep until the yawning squeal of metallic brakes roused me at dawn.

Fifty Japanese schoolgirls filled the morning air with song and the syncopated clatter of their prancing wooden ketas along the platform beside the flung-open windows of our carriage. In brilliantly patterned kimonos their slate-black hair undulated as sea reeds around their delicate porcelain-like faces during their dragon dance beneath the twin pole banners that a pair of implacable ten-year-old boys held aloft with pride against the rays of a rising sun. The sleepy transfixed soldiers read aloud from the carried banners. "Good Luck in Korea, 7th Division G.I." I smiled: *So much for our secret move!*

The beauty and honor of the dance bestowed by yesterday's 'enemies' touched me deeply. I wondered if it was their traditional *Bushi* farewell for warriors who departed to China and Korea. G.I.s showered the bowing children with silver-wrapped slivers of gum as the train huffed and puffed its way out of the station. A soldier yawningly asked Richard if he really believed we were at war. Richard smiled, and replied, "Only if we see the Red Cross selling hot coffee and doughnuts when we get there." Campbell's voice filled the compartment when the train eventually stopped. "Last stop....everybody out!"

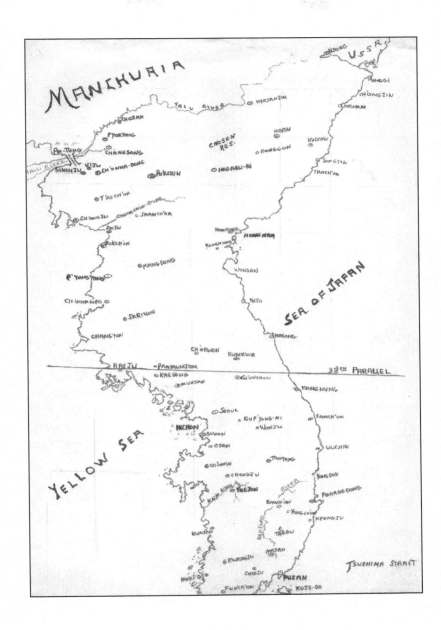

CHAPTER 9

Pusan

We marched into the nearby Fukuoka marshaling yards where some men slept, wrote letters home, or mingled with the other arrived troops awaiting shipment to Korea. Beneath the squawks of circling seagulls I walked past squads of laborers in old tattered Army caps and frayed uniforms to the end of an isolated pier and stared out over the Tsushima Straits: *Was it from here that Admiral Togo launched his attack against the Russian fleet fifty years ago?* The spell was broken by the distantly glimpsed sight of Frank and Richard waving from beside a crowded noodle shop. Inside, the overworked waitresses dashed between tables of hungry G.I.s with bowls of simmering noodles and rice cakes while we sat earnestly discussing the racked vessel tied up at the dock.

"It's either a cut-adrift Singaporean flophouse or salvaged Kamikaze target ship," said Richard, "probably named '*The Scratchy Maru.*'" Our discouragement mounted as some of the waiting 1st Cavalry Division soldiers staggered up the ship's splintered gangplank carrying leather golf bags, radios, guitars and duffle bags. One even had a leashed dog. "It sure doesn't look like we're going into combat," I said.

Once outside my glance shifted to the sleek long-legged young USO hostess that moved towards the ship's gangplank, where she smiled and waved the homeward bound letters the topside troops had entrusted her to mail. Her loosely fitted blouse and trousers failed to camouflage her bouncy agile body. I approached the back of her flaxen-head, with a wistful hope she'd turn with the mist of love in her eyes to my greeting.

"Hello," she echoed back, in monotone flat enough to tame my worst intentions just as Richard arrived. She noted we were twins and took our picture before our group began boarding the next ship in line. Once underway, and after a cold C-ration dinner, I walked aft to where the ship's propellers sent foamy *haiku farewells* to the fading coastline of Japan then later slept on the damp slick port quarter deck until a cry woke me at dawn: "Land Ho!"

Robert (left) with Richard (right) at Nagai, awaiting loading aboard the Scratchy Maru. 4 July 1950. The Korean War has begun.

I strained to see through the foggy drizzle as the ship glided into a murky veil of pungent cooking fats, fish and ship's oil and into Pusan's harbor; and through a sense of déjà vu that whispered the dying words of General Yang aboard his ill-fated junk. "My troop's faithful, they die with me."

As we debarked onto a dank and lifeless pier, Campbell called for volunteers to unload ammunition from the nearby anchored and deserted ships. I was one of forty or so that stepped forward to offset the local stevedore strike. To raise money issues during war was tantamount to treason and I felt it also stained Asia's shield of martial honor. After a Korean MP press gang with a collection of docile laborers relieved us we marched through the morning's ox-cart traffic. Up narrow winding streets we went, past rows of smudgy stucco and rough-hewn wooden houses that proudly flew their national flag.

Glimpses of their interiors showed them to be as worn as the squatting laborers who blankly gazed at our passing column while puffing on arm-length long reed pipes. Ragamuffin urchins begged for food and gum at every turn. Middle-aged women with downcast eyes glided by with bundled wash or unglazed clay pots balanced on their heads. Others sat with suckling babes pressed to their breasts, or nervously smiled through rows of silver-capped or partially missing teeth. I suspected that the poverty-racked country's history of pogroms dictated they hide all attractive women...if there were any.

There were no guards posted around the two-foot-thick walls of the open-gated compound that we walked into, or the enclosed two-storied wood-framed building that was the 24th Division's temporary headquarters. The wall's shadows seemed a temporary escape from the blistering sun, but not the ravenous flies drawn to the serving tables centered in the enclosure and laden with open vats of watery powdered eggs, white bread, green apples and urns of over-boiled coffee. Richard, Frank and I propped up against the wall, awaited the 1100 hours GHQ briefing and joked about the Army's latest social endeavor, 'Operation Flush.'

"Yeah," Richard said, "they released two hundred and fifty G.I.s from the stockades to serve on the line."

Suddenly a voice shouted, "Halt! Halt! Stop that man!" By instinct I bolted to my feet and framed my sights onto the back of the sturdy Korean who momentarily paused atop the far end of the compound wall. Doubt froze my adrenaline and trigger finger, wondering what he'd done and if I'd be court martialed for killing him. I followed him over the wall with shouts to halt as he wove through the surging crowds, *"Tomari, tomari!"*

Catching up, I tackled, then jerked him to his feet, and with a right cross sent him tumbling back head-over-heels down sixty feet of cobblestone steps. He ricocheted off all the walls down to the bottom. My eyes widened in disbelief as he jumped up. Without pause he sprang back up three steps at a time until he stood at my side. I rested my hand on the holstered pistol. He smiled and 'daintily' squeezed the muscles of my other arm. "Ohhhhh, you *verrrry* strong!" He then spun like a dancing Dervish back down the lengthy cobblestone steps and disappeared in a labyrinth of alleyways below. I exhaled and thought, *this is going to be a very long war.*

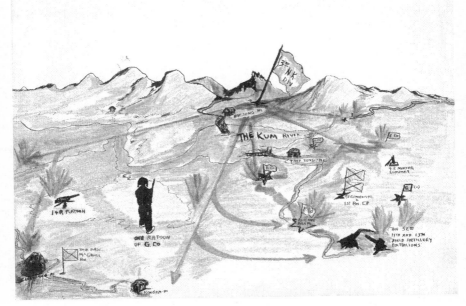

At the Kum River.

Two hours later, a class A uniformed Tokyo GHQ captain arrived with an NCO aide at his side. He motioned us to gather round him, and with a Texas drawl he said: "Stand at ease, men and smoke if you've got 'em. As of 0900 hours this morning there's been no reported contact with any North Koreans. The 1st Battalion of the 24th Division's 21st Regiment was flown in a few days ago. Right now they're tying in with the South Korean army to form a line north of the Kum River, near a town called Osan-ni. They're our most forward unit, but most of you men will be going to the 19th and 34th Regiments, both of which are in reserve. Quite frankly, men, this doesn't look like it's going to develop into much. Nevertheless, you'll all be getting a service ribbon just for being here in Korea, but from the looks of things, that won't be for long."

Muted whistles and rebel yells mingled with sighs of relief from the grinning troops. One of them must have been blindfolded as they passed through town because he asked, "What are the chances of getting a pass, sir, and taking in some Pusan night life?"

An NCO shouted, "Sir, have any South Koreans made contact with the Reds yet?"

The captain grinned broadly. "Not as far as I know." Cheers went up again and the captain continued. "Our intelligence reports that a group of NKs were spotted crossing the 38th Parallel, a bunch of college-aged kids and some younger ones. They apparently decided to come south to raise a little hell. Commies... just tryin' to stir up a fuss before hightailing it back up north."

Another G.I. questioned, "Sir, were they armed?"

The captain smiled. "Well, some of those boys were reported to be carrying sticks and stones, with maybe a few rusted World War II Jap M38 carbines thrown in. And the sons of bitches have an old beat-up truck that they'll be needin' to carry their sorry bruised butts back north, if we catch up with them!" The captain proudly pointed up to the compound's limply hanging stars and stripes. "When they see that flag and your uniforms, those NKs will hightail their pinko asses out of here so goddamn fast we won't even know they'd been here!" A cascade of applauses, rebel yells and laughter roared through the compound.

The captain departed and I turned to Richard and Frank. "The situation doesn't look good. We've got to find a way to get up to the 21st Regiment!" We burst into Campbell's office, made our request and his reply was uncharacteristically modest.

"I don't have any control over how battalion cuts orders. You'll just have to go to where you're told."

"What are our chances of seeing combat with a reserve unit," I asked.

He grinned. "Don't worry, Mercy. If and when the shit hits the fan, there ain't nobody gonna be in reserves for long." That breathed life into my *raison d'etre*.

The true undisclosed intelligence reports of 5 July 1950 told a different story. The few "kids" the captain referred to, were the entire 200,000 man NKPA [North Korean People's Army] and they were all—newest recruits included—in a state of high morale, and eager to taste the intoxicating nectar of battle. Many of them had fled Japanese annexation for the USSR throughout the 1930s. They trained and served under fire with the Russian army from Stalingrad right up to the gates of Berlin.

Others had joined Mao Tse-tung's guerrilla army in northern China and fought both the long-hated Japanese and General Chiang Kai-shek's nationalist forces for over a decade. Several thousand of those troops had just returned from an extensive three-year training program in the USSR. Their division and corps commanders had, as junior officers, served with credit in most of the major battles in World War II. Twenty-seven Soviet army advisors were assigned to the ten attacking NKPA divisions and it was their General Vasiley who gave the order to attack the previous week.

The official GHQ estimate of the NK weapons capacity somewhat exceeded the captain's tally. They'd mustered eight full-strength divisions, two additional understrength infantry divisions, a motorcycle reconnaissance regiment, an armored brigade and a brigade of border constabulary. In addition to their individual and crew-served weapons, which included 120mm mortars, they also had divisions of heavy artillery.

The previous Sunday's predawn salvo at 0430 hours on 25 June came from the NKs entire inventory of 122mm and 76mm artillery, which literally stretched from one coastline to the other. By midday, one hundred and twenty-four of their 280 T-34 tanks were within four miles of Seoul. They had committed 180 new aircraft, including forty Yaks and seventy attack bombers, with more of both in reserve. The Yak fighters had destroyed every American plane on the ground at the Kimpo airfield then strafed and bombed the disintegrating ROK army as it fled south.

On 28 June as the NK army approached the Hangank Bridge that spanned the Han River. ROK engineers prepared to detonate charges to deny the enemy easy access to Seoul. General Pak Il ROK Deputy Chief of Staff ordered the bridge destroyed at 0215 hours, while thousands were queued up to cross over and more than five hundred desperate to escape soldiers and civilians were on the two spans that were exploded. They fell 75 feet to their deaths into the river amid smoldering timbers and twisted steel girders. Blame for the 'mistake' was placed on the ROK chief engineer, a Colonel Choi Chang-sik who was later executed by a firing squad in the staff cover up. By the end of the first week in July the already understrength South Korean army of ninety-five thousand men was reduced to twenty-two thousand. They had been killed, captured or pressed into the North Korean army that was a hundred miles from Pusan. Their high command predicted victory and the total annihilation of all American and "puppet" troops within three weeks. This seemed a reasonable assessment even by our State Department and the Pentagon who feared this was the prelude to an attack on Japan and/or Taiwan by Russia and Red China. President Harry Truman signed an order for the use of atomic weapons if they did, but publically denied that fact. The Joint Chiefs of Staff made hasty preparations for the defense of both and were ready to launch World War III if necessary.

From the end of WWII in August of 1945 communist agitation had made it politically difficult for the newly formed republic. In the five years preceding hostilities there was a major insurrection throughout South Korea with serious clashes along the 38th Parallel and over 100,000 people had died in 'political disturbances,' guerrilla warfare and border clashes. The newly formed South Korean army was grossly underpaid, poorly led, and low on morale. The United States had not supplied them with heavy artillery, tanks, anti-tank weapons or air power for fear that their firebrand president Syngman Rhee might invade the North. They were given only enough ammunition and provisions to maintain them in the field for fifteen days and most of this was lost during the first few hours of combat.

Treachery, such as had occurred two years earlier on the southern Island of Cheju-do, was a concern too. Several hundred members of the South Korean 11th Constabulary Regiment had mutinied in April of 1948 and the fighting lasted until May of '49. Estimated death toll on civilian and military combatants was 60,000. It was brutally suppressed by the South Korean army and all the captured officers and many enlisted ranks of the mutiny were executed, some quite imaginatively. The luckier ones strangled on the gallows and received full volleys from the firing squads stationed beneath the trapdoor. Others terminated under prolonged and agonizing interrogations. It was forbidden by national decree for any citizen to make mention of this uprising under penalty of arrest, torture and/or death. Elsewhere, hundreds of other North Korean instigators and provocateurs were purged from the ROK army, usually by firing squads.

Arrayed against this Asian juggernaut would be our just arrived and understrength 24th Infantry Division of less than nine thousand acutely undertrained men. Ninety-five percent of them had no combat experience and we came without tanks, heavy artillery or even adequate supplies of fresh ammunition; or the trust and confidence of the Commander in Chief and our own officers who didn't or couldn't trust us with the truth of the tactical situation.

Later Richard, Frank and I found a bathhouse in a remote corner of the squalor-racked city to wash off the residual grime and sweat from the ship and troop train. We left our uniforms and boots by the door. Our pistols were within easy reach of the near scalding communal tub that invoked some fond and steamy recollections of Japan, until Frank pointed and shouted, "There!"

His call startled the furtive Korean who'd surely entered to steal our money, uniforms and weapons if he could. My three shots snapped around his head as he flew empty-handed back through the front door. I wasn't sure if it was the tight group shot in Mama-san's rice paper paneling that made her scream, or the sight of our naked bodies giving chase up to the doorway. My inward curses for having twice failed to kill in one day, when I had both the chance and justification, went unheard by the others.

We were on the troop train when it left at 0900 hours for the newly established provincial capital in Taejon, and we returned the appreciative cheers and waves of the Korean MPs that lined the station's tracks. Our dilapidated train steamed into a shimmering countryside of rice fields, and lush green mountains before it slowed to inch its way across a gorge-spanning wooden trestle bridge. Stern-faced guards in raised makeshift towers at both ends of the bridge watched us inch across its yawning rocky chasms. Hours later, Sgt. Campbell's voice echoed throughout the car. "Taejon. Last stop. Everybody off. Taejon!"

CHAPTER 10

Taejon and the Kum

All that was missing in my glimpse through the soot-streaked window was hearing the reverberating clash of the gigantic gong J. Arthur Rank used to open all his adventure movies. Hundreds of chaotic natives desperately surged around the corrugated tin-roofed station to escape on nonexistent southbound trains. Stern-faced Korean MPs with carbines resting on their hips snapped harsh commands at men, dowdy women, children and even the watery-eyed venerable white-bearded elders who uncomprehendingly glared out from beneath their traditional black stovepipe hats. No one was above suspicion. I shouldered my rifle and pack and stepped out into the oppressive heat and pungent smells of the frightened city.

The confused and apprehensive throng waved and cheered with unfathomable words of thanks to our sweat-stained columns, as we marched through streets swarming with ravenous insects and countless refugees. Some lumbered like cattle, pulling overloaded carts filled with the possessions of generations. Fearful women clutched at their infants and children. Excited squads of ragtag boys and bewildered middle-aged men, carrying knives, rusted *Samurai* swords or ancient spears aimlessly milled about in the warlike atmosphere.

Just ahead, the division's repo-depot (replacement center) lay under a blanket of rust-tinged dust from trucks that shuttled troops up to the ever-closer frontlines. I immediately filled my cartridge belt and took extra bandoleers from a supply table. The 110° temperature overrode the order to remain in the immediate area and drove several of us to the nearby Kum River Bridge. I stood watch beneath its iron girders while the others splashed through the rippling downcast shadows of troops, vehicles and hundreds of civilians fleeing south. I compulsively checked and rechecked my rifle's chambered round while a knot of civilian men meandered about a hundred yards out. My thoughts flew back to that rainy night in Sendai and the dog I shot while on guard duty: *Harden yourself for combat...if you can kill an innocent dog...people should prove easier.* That tested ethos had left my heart more saddened than steeled. The whistling heat and Richard's shout snapped me back. "Hey, it's your turn to swim."

Forty miles away NK divisions besieged the South Korean lines while American and Australian fighter planes mistakenly bombed and strafed ROK ammunition trains and road-bound troops who'd never seen a tank before the Russian-built T-34s smashed across their border. Most fled in wild panicky retreat, but a few emulated their despised Nipponese cousins and dove with high explosives strapped on their backs beneath the thrashing treads of the enemy's perusing armor.

As I swam, thirty-three T-34s reached the not too distant town of Osan-ni and outflanked Colonel Smith's recently arrived task force. His two rifle companies, a total of 400 men from the 21st Regiment's 1st Battalion, were rumored to be the lowest-disciplined and most non-combat-ready unit throughout all of occupied Japan. Colonel Smith was wounded and a hundred G.I.s died, as did the left-behind wounded who were shot and/or bayoneted. News that the NKs weren't taking prisoners spread like wildfire back to U.S. positions on the north side of the Kum River where the 34th Infantry Regiment dug in around P'yong'taek.

When we returned to the repo-depo compound from our swim we listened to a corporal who stood on a box as he read aloud from his roster. "Korbell, the 34th, Sgt. Campbell the 21st, the Mercy brothers, the 19th..." Another two dozen soldiers were also assigned to the "Rock of Chickamauga" regiment, which was in division reserve eight miles north of Taejon near the winding Kum River. After he informed us that it would be hours before we departed I felt there was enough time to follow an urgent impulse to go back into Taejon alone. The city had changed and swelled into a mosaic of frightened, tired and often treacherous eyes that seemingly sensed its own doom. I waded in blessed ignorance through a parting sea of white linen-clad refugees and probably more than a few NK agents, guerrillas and political provocateurs.

My newly acquired M3 grease gun hung from my neck. My shouldered M1, two bandoleers, bayonet, boot knife and a western-holstered pistol added to my sense of security, as did the .32 Mauser and blackjack concealed under my fatigue jacket. I providently knocked on the building's door where some ROK soldiers had just entered. It turned out to be a district stationhouse for the Draconian National Police.

A poised young lieutenant answered. He studied me from head to toe then returned the salute with his eyes glued to my grease gun and invited me into his sparse quarters for conversation and tea. The room held an antique wooden chair, a small mahogany table, a calligraphy scroll and an acetate-covered area map pinned to one wall. His ammo, carbine and helmet rested against the other. He clapped his long tapered hands twice as we sat on the matted floor and a boyish soldier of about fifteen entered. His bow was shrouded in respectful silence and with downcast eyes placed a steaming teapot tray with two cups between us then exited without a glance.

My eyes swept past the lieutenant's shoulder, out the open rear window and onto a gray pockmarked wall in the enclosed courtyards. Parked outside the opened back gate were two flatbed trucks, with a cargo of twenty kneeling, rope-tied civilian prisoners on each. The wicker dunce cap-like basket hats each wore obscured their bowed heads. Angry sneering guards stood over them with fixed and readied bayonets. The lieutenant's question drew my gaze from the window. "And how did you happen to become a soldier?" He nodded appreciatively over my summarized history. "Well, thirteen is rather young for military duty with Westerners, isn't it?"

I felt flattered. "True, sir, but it's been my lifelong dream to serve here in Asia." We smiled and our raised piping hot cups of tea clinked in salute. *He looks like Richard Loo, the actor in The Purple Heart.* A sudden shrill cry rang up from the courtyard. "*Charyott* [Attention]!"

Behind him, below in the yard, six civilians lined themselves up against the wall as he politely locked his gaze on my grease gun. A command sounded and a volley rang out then another six quietly took their place at the wall, *Just like in that film, Dragon Seed.* I smiled over that quick remembrance. The lieutenant cooed, "Hmm, I see you approve of our handling of these communists" then dipped his teacup towards my gun. "How much easier my work would be if I had such a weapon," he sighed.

I sipped loudly, gesturing an appreciation of both his tea and sentiments and my mind raced: *These prisoners will die either way... if I complied Asian etiquette required that he reward me with something of 'equal value'... I've always wanted to be on a firing squad... with my grease gun, I could do the job alone...it could be my baptism of fire, harden me up as a soldier...no hesitation, a killer even before I hit the line!* His thin lips curled in self-satisfaction. I was sure he'd read my mind as the cry of "*Charyott*" rang out again. The next volley seemed to echo with threats of divine retribution should I fulfill my fantasies and that sudden uncovered sense of consciousness might prove troublesome. The impatient lieutenant's repressed tensions spewed out as more civilians stepped over the mound of dead to silently take their place against the blood-speckled wall.

"But, you … you already have two other fine guns! Surely, you could leave one with me?" When the third courtyard volley rang, I struck a match to light my cigarette and its flare reflected from the lieutenant's eyes the degree of "face" I'd lost. His body stiffened then fanned away the pack of Lucky Strikes I offered and in a wounded voice whispered, "No, no, I am Christian." I quickly butted out the cigarette, bowed apologies and raised my tepid cup in a farewell salute. I felt as disillusioned as he seemed to be over my newly discovered weakness. Nevertheless we exchanged farewell bows at the door where he longingly glanced again at the departing grease gun. "I wish you luck in Korea, G.I. soldier."

Back at the depot I had time to spare before Richard and I, along with fifteen others departed on the truck. When it delivered us to our destination a large swarthy NCO stood in the center of the road. Between his jutting jaw and bushy eyebrows sat black angry eyes that seemed to appraise our worth.

"I'm Sergeant Hungerford, and I wanna welcome you men to George Company, the best goddamned line outfit in the regiment!"

I smiled: *He'd be perfect as Sergeant Markoff in Beau Geste!*

Then he nodded towards a nearby table and the assorted weapons and ammunition that shimmered in the late day sun. "If any of you men feel up to carrying a BAR then help yourselves and take whatever else you might like, too." It all seemed so familiar, the officers and NCOs hunched together over outstretched maps in the nearby hut and the helmetless troops that lazily lounged against rocks and trees writing letters home. *It's like every war movie I've ever seen.*

Hungerford barked, "A-TEENN-SSHUN!" and looked as though he was witnessing the second coming as a lean six-foot-two officer approached. The dark penetrating eyes that flashed across our openly expectant faces seemed familiar with war and his voice was resonant.

"Stand at ease, men. I'm Captain Michael Barszcz, and we're going into what might turn out to be... war." He paused while two other officers arrived at his side. "That's right, men. War. That means fighting and dying; and this story may well be written in 'blood, sweat and tears' before it's over."

The files of ragtag troops that passed on the nearby southbound road drew our riveted gazes. Most were without weapons, others wore them like beach towels slung around their neck. Some sported native straw hats, were barefoot and looked nothing like the battle-weary film heroes I remembered of Bataan and Corregidor that stoically marched with their walking wounded. The prideless column drew our dismayed whispers. "Who and what are those sorry-looking people? What could have driven American soldiers into that kind of pathetic retreat?"

Major Melecio J. Monteclaros (S-319th Infantry, left) and Captain Michael Barszcz, Jr. ("G" Company commander, right).

Sgt. Hungerford's snarl broke the demoralizing spell. "Don't look at those goddamned disgraceful bug-outs—they dishonor us all!" The captain's lip twitched into a sardonic sneer. Crimson-faced, Hungerford bellowed again. "They're bug-outs, and that's one thing this here goddamned company ain't never gonna do!" He spat and turned his back on what were Task Force Smith survivors from Osan-ni, and the stragglers who'd deserted the 34th Regiment at the village of P'yong'taek. Our heads hung in shame until they passed and when the captain left Lieutenant Robert L. Herbert of the 2nd Platoon took his place.

He was in his mid-twenties, slight of build, with a square jaw and a saber-like scar across one cheek: *He looks Germanic, perfect for the role of Michael in The Prisoner of Zenda*. His pale blue eyes stared blankly as he gestured broadly and less articulately than the captain. "Sixteen BARs men, one for each squad. Machine guns, mortars—you name it, we got it—and the enemy will rue the day they run into us. And one more thing, men—I expect each and every one of you to do his duty!" Richard and I nodded approval to each other. Later we discussed the pros and cons of carrying a sixteen-pound Browning automatic rifle that unappealingly lacked a bayonet stud.

We talked while we field stripped and cleaned our weapons as another retreating column passed by. We agreed on its possible causes, the Army's overemphasis on sports in lieu of training, which for soldiers meant doing nothing but playing ball, devouring steaks and milkshakes, and titillating some officers' wives.

The voice of our new platoon sergeant, Sergeant Grenno, scoffed out from behind us. "Y'all ain't seriously thinkin' about carryin' all that there shit are yah?"

There's some truth about first impressions.

"You bet your ass, Sarge," I said, "I'm hoping to draw a lot of fire."

He remained expressionless. "Well don't do it around me. The captain was gonna split you two up, but seein' as how this here thing's gonna be all over in another week or two he figured it'd be okay keepin' y'all together."

Near nightfall I wondered what tomorrow would bring while watching the perimeter guards being posted and strangely thought of Ronald Coleman in *A Tale of Two Cities*. I whispered his famous line: "Tis a far, far better place I go than I have ever known..."

Canteen water doused out our small fires and streaked the dawning sky with puffs of grey smoke. Richard shouldered his new BAR and waved from the squad ahead as George Company took its first step into the Korean War. Happily I marched in cadence to the rhythmical clanging of my multiple bandoleers until the shots that rang out ahead started the company across the open paddies on our left flank. My heart beat faster and I felt it pulsing in my hand when I slammed the unsheathed bayonet onto the rifle's stud; and thought of every cinematic charge I'd ever seen. I slogged a few yards ahead then stopped in mid-splash: *Something's missing...what? It's...the musical soundtrack!* I whispered aloud: "I HEAR NO BUGLES!"

That's when the growing tempo of fire sent me leaping behind a paddy wall and shouting thirty yards ahead to Greeno. "I'll cover you, Sarge!" His back was stiffly pressed to the rear wall of the single hut just ahead and his eyes, like a lighthouse beacon, swept shafts of fear from side to side. He'd signaled me forward into the company's forming line of outgoing fire where I wondered why the Gooks weren't shooting back. Then I recognized the South Korean flag being desperately waved by one of the hilltop soldiers 250 yards away. My thrice screamed call to cease fire went unheeded. The overzealous troop's lack of fire discipline proved equal to their marksmanship, which failed to hit a single ROK within their tightly packed formation. When we pulled back to the road, my head buzzed with questions: *Why would a WWII veteran like Greeno freeze up. Why didn't they recognize the flag we're here to defend? More importantly, how did so many bad shots find their way into this company?*

The next day the captain pulled me out of the company's strung-out column when it began its upward climb into bushy low-lying hills; where I stood drenched in sweat listening for his orders. He pointed into the deepening blackness of the night shrouded fields then told me to dig in, and not let a living thing get through.

His trust in me to singly guard the company's isolated flank filled me with pride and got me through the night's attack of grasshopper-sized mosquitoes. Those monsters penetrated my fatigue jacket, pants and even the thick gobs of putrid rice paddy mud I'd smeared across my face, neck and hands. At sun rise their welts oozed a sticky white resin. One G.I., driven mad by the attacking swarms, was still trying to escape into an empty C-ration carton case, when the medics arrived to cart him off.

We maneuvered through more of the heat-stifling days and nights and my annoyance with the Army and G Company grew. I wondered why we didn't stand and fight the phantom NKs that were encircling us and whether I'd ever get to fight in combat. I discarded all but two of my bandoleers, suspecting they'd never be used.

North of Chongsan, we crossed a dry riverbed and the captain remarked on the olive drab handkerchief pinned Japanese style to the back of my helmet. "You look like a goddamned Arab, Mercy."

I smirked and the words were out of my mouth before I knew. "It's in keeping with the company's bug-out tactics, sir."

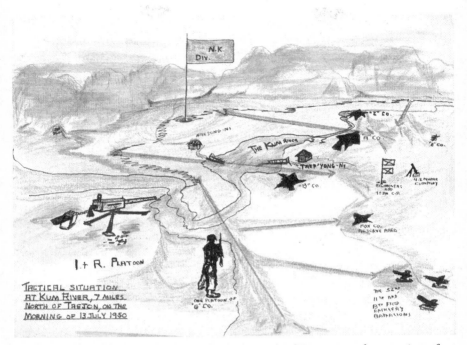

Tactical situation at Kum River, 7 miles north of Taejon, on the morning of 13 July 1950.

Richard crossed swords with him on the following day as the company dug in four hundred yards from a NK unit that leisurely sniped at us. Barszczs ordered his men to cease fire, but Richard insubordinately squeezed off a full clip then leapt from his foxhole.

The astonished captain shouted, "Where in hell do you think you're going?"

Richard pointed down the reverse slope to the tree next to the CP. "Right over there, sir, 'til I'm allowed to shoot back."

We surmised, after the unmolested North Koreans pulled out, that Washington was perhaps hoping to gain a truce by keeping the NK casualty count down.

Torrential rains and flash floods swamped our mess kits and turned the roads into flowing rivers of sludge. All planes were grounded. The NKs moved no less quickly to deliver their supplies to the Kum River than the dysentery I had after foolishly drinking from Asia's polluted fields. Rudyard Kipling was wrong when he penned in *Gunga Din*, "tis better this, than none."

After tightening up my pistol belt two more notches I moved with the

73

platoon through a squall of incoming 120mm mortar shells. Then dug in and held a female target in my sights, convinced she was the enemy's forward artillery observer. Squatting alone 150 yards out on the road, she was indifferent to the shelling. She stared and mouthed out words as she gazed up at our hill. I would have bet she had a radio strapped to her thighs. After I'd called to Sergeant Mayes for permission to kill her he studied her through field glasses. "Forget it, Mercy, she ain't doin' nothing."

Two more 120 rounds screamed in.

I stared at him blankly. "Sure, any nitwit can see that she ain't doin' nothing!" The dust cleared, and 'Komrade Heroine' was gone: *How did we ever win World War II?*

Early the next morning low flying B-26s dropped strings of five-hundred-pound bombs on the high ground directly across the river we'd approached, sending up clouds of black smoke, shredded trees, rocks and bodies. I shouted to the planes, "Save some for us!" Then we dug in a few miles from the steel girder bridge at Tapp'yong-ni, while eight miles back in Taejon, General Dean labored over how to hold the line for five more days as General MacArthur had ordered. Outside his headquarters were a platoon of riflemen, a company of M4 Sherman's from the 78th Tank Battalion and some batteries of anti-aircraft artillery. He was dismayed by the poor performance of his troops and incompetent officers in the widely dispersed and under strength regiments. He ordered the 649-man remnant of his badly mauled 21st Regiment to keep the divisional escape route south of Taejon open. They got strafed by Yak fighter planes through the day.

Our regiment, technically in reserve, had its 1st Battalion strung out for six miles along the river, a distance normally covered by two divisions. The 2nd and 3rd Battalions struggled to plug up the many punctures the NK made in our MLR (main line of resistance). Easy Company was six miles to the east and several miles below the 1st Battalion, near the village of Sinhung-ni and a critical railroad trestle bridge. They were tied in with the ROK 2nd Division on their right. Some 4.2" mortars and three batteries of 105mm howitzers were a few miles behind us.

P-51 planes attacked and barely scratched the enemy tanks dug in across the river. With their nine yard belts of ammunition expended they left and the NKs sent across a flotilla of reinforced infantry companies. They landed unscathed, thanks to the 34th Infantry's new S-3 officer. He didn't call in artillery fire because he was saving the diminished supply of 155mm rounds for the enemy's "big push." Once the NKs gained a toehold, he and the entire battalion S-2 staff (Intelligence), along with all of King Company (heavy weapons), came down with a contagious case of 'combat fatigue' and left!

My platoon was rushed by trucks to block an enemy breakthrough in the nearly-disintegrated 34th Infantry Regiment's lines. There, platoons of heavily camouflaged NKs were maneuvering in behind mortar barrages to cut off the fleeing G.I.s as we arrived. I fired eighty tracer rounds at maximum range, which drew in some unwanted mortar fire. We broke for the trucks that 'red-balled' back to George Company's shrinking perimeter just behind the 1st Battalion line. Hours later the proverbial dam on the southern banks of the Kum River disintegrated under the crushing flood of NK regiments that all but annihilated our mortar and field artillery positions. The howitzers they captured were used to cut off forward troops at roadblocks, who were still unaware of the overall situation. The rear areas were in total panic.

Three North Korean divisions rapidly closed in on the decimated 24th Division. A fourth enemy division broke through the ROK division on our right and an hour later our division's fate was sealed. The NKs set up a roadblock on what was our only assessable escape route, six miles south of the city. Shock and denial swept through headquarters. They chose to believe that the encircling troops were 'friendlies'—all forty thousand of them! Distant cousins to the mild-mannered Apache, the ruthless NKs attacked with tanks, artillery, and mortars and took no prisoners. The numerical odds were five to one and climbing.

Enemy fire destroyed all our artillery communication trucks and other radios. From headquarters on down what equipment remained, including crew-served individual weapons, were all WWII worn out junk. There was no ammo for the 57mm recoilless rifles, and no armor piercing shells for what 105mm Howitzer batteries were left. The 2.63" bazooka rounds bounced off the heavily armored T-34 tanks, M1 rounds too often failed to fire and hand grenades were nonexistent. Air support was spread wafer-thin and was usually "badly needed somewhere else." Morale was low and confusion high, and was it not for the time-honored custom of keeping troops totally uninformed absolute panic would have ensued. Washington and GHQ in Tokyo were willing to pay the price of one lost U.S. division, with a skeletal ROK army thrown in, to buy the time General 'Bull' Walker would need to build up defenses and hold the port at Pusan.

The company dug in on the hilly terrain west of the Taejon airstrip, while air strikes hit on both sides of the river. A fiery mass of burning huts set the night sky aglow and the clatter of rifles and machine guns were everywhere. A brief quiet followed, but a predawn flare ignited the firmament anew. The NKs crossed the river in force and quickly

75

annihilated most of Charlie Company's two hundred men. They easily breached the mile-wide gap between the 1st Battalion and what remained of the 34th Infantry Regiment's far right flank.

The captain and Hungerford were back in the city when two of the many T-34s loaded with infantry wiped out the headquarters' CP and an entire service company unit. They got pinned down amid squads of dead G.I.s. A steel sliver from the tank's 76mm gun pierced the back of Hungerford's skull. He refused medical treatment, little realizing that this wound would come back to haunt him in later years.

The scorching sun played havoc with my worsening dysentery. I left my rifle in the foxhole as Herbert ordered and made a series of round trips back up from the trucks parked along the road with twenty-gallon water cans in each hand while he carried nothing. His walkie-talkie crackled.

"The company was falling back," he said, but no shots had been fired. Herbert's self-appointed corporal's job was clearly to get him away from the approaching enemy and closer to the road on which to escape. He shouted, "Get up there and tell Sgt. Greeno I'm going back to look for a radio Jeep!"

I smirked as he ran down the hill knowing that a court martial board of his peers wouldn't find a fellow officer guilty of deserting his soon-to-be overrun platoon so he could fill some canteens and find a Jeep to aid his escape.

Greeno cleared the platoon off the ridgeline, and waved me back from retrieving my immaculately cleaned and freshly oiled rifle. I quickly found another discarded one on the road then boarded a waiting truck. We sped away as enemy artillery rounds and strings of machinegun fire cut through the sweltering air. We dismounted minutes later near the tail of the company column. A voice called back from up front, "We're heading for an NK roadblock that's got us locked in."

I snapped on my bayonet.

The NKs had dug in on both sides of the road for a mile and a half in depth, and their tanks rampaged a short distance behind us in the body-strewn streets of the ravaged city. Ahead, a stopped truck turned around and raced back down and through our parting columns. An MP Officer shouted from its fender, "TANKS! TANKS!"

That filled me with excitement, and a not fully acknowledged fear. I peered out from the roadside ditch with the rest of the company's dust-coated faces and awaited the arrival of the dreaded T-34s. A quick search of my memory bank couldn't recall a film that showed rifles stopping tanks, but did deliver one delusional stratagem: *If I could fire enough armor-piercing rounds into the tank's barrel, it might ignite the round in the breech, and blow it all sky high!*

When Hungerford bellowed, "Saddle up," we advanced to within four hundred yards of the obstacle, with squads from each platoon fanned out along the ridges. Then I fired at the concealed NK rifleman who opened up on Richard's platoon across the road and enjoyed the weapon's jolt, the sweet scented blowback of cordite, but cursed not knowing if my rounds tore through camouflaged men or genuine trees. In a blink the hillside erupted alive with staggering shrubbery.

Two ROK P-51s skimmed in low with all guns blazing and their rockets wreathed the foliage with severed arms and legs. I hoarsely shouted into its savage beauty. "Kill them all!" My thought was they were only the flank guards and not the MLR. The planes snapped off fewer rounds on their second run before winging off to help the nearly destroyed 1st Battalion.

A wall of NK fire then turned us back and left dead and wounded where they fell. I leapt into a roadside ditch and one good whiff of my sweat-drenched fatigues, mingled with the gaseous scented blood that had coated my mouth for days, sent me into a gut-wrenching puking spasm. I dashed to the damaged Sherman tank that our regimental commander, Colonel Meloy, had commandeered and driven through the roadblock; and got close enough to hear him talking with Captain Barszcz.

"All communications with Taejon are cut, and the last anybody saw of Dean, he was chasing a T-34 with a bazooka. Those goddamn tankers wouldn't attack the gauntlet's machine gun positions, unless riflemen went with them. The bastards just buttoned up and crashed through the roadblock and deserted the pinned down infantry. Then the troops refused to attack! It's not like the old days, Mike, that's for sure. Oh, one more thing, the 21st Regiment failed to keep the division's escape route open."

Soldier down.

An ill-placed NK rifle round cut short Malloy's critique, which sent everyone splashing across the fetid fields in hot pursuit of some way out.

Back in the all but vanquished Taejon city, fear had broken down discipline and men deserted their disintegrating commands individually and in groups. A few hardcore soldiers fought with rifle and bayonet while a hundred other exhausted and trapped men foolishly chose to surrender. Others ran pell-mell into the enemy-infested hills after they wisely torched all their abandoned trucks. We later found the body of a chaplain who was bayoneted along with the fifty litter-bound G.I.s he would not leave.

The salty brine in my eyes blurred out the hillside targets. The fallen wounded cried out in anguish against the unbridled stampede for survival all around them. And I double checked the 'last round' in my rifle's butt plate. A fiery impact between my shoulders suddenly arched me backward as a. jet zoomed by overhead. I mistook its ejected 20mm cannon casing as 'the bullet that had my name on it.' Strangely enough I was calmer during the sporadic rain of bursting shells that followed and found joy through the clips of tracer rounds I emptied into the detachment of NKs doing their skin-peeling 'dance of death' in the consuming $1,000°$ flame of hissing napalm. We all cheered the stench of their burning flesh.

Suddenly there were trucks to board and we laid down cover fire for a dozen Baker Company survivors who slogged through the bullet-impacted paddies some one hundred yards ahead. The trucks geared back in reverse for half a mile to where Barszcz waved his pistol toward a roadside villa. Richard and I hacked a firing port through its outer wall. *Damn, it's almost like the film Beau Geste... with the Legionnaires at Fort Zinderneuf.* I smiled at Richard as I arranged my bandoleers and did an impression of Sgt. Markoff after he'd driven off the attacking Bedouins.

"They'll come. They'll come when I want them." Richard rolled his eyes.

Sgt. Hungerford bellowed, "Saddle up," shattering my last stand fantasies. I cursed aloud when I passed him and Barszcz along the road.

The captain pulled me aside. "Forget my rank for a minute and tell me what's bugging you?"

Six years of military conditioning evaporated in a flash. "Why don't we stand and fight them, sir? We could pile them up, Captain, if we really put our minds to it!"

His poker-faced stare betrayed nothing, including the fact that we were low on ammunition, out of radio contact with everyone and had six hundred dead in our regiment alone; and the three NK divisions who were in hot pursuit had us virtually boxed in on four sides The captain's voice was edgy when he said,. "You're a soldier, Mercy. You follow orders and do what you're told. Now get back to your squad and stop bitching!"

Only later did the gravity of the situation become clear when Barszcz allowed a junior lieutenant, who insisted that his men call him 'Joe,' talk to the company. "Listen, men, I think I can get us out, and the captain approves of me giving you this option. Escape with me by truck to Pusan, or stay here and die."

Richard and I wondered why thirty soldiers, who were never to be seen again, would follow any officer who'd surrendered his rank for the name of Joe.

Richard whispered, "You realize we haven't seen or heard a plane in over twenty-four hours?"

Barszcz shouted. "Saddle up!"

The captain headed north, and we dutifully followed.

CHAPTER 11

Which Way Out?

Dysentery and ravenous thirst plagued me during our muffled race through the ominous hills and sweat blurred my eyes as I searched for signs of ambush along the boulder-strewn trail. Then, in the swelter of high noon, an entire platoon mindlessly broke from the column with their open canteens loudly clanging to be filled from a nearby stream. The angry captain's carbine pointed at a pocket of men that emerged from the woods a hundred yards off. "God damn it men, we don't even know who they are!"

My sights remained on their point man's chest: *Uniforms off dead G.I.s had been used before to infiltrate our lines.* As they orbited closer, I wondered why they weren't pulled into our company to augment its firepower, but felt their anxiousness to escape would make them useless in a firefight.

A panicky Herbert ordered me to follow him up a flanking trail to an overturned .30-caliber water-cooled machine gun. I uprighted it, adjusted the sights and racked a round into the chamber.

"Stay here Mercy, and cover the company's retreat. NKs are coming up from behind!" *What was it about me that radiated expendability?* My mumbled curses and thoughts trailed behind him racing back towards the retreating column: *Why should I stay to die while they all run. Kill him. No... leave him wounded for the NKs to find.*

Curiously I remembered a touching scene from *For Whom the Bell Tolls,* showing a mortally-wounded Gary Copper who stayed behind with a machine gun to cover the escape of both his band of Spanish partisans and girlfriend Maria. Ingrid Bergman cried in anguish from the back of her galloping horse, "Roberto! Roberto!"

I threw the gun's firing mechanism, tripod and ammo in four directions then followed the familiar trail of abandoned equipment up to the rear of the moving column where Richard anxiously waited. We found it strange that U.S. troops behind enemy lines would throw away their ammo and weapons, blindly hoping that if captured without them they'd be spared: *If we run into real trouble...it would be just like Taejon...every man for himself.* Richard and I shared an uncommon luxury in the company, and possibly the entire Army. We knew we'd never desert each other.

Some of the greedier troops up forward had 'double-dipped' into the evening's C-rations as they were passed back, leaving a half dozen of us at the rear hungry and disillusioned; and disheartened enough so that we fell back as a self-appointed rear guard, and watched the company disappear into the gathering dusk before we continued on.

Near dusk a flash of movement in a nearing courtyard prompted me to scale the wall with an unpinned grenade, but nothing was found. Back on the road we quickened our pace beneath the stars that guided us south until the menacing sounds of running feet from behind drove us into the covering foliage of a roadside culvert from where I could literally feel the tension emanating from the approaching twenty soldiers. The first syllable of my whisper froze them into biblical-like columns of stone. "Pssst, don't shoot... We're G.I.s."

All of them sighed with relief when we stepped onto the road and one spoke. "We spotted some Gooks an hour ago, but we don't think they picked up our trail. We're looking to tie in with a larger unit."

They left in happy pursuit of our company while we waited two hours in ambush for the unsuspecting NKs who never arrived. We marched on through a veil of hungry mosquitoes until 0200 hours when we dug in on a small hilltop above a truncated dirt road. I took the first watch and mused over how easily it had been of late to drift off between wakefulness and sleep, never quite sure of which state I was in.

Suddenly, it was dawn, and I noticed Richard and the others cautiously peering up from their flanking shallow foxholes. "What's up, Richard?"

He paused then whispered, "What's up? Damn!" Then correctly concluded to the others what had happened. In my restless sleep I'd called out, "BARs to the right," and remained alert through the hours that passed. No one smiled as they moved down onto level ground and heated coffee over a twig fire while I headed off some forty yards to scan the winding road. There was no telling how close the NKs might have gotten during the night.

The preoccupied squad amazingly took no notice of the nine white-clad young men that approached in a quasi-column of twos formation, with total suppression of normal arm swing—in a failed hope of appearing nonmilitary. The butt plate of my rifle rested on one hip as they halted five feet away.

Their devious leader coyly cooed, "Oh, nice rifle—me see?"

Those words would be your last if I were a Jap or Korean... and could be yet, too, for thinking me as dumb as those assholes by the fire. I replied, "Okay."

He beamed broadly until I loudly ejected the ammo clip and flipped him the empty piece. Anxiety emanated from his motionless column and their fearful eyes looked neither left nor right. No one knew what would happen next. All those tensions still went unnoticed by Richard and the others while I inwardly deliberated the risks of firing my M1, or how far their screams might be heard if we either bayoneted them, or just cut their throats. What would we do with their bodies? If the Gooks showed up and found them they could pick up our trail, or maybe radio ahead someplace to cut us off. We'd be in deep dung and taking them prisoners would be a problem, too: *...but any fast moves from them and they'd all be dead meat.*

In the silent minutes that passed they'd wisely chosen not to jump me. I smirked at the enigma, thinking that those sons of bitches must have done a lot of chanting to Buddha as I watched them walk away unscathed. Maybe if I had joined the lieutenant's firing squad back in Taejon, this would have turned out differently. Yet, you can't trust the Army, the country and much less the politicians to back you up, should some action you take become 'controversial.' All those entities wanted to be seen on the moral high ground: *We should be more like the Japanese and Germans and just shoot suspects on sight!* It was a moral battle between instinct, norms and the fear of punishment.

At midday in a deserted village I questioned a grinning old toothless woman who told me in Japanese that she'd seen no NK soldiers. Behind her the squad gently ransacked the hut for food and the ever illusory case of cold beer. We made do with the unearthed bottle of milk saké she gifted to us as we left. It helped fuel the chase of a wild goose we caught, and later traded off for a helmet full of cold bland low-grade rice to the sole occupant of the next hamlet. Each man got one sticky handful.

Near dusk in another abandoned village Richard and I broke into a barbershop where he began to shave me in the establishment's solitary worn out chair. The elderly Korean who'd suddenly burst through the door pointed his wizened finger back towards the road we'd come in on; and we noticed the not too distantly rising cloud of khaki tinted red dust. We exhaled in unison: "T-34 tanks!"

Following my hasty bow of thanks for a gesture that had it been seen by an enemy, would have forfeited the Korean's life. We double-timed with the squad through the night and only stopped occasionally to press our ears to the ground, hoping not to hear the sounds of running feet or rumbling armor. By chance we overtook a small group of G.I.s who were just ahead. After a quick exchange of names, companies and regiments I cautioned them against 'bugging-out' in the event of trouble. That prompted a headquarters clerk to hand me the two maps he said he'd taken off a dead Gook.

Richard and I took point when we moved out at dawn and then studied the official looking two-storied wooden building that sat 200 yards ahead. No signs of life showed around or from within its low stucco walls, but the dirt road gave indications of recent traffic. We closed in with the squad and found a stony-faced South Korean soldier walking his post inside the shadowy courtyard. His unfriendly glare cautioned against blindly entering where unseen guns could have wiped us out in a blink: *Could be an NK dressed in a captured uniform...or covering for a bunch of deserters...who might have killed their officers.*

Richard withdrew backward with a leveled BAR, covering our quickened pace down the desolate road that eventually led to the banks of a fast moving river. We'd discovered that the raft we made from tree limbs bound together wouldn't stay afloat under the weight of more than one man. My rifle and ammo dangled from my neck as Richard launched my solo downstream voyage with a wish: "Hope you don't draw any enemy fire."

Within the hour I was unceremoniously beached where the squad later found me sopping wet then joked about it until dusk. That's when we met the Buddha on the road.

"Where's North Korean army?" I asked the humble farmer.

His eyes twinkled as he pointed behind him, *"Iie, Iie, G.I. asoko desu* [No, no, G.I. is there]!"

It was a relief to reach the American lines, such as they were, without foxholes, tanks or artillery. From the unprepared looks of it I wasn't surprised that no reconnaissance or combat patrols had been sent out. Inside the compound the soldier-clerk who'd given me the maps the previous night asked to have them back. Clearly, they had been given as a precaution against his torture, had we fallen into enemy hands. I suspected he imagined winning a Bronze Star and maybe a cushy rear-echelon job for his heroic find. When he asked for the maps again I told him to shut up or I'd step on his worthless face.

Richard and the others searched for food while I gave a snappy salute and the captured maps to a neatly dressed second lieutenant inside the battalion HQ tent.

"Private Mercy, Robert, W. reporting in with eleven men for duty, sir."

His glance shifted from the maps to my holstered revolver as he told me about his cavalry unit's unopposed landing at Pohang, before he switched into his best used-car salesman's pitch.

"You're safe now. You won't need that pistol."

My eyeballs banked off his upturned palm and looked into his conniving eyes. "Sir, I'll surrender my rifle, if ordered, but not the pistol. That's private property." *Another goddamned thieving officer!*

He took the M1 and I headed off for the boxes of supplies I'd noticed stacked in the ambulance parking area. Once cushioned between some crates I stared back down the road we'd traveled. Then an unwanted cataleptic sleep overtook me, in which I could not move, speak nor close my eyes; but somehow remained consciously alert—though appearing dead to any casual observer. I was keenly aware of the two medics who approached and looked into my unblinking eyes. "Holy shit, he's dead!"

"Naw,"answered the second medic after drawing closer to my face. "The poor son of a bitch is only asleep."

Then they left. My vision encompassed the shadowy gray road beneath the star-studded sky: *The NKs wouldn't take me by surprise.*

CHAPTER 12

When Do We Hold

The night's tortured vigil had left me near exhausted but I found Richard and the others in the mess tent, catching up on lost meals and stateside news from the newly arrived troops.

"We heard the 24th Division had fallen back to 'alternative' positions," said one soldier.

"There's nothing alternative about a route," I yawned.

Another said, "Most articles and editorials back home are on which politician is soft or hard on communism, sports scores and crime reports."

Another voice laughed, "Yeah, and who's sleeping with who, and what, in Hollywood."

Then one G.I. asked about the NKs. "Never surrender or take one of them alive," I advised.

After evening chow a truck brought us back to the nearby 19th Infantry straggler collection point and while the others searched for their platoons I isolated myself by a solitary tree and risked another smell test of my fetid fatigues. I got the same regurgitating results. I gargled water, dusted off my boots, then reported in to the dour faced Barszcz and Hungerford duo. They were hunched over the hood of a Jeep, studying a map. The captain ignored my braced salute and held his accusing eyes on my weaponless shoulder. I answered the voiceless charge. "Sir, a cavalry officer confiscated my rifle."

Hungerford caustically sneered, "Sure...we *knew* you two would make it back."

I stood motionless: *Contemptuous bastard...why don't I just go and ride the sick-book all the way back to Pusan...but then I might miss out on a good firefight...screw 'em both...*

Next morning Sergeant Greeno handed me a canvas vest filled with bottled gasoline wrapped in oil soaked rags and told me that if we run into any T-34s I was to smash one of these against its hull

I thanked him with a smile and suggested that if he'd set the example I'd happily give him covering fire. When his eyes narrowed I suggested he remind the captain that Molotov cocktails weren't part of any company's TO&E (Table of Organization and Equipment); and that it was strictly a volunteer job, which nobody else seemed to want, so why should I. He wordlessly turned and left.

The night's artillery thundered along the encircling horizon and sent their iridescent bolts flashing and throbbing through the grey rain-drenched sky while the company moved within a rail-marshaling yard and boarded a waiting train. There were no medics to attend the already on board walking wounded or Richard's surfaced malaria. He shivered and some others moaned through long hours of stifling heat. The fearful engineers knowing guerrillas and saboteurs lurked just beyond the blackened yard wouldn't move the train.

A quick remembrance of a scene from the 1930s film *Shanghai Express* prompted me to reenact it in the engineer's cabin. "Move train," I bellowed in harsh Japanese to the alarmed engineer and pressed my pistol's muzzle into his flared nostril, with my body angled as though to avoid his soon-to-be splattered out brains. His heart skipped more than a few beats and after the train jolted forward I returned to my car. At dawn we discovered the compliant engineer had throughout the night merely shunted around the marshaling yard and gone nowhere: *how would General Yang have handled this?*

Two of the onboard but previously unnoticed French war correspondents were drawn in by Richard's delirium. They seemed disappointed that he wasn't bleeding to death, which deprived them, I suspected, of that definitive war photo which guarantees journalistic acclaim. Later when the cramped train made an unexpected stop three other G.I.s and I propped Richard up between us and carried him back to the last boxcar in hopes it would be miraculously deserted. My gentle knock drew a whispered reply to enter into the all but vacant car: *He's got to be a full colonel to rate a private car. Maybe it's the regimental C.O.?*

In appreciation and remembrance of *The General Dies at Dawn* I offered that we serve as his personal guard. Richard and the others slept at one end of the car, while at the other the still obscured and seated figure seemed to smolder in the shafts of pale blinking moonlight that slashed through the slats of the mud-caked car as the train rolled on. Seated for hours in the open doorway I watched the dark silhouettes of trees and huts fly by until the hypnotic clack of the train's rhythmical wheels ground to a silent halt in a desolate inky black station.

No ambulances waited for the sick and wounded, only the posted ROK soldier who pointed me towards a hospital two miles away. With Richard's pistol cross-strapped to my hip and he and his rifle over my shoulders, I staggered under the two hundred pounds of dead weight through a series of silent hamlets. Two hours later I saw the flashlight-swept perimeter of the hospital.

Up on the second floor, I put Richard on a stretcher and placed his pistol and full canteen next to him where I fell asleep to be awakened later by gunfire. I raced outside to where a G.I. shouted from a ditch, "They're over there!"

The eight rounds he frantically fired ricocheted through the nearby deathly silent hamlet. In an instant a half dozen other perimeter guards gleefully added their firepower to the psychotic clash against their nonexistent phantom army. Inside the fearful patients, and possibly the villagers, prayed they weren't being overrun. Unsurprisingly, no curious officers or NCOs responded to any of this and only the known fickleness of court martial boards kept me from restoring order with the threat of my pistol.

Near dawn I left Richard some extra pistol ammo and hitched an ambulance ride back to the rail siding. The driver confided that it wasn't safe to transport wounded at night, proudly pointing to the single bullet hole found in most windshields in Korea. I thought it interesting that those drafty punctures were never even near the driver's side.

The Korean station guards jostled between the idling train and the matronly women who hawked apples from the platform. One guard snatched a fruit basket and gave it to some hungry G.I.s. I was grateful the train hadn't left as my actions would have been hard to explain. Later that afternoon, after we unloaded and started marching, we passed an elderly woman who bowed and chanted, "Thank you, American soldier...thank you."

Somewhere between Chonju and Taegu my carping to Sergeant Greeno about the lack of combat got me transferred out to the 2nd Platoon, run by Lieutenant Robert 'Fearless' Herbert and Sergeant 'Combat Joe' Wyland. 'Combat Joe,' a small-framed Midwestern vet from WWII, served with the company back in Sasebo, Japan, as did the platoon's least savory character Private Krocheck. He was Herbert's 'dog-robber,' meaning he'd perform whatever menial, and/or unauthorized jobs his patron might ask.

Evident the next morning was what little influence 'Combat Joe' had on Herbert's known propensity to take flight when our platoon, detached from the company, dug in above the road that led back to the battalion CP about a mile and a half away. Outgoing artillery whizzed overhead. While noting the many draws and gullies to our front that the NKs might use to maneuver up the hill, I glimpsed Herbert and his 'faithful shadow' leap over the skyline and run down the reverse slope. Wyland wordlessly watched them too, before continuing on down the line to the right of my anchor position.

Robertson (left) and Richard (right) crossing the skyline on patrol. Note Robertson's torn right sleeve from earlier mortar shrapnel.

Some minutes later Herbert's tense voice rang up from the valley. "They're out front, Wyland—they're out to your front!"

For the second time within a month I held them both in my sights and battled the inner voice that bade me not to fire. Disgruntled, I turned away and then found myself looking down into the unexpected spellbinding tide of camouflage uniforms that were stealthily working their way up the slope. I furiously fired into the crested wave not seventy yards away.

Blistering heat from my rapidly firing rifle made it difficult to hold, and threw back blue-tinged smoke and boiling linseed oil onto my face and eyes. Struggling for more accurate aim, I noted that my bandoleer was nearly emptied and that my weapon was the only one firing from our side of the line—'Combat Joe' had silently pulled back the platoon! When Burp gun rounds splattered all around me a scene from the film *Bataan* flashed through my brain.

I pitched over a grenade, catapulted the crest and rolled down to the base of the hill. There was no sign of the platoon, or NKs! *I should have killed Herbert and Krocheck when I had the chance...maybe I'm cut off?*

My determined dash through the underbrush eventually brought me before a captain at the battalion CP tent and I related the incident. "Sir, I want to charge an officer and NCO with desertion under fire."

He exploded. "*You're* the one who's going to face charges, because no such action ever took place! God damn it, making baseless accusations like that against a superior officer is a serious offense!" He caught his breath. "Now get back up on that goddamned hill!"

I answered quietly, "Sir, I'd like the captain to accompany me, sir, so he can see for himself that the Gooks are up on that ridge."

His thick inflexible Irish face reddened and bellowed to a sergeant clerk at his field desk. "Drive this sorry-ass excuse for a soldier back up to that hill position; and if he refuses to go up, shoot him!"

Parked in a clearing near the hill the sergeant scanned the lifeless skyline. "Looks pretty deserted up there to me. You better get your ass back up there now, soldier." He made no move toward his holster.

"Aren't you going up there with me Sarge?" He wordlessly drove away.

I slept well into the night under an overturned Jeep then walked unchallenged down the dark deserted road back to an aid station tent. Outside, a corpulent NCO droned on to a starry-eyed group of young medics roasting C-ration frankfurters over a small open fire.

"This is no war;" he said dismissively, "the last war, now *that* was a war!"

Toxic anger cancelled out my appetite. "If you think it's so fuckin' easy, why don't you get off your fat comfortable asses and hit the goddamn line for a few days!" He squinted through the flames, but couldn't penetrate the shadows that covered my return back to where I'd slept through the night.

Along the roadway at dawn I saluted the frowning captain. "Where've you been this time, Mercy?"

I answered evenly. "Sir, I got cut off from the platoon when they bugged out." He stared dismissively. "Get back to your platoon, Mercy, and try to stay put."

Alone at the road's edge and against the loud protests from my churning intestinal track, I wolfed down spoonful's of greasy cold C-rations until a sudden squirt of blood snapped across my face and chest from the quarter-ton truck that halted in front of me. Its cargo was stacked bodies of dead G.I.s. Curiosity overcame my resistance to look into their startled eyes for some imagined insightful clue about death: *They don't look like they do in movies: Heroic, proud and peacefully asleep.*

The shuffling passage of Sergeant Mayes' 1st Platoon, along with the first live NK prisoner I'd seen, broke my spell. The POW, looking like any Jap out of any WWII newsreel and suddenly became the lightning rod for every ill feeling I had…and before I knew it the blade of my throwing knife was in my cocked-back hand.

Mayes cried out over his half raised rifle. "You could get shot for that, Mercy." His furtive eye fused all my passions.

I flipped the dagger, laughing over the short distance between us, "This will be in your throat before you can click off your safety." Our mutual years of discipline checkmated our passions and kept us both motionless—unless the other twitched.

Fate, in the guise of WWII veteran Sergeant 'Gabby' Singhurst, taunted me again the next day. His prematurely grayed hair, stubble chin and uncanny resemblance to the old cowboy actor Gabby Hayes won him the nickname.

"Get your ass down the hill and bring up all those stacked up C-ration cases from the road," he said, "then distribute them to the platoons."

I spun my freshly oiled .45 back into its holster. "No. It's somebody else's turn."

A startled Singhurst jolted and stammered then stared over his half-raised rifle into the muzzle of the cocked pistol that I drew in response. "You'll get twenty years for this, Mercy!"

Several of his own men menacingly crowded in and whispered, "Kill the son of a bitch, Mercy."

This cut him deeply, "God damn you, Mercy, you'll get a firing squad for this." He left, cursing his way back to the CP.

I didn't know, nor had 'Gabby' noticed that the pistol's cylinder was empty. It was a lifetime first for me not to reload after cleaning a weapon and the lack of reaction from the company CP was equally surprising. The 'let the new guy do it' cycle was seemingly broken until the next day when Lieutenant Herbert's dog-robber Krocheck gave me a direct order to unload a supply truck; and he got his long overdue bloody nose.

Herbert later barked in my face, "Mercy, if you make another of my men cry, I'm going to personally send you home!"

My growing illness and frustration compounded when the company pulled back to Anu and went into reserve, where I momentarily considered a self-inflicted wound; but loathing for the cowardly practice kept me from it.

I also avoided sick call, for fear I'd miss out on a good firefight. A transfer to another unit was a consideration and I posed that question to my mess hall buddy Rundell. "Let's take off and join your old outfit, the 2nd Indian Head Division. I heard they landed here last week."

"Calm down," he said. "Your brother's back from the hospital, and assigned to the 3rd Platoon." I turned to leave and ran into a short stocky replacement named Casalucci who I discovered had lived down around Mott Street in Manhattan. His narrowed black eyes scanned the oblivious faces around us. He spat to one side and unconsciously gripped his groin. "Hey, Merc, who da fuck do we gotta watch out fer in da company?"

I whispered. "One guy for sure, his name is Krocheck."

He leaned in, and whispered back conspiratorially, "Ohhh, y-e-a-h?"

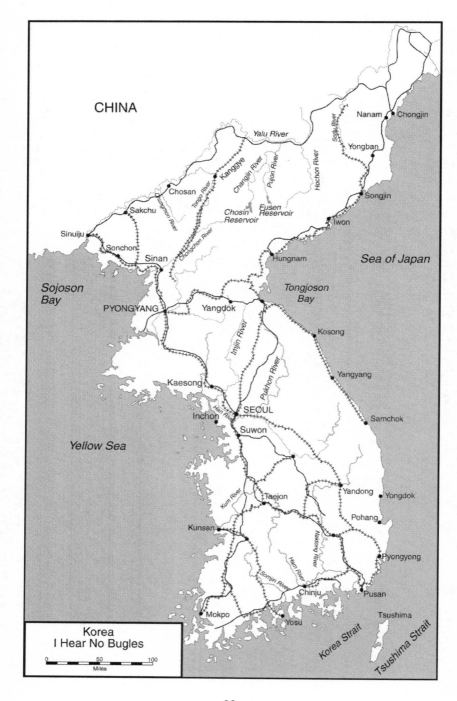

CHINA

Yalu River

Nanam · Chongjin

Yongban

Chosan

Kanggye

Changjin River

Pujon River

Hochon River

Songjin

Sakchu

Tongo River

Fusen Reservoir

Sinuiju

Chosin Reservoir

Iwon

Sonchon

Sinan

Chongchon River

Hungnam

Sea of Japan

Sojoson Bay

PYONGYANG

Yangdok

Tongjoson Bay

Imjin River

Kosong

Kaesong

Pukhon River

Yangyang

Inchon

SEOUL

Samchok

Suwon

Yellow Sea

Kum River

Taejon

Yandong

Yongdok

Pohang

Kunsan

Naktong River

Pyongyong

Han River

Chinju

Pusan

Somjin River

Mokpo

Yosu

Tsushima

Korea Strait

Tsushima Strait

Korea
I Hear No Bugles

0   50   100
Miles

CHAPTER 13

First Blood

North Korean guerrillas had set up roadblocks to our southwest while the undertrained Okinawan based 29th Infantry arrived without artillery ammunition, communications or mortars and took over our reserves position. George Company headed south to a T-intersection near a small twin-peaked hill at the edge of the rain-swollen Nam River. The 2nd and 3rd Platoons, with Casalucci in one and me in the other, marched towards the ridge. My brother's 1st Platoon and the 4th peeled off to an unknown destination to the west.

Sergeant 'Combat Joe' stood in the saddle of the heights and shouted for the 3rd Platoon to dig in on the left and 2nd Platoon on the right. I took the far right flank position and saw that it was devoid of any tie-in unit for as far as the eye could see. My right flank 'tie in' hill sat five hundred yards across a grassy field and stretched east along the river: *It's the company's blind spot...I'll need an LMG to cover all that ground.* Behind me on a right angle 200 yards away stood a small wooden bridge that spanned the river. On its far side was a dirt trail that led up to the winding southwest road that ran to Chinju.

Near dark the slash of our entrenching tools silenced the marsh crickets and I slept camouflaged until dawn. I estimated range points along the high ground to the north which tapered down into a distant misty cloud of umber in the west. On my left, about a hundred yards away, a brook ran past a small tree-shaded farmhouse, which was situated eighty yards forward of Barszcz' CP and directly in our line of fire. It didn't look like we were intending to stay there long. A sudden crunch of gravel on the reverse slope put Krocheck in my sights when he cleared the crest to tell me that the lieutenant wanted me for a patrol briefing in twenty minutes.

My stomach cramps kicked into high gear as I marched toward Cass, Krocheck and the awaiting squad. I bellowed over my raised rifle salute to Herbert, "Private Mercy reporting for duty, sir." When he nervously returned the salute, I gave such a thunderous slap to the upper hand in coming to Order Arms that it should have been heard in Pyongyang or, in my bad frame of mind, by any officer-hunting NK sniper on the high ground.

Herbert's outstretched hand traced the curvature of the ridge. "We'll move up along that hill and follow it down for a few miles to a small village. We're looking to capture some NKs for G-2 to interrogate. Are there any questions?"

When I'd asked what we'd do if we got into a fight Herbert stiffened and reminded us that we were on a recon patrol and there'd be no firefights. "Remember that, Mercy," he added, "and if we do hit trouble my walkie-talkie can get us some mortar support."

I whispered to Cass that this patrol isn't anything like Errol Flynn's in *Objective Burma*. His blank stare told me he hadn't seen the movie. We took point, with Herbert and Krocheck trailing behind the patrol.

Hours later we'd taken cover on the rocky sunbaked crest above the objective, a village of six huts. Women were doing laundry in a stream while nearby a half-dozen men stoop-walked to straighten the rice field's half-submerged shafts. The adjacent dirt road showed no sign of troop, tanks, or truck movement. The patrol's arrival was announced by the bouncing clang of bandoleers and canteens before Herbert slid by our side with raised field glasses. His faithful 'shadow' dutifully parted the grass to clear his frontal view.

"You two go down to the road, set up a checkpoint, and get any information you can."

I beamed. "Okay, sir, I'll set up some covering fire and send out flank guards."

"Stay alert," he said, "cause if we spot anything coming we'll only be able to give you arm and hand signals."

Cass and I exchanged disbelieving glances. "Arm and hand signals, sir?"

He replied, "Yes, and if you don't see them, you'll be out of luck."

To simultaneously watch him hiding in the tall grass and then to also watch the road, was an impractical task. As we walked down the hill I heard Cass mumble, "I'd like to give him an arm and hand signal, right in his mouth: *A fung gu, Lu-ten-niti... Capitano ... fung gu a tuti ogenumo*! Hey, why don't we just kill the bastards right now?"

I appealed to his Sicilian compassion with a wink. "Naw, better to leave them wounded for the Gooks to find…capiche?"

His eyes glimmered. "Yeah, *marone*, dats a great idea, Merc!"

I continued more in humor than conviction, "If we scratched them now, there's no telling who might suddenly find Jesus on this patrol, and we'd be facing a court martial."

Cass' thumb nimbly etched the sign of the cross on his forehead. "Yeah, you're right."

"Yeah," I added, "one of these guys might write a book someday, too, and that could spell trouble."

Cass sighed. "Hey, I'll cut off all his fingers."

When a dozen civilians had passed and before the late noonday shadows had stretched from the huts I saw a glitter of light reflect from a distant hill. I'd thrown a stone to get the attention of the flank guards then pulled in the checkpoint. When we reached the grassy knoll, Herbert and Krocheck were gone. I wondered how he'd manage not to get busted in rank and cashiered out of the Army for his unfailing cowardice. On the reverse slope Krocheck shamelessly popped out of a weed patch, asking if we'd seen anything. I didn't reply as he led me to Herbert, who was found leaning up against a tree with a cigarette in his mouth.

"Give me your report, Mercy."

I exhaled. "Sir, the immediate area looked clear, except for a reflection of something on a distant hill. If I'd had the radio, sir, I could have called in a few rounds of WP."

Animosity simmered in his eyes as he bellowed to Krocheck to get the patrol ready to move out. Halfway back to the company area I overheard part of his walkie-talkie conversation with the company commander.

"Yes, sir, Captain, the men didn't find anything, but I saw something move on a distant hill. Yes sir, over and out."

The captain showered Herbert with congratulations on our return while Krocheck struggled desperately for inclusion. Back up on the reverse slope I stared glassy-eyed down into the babbling river as Cass joked, "Hey, Merc, I bet Herbert puts himself in for a Silver Star!"

I couldn't resist doing an impression of Humphrey Bogart reading out his citation "And for conspicuous gallantry and being able to find your way back to the company without ever firing a single shot, you are hereby awarded the-blah-blah-blah."

The squad laughed just as Krocheck suddenly appeared from out of nowhere and unceremoniously dropped a carton of C-rations in our midst. Within a minute we'd opened our individual ration box and my mouth salivated for its prized content—the miniature tin of sweet fruit. Seconds later Lieutenant Herbert swooped in and snatched those delicacies out of each soldier's hand, which he then flipped into the emptied carton held by Krocheck. Herbert defiantly grinned at our silent disbelief before they both dashed back over the ridge: *A United States Infantry Officer stealing food out of the hands of his troops! Amazing...never saw that in any movie...*

Our cans of greasy sausage patties and franks & beans heated over a small twig fire while Cass cursed then pierced his can of spaghetti with a bayonet before he walked towards the crest flipping a grenade from hand-to-hand.

I called out. "Hey, Cass, you heard about how the surrounded German army at Stalingrad would shoot any officer, regardless of rank, who stole food from the troops, right?" The image momentarily pacified him and he rejoined the circle doing a convincing impression of an Italian gangster. "Yeah, but in dis here Army, we gotta make-a look like-a accidenti!"

Their laughter lessened over my next story of the hot summer night up along the Kum River. On that night, Herbert had the platoon's lister bag brought to his CP where he and his dog-robber laughed as they guzzled down endless cups of water. The rest of us had been rationed to one canteen per day. Under a whiz of outgoing artillery, I stoked the conversation with little-known tidbits on military mutinies—which was a thousand light years from our consciousness, before we all went to sleep.

Jets zoomed in through the dawn's clear sky to napalm and strafe the hill directly ahead. I leapt into the next foxhole to enjoy the show over some freshly brewed coffee with Cass and a guy named Buford.

"So what do you think, Merc," Cass asked? "We gonna hold here or what?"

Buford chimed in, "Ol' General 'Bull' Walker said we'd stand and fight here."

I looked over the indefensible terrain and told them about the captured G.I. up at the Kum River. "His hands were tied behind him and they ran a cord through his nose and knotted it to the back of a T-34. His face was half pulled off when he couldn't keep up."

"Marone," Cass whispered, "I'll remember dat when they get here."

A 120mm round swooshed in, and sent up a plume of black smoke near the CP tree. Barszcz and the others scurried for cover. No follow-up rounds came in: *They must be short on ammo...but they'll be up here tonight for sure...*

It was difficult staying awake back in my foxhole, cleaning and oiling my rifle, bayonet, and 'last round' in the draining 100° temperature. A pebble thrown near me by a G.I. broke my drug-like trance. My cocked pistol pointed into his startled face.

96

"Whoa," he said, "I'm Pat. 'Combat Joe' sent me to buddy-up with you." He carried only one bandoleer, no bayonet and his dust-covered rifle wasn't to my liking. "I clerked at battalion and volunteered for the line to get material for a future book."

Suddenly, we heard a shot, and our eyes flicked down to 'Combat Joe's' position. His string of carbine rounds drove a farmer to hide behind a fallen tree: *It looks like an easy kill...* The Korean's head was on the stem of my front sight as unconvincing rationales flew through my mind: *Maybe he's the Gook's FO...maybe Wyland saw him planting a booby trap...or maybe he's just toying with him...not even he could miss at sixty yards...must be an NK...this is my real baptism of fire, a clear kill.* An inner voice then loudly pleaded not to do it. The rifle bucked hard, and I was thankful I'd missed. When a flicker of unwanted compassion emerged I inwardly cursed my weakness; and though I took up the trigger slack with enforced determination, I still ached to hear 'Combat Joe,' Barszcz (or God Himself) command me to cease fire!

The bullet splintered tree bark inches below his terror stricken face—he turned in a desperate dash for home. I clearly heard my inner voice tinged with panic when it shouted out for him to stop: "No! No! Stay down...stay down!!" My rifle's thunderous recoil proved more violent than any other I could recall. Through unblinking eyes I watched as the impacting bullet froze him in place with arms outstretched...as though crucified on a cross of air. The sweet scented cordite that wafted back into my face brought with it the recalled voice of Ronald Coleman in *The Light That Failed. "Ah, perfume of the Queen of battle."* A woman's shrill shriek shredded the last reverberated echoes of my fired shot. I watched her tearful frantic race from out of the nearby hut to where she knelt choked with sobs and cradled the lifeless body to her breasts. In every searing detail I watched Michelangelo's Pieta transformed into living, breathing life.

Pat sneered, "Feel better?"

I struggled to repress the unexpected burgeoning sense of guilt and the yawning abyss of emptiness that followed, in which I could not find a rationale to appease the unwelcomed truth, of what I'd done. "Yeah," I said, "and go find yourself a new home while you're at it." Grateful to be alone I sank into the foxhole and the disheartening reality that killing hadn't hardened me, or my heart, at all...

An hour later providential thunder cracked out of the four .50-caliber gun barrels on the M16 half-track stationed at the road intersection 150 yards away. Sergeant Gay leapt into my foxhole; his field glasses followed the gun's line of fire back down to the left on the parallel road and whispered, "There...see...seven hundred yards out!" Another burst streamed through the distant troop column, sent tracers ricocheting skyward and bowled men down into the flanking paddies.

"Jesus Christ," I yelled, "they're G.I.s!"

Two-dozen more rounds cut through the still swirling gust from the previous burst. Then Gay murmured, "Somebody better stop 'em."

A churning remorse catapulted me to my feet and with the poncho I ripped from my ammo belt, I started frantically waving towards the quad-fifties startled crew. The electrical current from the turning turret gave a cobra-like hiss as the gun's smoky fangs rose to spit; and I cried out an unmistakable American idiom: "Cease fire, you dumb stupid-ass sons of bitches, they're goddamned fucking G.I.s!"

After a breathless minute ticked by, the guns lazily recoiled and swayed north. The pinned down company rose miraculously without a single casualty and hurled angry curses when they passed the shamefaced halftrack crew as they headed towards the river's bridge.

During the night, a cry from the crest pulled me from a troubled sleep "Replacements coming in." Silhouetted against the night's artillery flared sky they scurried to find positions along the forward slope. Dawn neared and two grenades exploded. I waited the expected attack. At first light jets dove in full throttle and fumed the cool pristine skies with malodorous napalm and cannon fire. A barrage of artillery soon followed. Buford in the next position saluted with a raised steaming coffee cup as I leapt into his foxhole.

"I thought for *sure* the Gooks were up here last night," I said.

He laughed, "Oh, you mean those grenades? You ain't gonna believe this Mercy, but 'Combat Joe' buddied up some of them new replacements with older guys. He told 'em not to go shooting up the goddamned place but use grenades if anything moved. Well, wouldn't you know, one dumb bastard, and I'm sure glad he wasn't in here with me, pulled the pins out of his grenades so he'd have 'em ready—then set 'em up on the lip of his fox hole, so they'd be set to throw! Ka-boom!"

Casalucci and 'Combat Joe' raced towards me across the late day skyline. 'Combat Joe' barked, "Get ready to pull out."

I mumbled, "That figures."

Buford cried, "I'm ready to roll."

'Combat Joe' threw him a steely-eyed look. "You'll stand fast until I give you the goddamned word, and *you*, Mercy, stay behind with Casalucci. Cover the platoons until we're across the river."

Cass' thumb flicked from the edge of his teeth. *"Ah grazie, Sargenti."*

I cut in, asking for a couple of BARs.

His field glasses scanned the front. "Can't do it, Mercy, might need 'em on the other side."

Cass and I tapped down our ammo clips and un-crimped grenades pins for easy pulls and throws while 'Combat Joe' led the wading platoons across the river. In the thickening dusk Cass nudged me awake to see a lava-like flow of camouflaged uniforms stretch down the opposite ridge. "Here dey come," he said.

Our rifles bucked, blood gushed from bodies as they spun out of the narrow apertures of our sights. We played dead a full minute when heavy MG fire peppered the ground around us. Returned to life we fired back, and strings of burp gun rounds trailed our heels to the crest.

Cass laughed. "Hey, Merc, this is a real kick in the ass. I ain't had this much fun since Coney Island!"

Heavy small arms fire broke out first then rapid firing artillery on the far side of the river, somewhere just beyond the bridge. The NKs were behind us! We launched ourselves like christened ships down into the oil-slicked water as NK rounds thumped and snapped in around us. The quick currents filled my boots with sand in our armpit-deep wade to the other side as darkness fell.

We raced towards the dozen leaderless men huddled beneath the swaying ghostly glare from drifting flares and distant bursting shells. I drew my pistol.

"I'm an NCO. We don't have much time. Stay together as a team, that's our best bet to get out alive. And no bugging out! I fucking mean it!"

I posted flank guards and a point man from what was mostly part of last night's replacements. Regiment had deployed seven hundred inexperienced new troops over the objections from company commanders.

Just yards from the main Chinju road a lieutenant staggered out of the darkness, fell by our feet and gasped, "Tanks, tanks! The Gooks swarmed over our batteries, killed everybody. They're right behind me. Move out, pronto."

He pointed back three hundred yards to the flaring exchange between M1s and Burp guns. We dashed forward a hundred yards into a small cul-de-sac. The troops, Cass and the exhausted lieutenant sank into the foliage of a nearby hillside. I dove behind the last of three isolated huts as the lead NK tank jolted to a stop on the road fifty yards behind. Its menacing 85mm gun traversed over the pocket where I lay. My heart pounded: *Had I been spotted?* Four soldiers leaped from the silhouetted hull and headed my way. It was too late to run. I quickly splattered my face with mud, and wedged my head out against the edge of the shack hoping it would pass for a rock or clump of clay.

They laughed as they casually strolled up to the hut's wall and urinated not eight feet away from me. I slowly clutched my brass-knuckled bayonet, hoped none of them would need more privacy behind the house. I sighed with relief as they started back towards the road just as another leather-helmeted figure suddenly emerged from the darkness. He returned the salutes of the other two and took his turn at the wall.

This is like watching a French art movie from the first row...fucking Commies seem more 'democratic' than our officers...who wouldn't dream of pissing on the same wall used by an enlisted man...the T-34s will drown out any sound the lone officer might make if I kill him. He turned and I smiled imagining the puzzlement of his crew: *Maybe they'll think he deserted...or maybe ran into some unseen... treacherous G.I.?*

Remembered film sequences of enemy sentries being knifed, the countless boyhood hours I'd practiced for it, fueled my half-raised body to spring just as yet another Korean emerged from the far end of the hut! The NKs laughed, pointed to the high ground behind me while my braced arms quivered beneath me. Their quiet departure frustrated my intent, but fed my mind's eye a scene from *For Whom the Bell Tolls.*

I'll knock out all the tanks. That exhausted lieutenant with the troops up on the hill would see it, and he'd put me in for a Congressional Medal of Honor! An instant flash of heroic Marines, unhesitant *Bushido* warriors and a plan of attack filled my mind: *I'll get across the road unseen and pitch a grenade into the lead tank's open hatch. Its full ammo racks will blow it to hell, and in the mass confusion I'll knock out the other three tanks!* I could visualize the entire column in flame, the screams of dismembered NK bodies thrown into the night's blood red sky. Unstoppable, I imagined myself shooting and bayoneting whoever is left: *Do it, do it, you can do it!*

Inexplicably the images in my mind suddenly changed. Instead, I imagined a hail of burp gun fire ripping through my body. Unable to move, I'm bayoneted. Next, I'm being buried in Arlington National Cemetery. After the president lauds my bravery, he respectfully presents my posthumous CMH to Richard. MGM casts Tony Curtis to play my life story. I am venerated by my old alma mater, Brooklyn's East New York Vocational High. The teacher's prophecies are disproved. I didn't die in the electric chair.

Shouts and the clang of enemy armor headed south towards Chinju snapped me back to reality with a remorseful heart. I hadn't tried to stop them. I reached the hill where the others had escaped and whispered into the humid silence for the lieutenant, Cass, anybody, but there was no reply. Well, so much for witnesses for my CMH!

100

I paused at the crest. Below, flashes of burp gun fire flickered through the darkened cordite-shrouded valley where the captured wounded were executed. I picked up the growingly familiar trail of discarded weapons, ammunitions and God-sent canteens and gratefully drained them dry. I wondered what those G.I.s would do without rifles, ammo, and water when the sun rose.

CHAPTER 14

Run to Chinju

I made my way beneath the dawn-tinged pines along the skyline towards the dim sound of equipment rustling somewhere ahead. The last man in the column was startled.

"Hey, Mercy, where the hell did you come from?" My pale skinned, 110-pound fellow New Yorker in the 3rd Platoon flashed his uneven hound-dog toothed smile.

"That's what you get for not checking to your rear, BB," I said. We scanned the sky for the reassuring signs of a plane and saw only plumes of black smoke swirling up on the right flank. The NK tanks had captured Chinju. Unseen was their fast moving division on our left headed for the city of Mason, only fifteen miles from Pusan—we were sandwiched in between two forces.

Ahead, the single file column rounded a huge lime green boulder and walked down into a narrow boxlike gorge. "There's less than sixty men there, BB, where's the rest of the company?"

He shrugged. "Who knows? These guys are a mixed bag. G Company men, replacements from last night and God knows what else."

Concerned, I asked, "What about my brother's platoon? Barszcz, and Hungerford; and our weapons section?"

He stared blankly. "Beats the hell outta me. The company got separated last night when some nit in the middle of the column stopped and the troops behind thought either somebody up front heard something, or it was a rest break. Finally the guy directly behind him asked 'why did you stop?' The fucking hillbilly turns around and says, 'I'm just a-restin' up.'"

I eyed him suspiciously. "BB, you're making this up, right?"

He got defensive. "No, honest, Merc, it's the truth. When we finally pulled out the troops ahead of us were gone. Nobody called out because of being afraid the Gooks might be around…you know what I mean?"

"Sure," I nodded, "that guy had to feel a little stupid, too, for losing what's left of the company."

I felt apprehensive looking down the slope's sixty-yard decline into the sandy weed-filled ravine we'd have to cross. A smooth flat-faced cliff on our immediate left fell straight down into a basin that was rounded out like the interior of a stone cup with thirty-foot high walls on three sides. Its only exit out was a narrow sixty-yard long S-shaped curve that sliced between our hill and the adjoining slope that stretched four hundred yards up to a rocky moonscape summit.

Exhausted by worsening dysentery and the record-breaking humid heat I decided to rest in the small swatch of cool shade near the lopsided boulder: *I'll catch up with the column on the next ridge…or maybe tonight…when it's cooler.* I camouflaged myself beneath a swept up pile of leaves and, while watching BB follow the column down, I drowsily sank into unconsciousness from where an inner voice later bellowed: *Wake up or die!*

Startled, unfocused I thought it was a dream until seconds later machine gun fire sent me into a long seemingly slow motion dive into the ravine. The gun's position, some thirty yards beyond the boulder where I'd dozed, was impossible to see. They'd walked right by me, not four feet away along the crest. The same hallmark trail of discarded equipment that I'd followed led them to us.

Another burst fractured rocks above the S-shaped curve, severed dead trees and burned into the back of the desperate column headed up to the high ground. My search for the roaring gun intensified in paces with the inescapable screams that come from the wounded and the dying: One burst blew open the torso of a G.I. from groin to chin. Another's legs were pulverized and the last man in the column, where I would have been, was near decapitated: *Was that BB?*

A final withering leaden gale raised gusts of blood-stippled dust into a sudden eerie silence, save for the metallic jangle of the dead G.I.'s helmets that rolled back onto the valley floor. The NKs, with their nasty screwdriver-tipped bayonets, would soon be down to mop up. I snake-bolted through the high grass, coming face to face with a racked-with-fear sweat drenched 200-pound teenager with a bullet wound in each leg.

He cried out, "In God's name, please! Take me out!"

I nodded then dashed towards the nearby tapered fissure I'd spotted running up the face of the rock wall. I squinted up its constricted thirty-foot shaft. It sprouted some twigs, a few inch-wide stone protrusions and showered down dust from the machine gun vaporized rocks above. Drawn back to the wounded soldier who saw the improbability of the climb written on my face, he whispered, "Please, don't let them get me!"

I unhitched one of the two grenades from my cartridge belt and flipped it to his side. "This is the best I can do." I'll never forget the tortured anguish and fear that churned in his eyes before his head lowered in despair. "Hail Mary, full of grace," he began and I, unseen, drew my pistol: *Will God punish me if I kill...or leave him...and...will the shot give away our position?* I suddenly recalled a film clip of a WWI soldier shooting his friend to spare him the torture he'd expected.

I made the nauseating nightmarish choice, and crawled up the funnel to the ridge, which violated every belief and cherished honor code I held. I reached the crest where burp gun rounds pelted down around me then crumbled as though hit and rolled to the edge of the precipice. When the enemy fire shifted the wounded soldier's head was in my sights for the *coup de grace* I earnestly wanted to give; but was appalled instead by my inability to shoot: *Would I ever know why?*

A quick glance up and down the ridge revealed that I'd surfaced somewhere in the extended middle of what was left of the escaping disbursed column; and saw slack-jawed BB whom I joined beside a boulder, and fired six clips into the advancing NK line. Their return fire drove us up the hill past fallen bodies and discarded rifles. I cursed the forward G.I.s. "God damn you! Stand and fire!" Then wondered if the Gooks were already up and waiting for us on the reverse slope.

We drew up to a group of G.I.s huddled over a supine and wide-eyed black soldier who, in his agitated fugue state, rocked from side to side and clicked his empty rifle against a vacant sky to kill the demons that overran his disintegrated mind; and he moaned, "Ah, man, ah, man, ah, man!"

One G.I. waved dismissively. "We ain't got no coloreds in George Company, 'cept for Johnston the medic and this ain't him."

Another said, "Probably some bug-out truck driver."

Someone else added. "Fuck, leave 'em." I thought my drop kick to his jaw would sever his hysteria, but he neither blinked nor changed cadence in his rhyme. "Ah, man, ah, man, ah, man..."

A wave of ricocheting NK tracers pushed us to the summit. BB cleared it with a shout. "Let's go Mercy!"

While firing back down into the advancing NKs, I was suddenly wrapped within a very real—or insanely imagined—thin gauzy mist; and equally mysterious was my total insensibility of the present moment. I somehow was whisked back through time to when I was a Hessian soldier aiming my flintlock at a dark horizon. Then just as suddenly I was back in reality, with goose bumps tingling across my shoulders: *I've done this before! I've done this before!*

I glimpsed an older NCO near the crest facing twenty seated G.I.s, with rifles passively resting at their sides. They carelessly munched C-ration candies, oblivious to what the NCO's obvious intent of *en masse* surrender will bring.

I shouted, "Are you out of your fucking minds!" They stared blankly: *Should I shoot him...and save them for what the day will bring? No court martial board would convict me...or would they?*

Men flew down the rocky reverse slope, some tearing off their fatigue jackets and cartridge belts to leap up into the illusory cover of small trees. I ran full tilt thinking of Henry Fonda outrunning pursuing Indians for two days in *Drums along the Mohawk;* and added up all the rounds in my cartridge belt and bandoleers: *One hundred ninety...one in the butt plate...fifty rounds of .45...with good cover and luck, I could knock off a reinforced company...go out like a soldier!*

I splashed through a hundred yards of cool dung-soaked paddies towards four G.I.s. They were standing thirty yards forward of a fence made of woven branches that ringed in a dozen huts. Surprisingly one soldier was my old basic training buddy George Cronin who arrived with last night's replacements. BB, Sergeant Gay and Ed Sieto stood at his side. Sieto had to avoid capture in any firefight with the psychotic and Japanese hating NKs and that made him worth his weight in gold. A string of burp gun rounds slammed into the drainage ditch, making us dive for cover.

One of the heavily camouflaged shooters charged right into my two M1 rounds and splashed back into the green slime. Sieto feigned shock, "Mercy me," then I nailed two more NKs on a paddy wall at 100 yards out. A whistle shrilled: *The Gooks had circled the hill...they're closing in.*

All but Sergeant Gay fixed bayonets as a quarter acre of what seemed to be weeds and trees rose up and walked toward us. Gay shouted, "Don't shoot!"

My defiantly fired rounds obliterated his hope that the NKs would be merciful if they suffered no more casualties. We dashed for the hamlet and Sieto shouted for us to freeze. The blade of my front sight trailed the swift swing of his hand, pointing to the old wrinkled head of a woman seated in an open doorway.

"I'm hungry," he said, "let's get Mama-san to make us up some rice."

I cursed through gritted teeth.

"Sieto, forget the goddamned chow! Are you out of your mind?!" A sudden burst of burp gun fire from the opposite flank didn't affect his impish pout. We fled.

Sergeant Gay, with the others a short distance behind, paused while I broke through the last fenced-in yard of the village. A sustained .30-caliber LMG burst snapped red tracers just above my head and set fire to the nearby thatched roof hut. It came from the elevated woody knoll seventy yards off on my right. Between my returned bursts, I glimpsed a white-clad figure coming out of the smoke billowing house behind me: *He's armed...use your bayonet!*

I hesitated and he stopped a foot away. The fifty-something farmer bowed and unrolled the *tatami* mat I had mistaken for a rifle, motioning that I lay on something more worthy than humble ground. I was moved by his touching madness and returned his cycle of ever deepening bows. He sobbed and struck the ground beside me with each round I blindly fired at the machine gun, until it suddenly went silent. Either he was out of ammo, or I had made one-in-a-million shot! I looked at the Korean's thankful weathered face feeling I'd known him all my life. He was the essence of filmdom's oppressed Asian villagers who had no one to take up their fight. I felt briefly ennobled.

Gay shouted, "Hold your fire, Mercy, we're coming in," and dashed with the others past the burning house to the far barrier wall.

I spoke with genuine concern to the farmer. "*Dozo, eki masho ka* [Please, will you come with us]?" He shook his head, and swept his gnarled hand from his heart to the ground. I bowed as deeply as he and then dashed to the bamboo fence. We all looked over the precipice's forty-foot deep incline at the single footpath that stretched out between the expansive paddy fields and beyond.

Gay jutted his chin and whispered less than startling news. "They're in the hamlet. Get on down there Mercy. See if you draw any fire."

I nodded disdainfully.

Sieto encouragingly jiggled his bayonet-affixed rifle and said, "*Banzai.*"

Sixty yards along the path a round fired from someplace just beyond the hamlet's high ground struck a foot ahead. I saw no telltale puff of smoke to fire back at. The next bullet struck just beneath my descending foot and I bellowed up to the hill, "Fuck you, you Gook son of a bitch!" The firing stopped. I covered three hundred yards to the east-west running road, and took cover behind a muddy embankment.

I sighted Sieto and other G.I.s drawing fire on the path I'd taken along the valley floor. I was distracted by a Jeep carrying three South Korean soldiers that stopped a few yards behind me; then concentrated on the

106

single soldier who headed towards me. He wore no helmet, rank or insignia, only a Band-Aid on his pinky and a .45 automatic tucked beneath his open field jacket: *He's in somebody's army, but whose? Why is he heading toward the shooting, alone?* My inner voice whispered: *"Kill all three!"*

He returned my greeting in Japanese and continued towards the hamlet where the shooting had since stopped. I walked past the Jeep and the other two inscrutable Koreans, with a readied rifle in one hand and a cocked pistol in the other. I pulled my tiring body up to the high ground that seemed a galaxy away. Below distant enemy columns moved across the body-strewn paddies: *Maybe I'm the only one who got out alive?*

Hours later I crawled to the first of the three fenced-in huts I had spotted just ahead, hoping to find food and water. The sudden sounds of laughing Koreans filled me with panic. My only hope was to kill them all by surprise. I peeked through the fence. A second lieutenant whose gold bars were as bright as the .50-caliber casing on his polished swagger stick was on the other side with a khaki-dressed platoon sitting around him.

I suppressed a hysterical laugh and shouted, *"Konichiwa, Gozari masu* [Good afternoon, sir]!" When he returned my salute, I asked in Japanese, "Where are the communist soldiers?"

His laughter roared, as he jutted his jaw in four directions. *"Sokora juni iru* [They're everywhere]!"

After they fed and gave me some water, I joined their march. As we crossed over a series of hills, not hearing any sounds of planes or duels between distant artilleries, I thought perhaps we'd lost the war. That set my mind to remain and fight alongside these Koreans until our Army returned, as in the Philippines. Suddenly, our point man shouted, "G.I.! G.I.!"

The lieutenant's swagger stick pointed to a distant highway shrouded by clouds of floating dust. We bowed and parted company there while troop-laden trucks sped by in both directions. I slept beneath a truck until dawn at the 19th Infantry's collection point then uneasily headed towards the CP recalling my last return after the fall of Taejon. I spotted Richard on the opposite side of the road, grateful he was alive. I called out a hello. He grunted out, "Hi," and passed without a second glance: *Why is everyone acting so strange?*

Hungerford and the steely-eyed captain looked up from their map spread across the hood of a Jeep and returned my braced salute with two limp fingers. Hungerford's venomous hiss would have turned a cobra green with envy. "We knew you'd make it back, Mercy."

In the platoon area I bloated myself with water and slept until noontime chow. Again, it was greasy bacon, burned bread and watery powdered eggs. Even my cook friend Rundell didn't recognize me. I found a quiet spot to read the long awaited first and only letter from my NY girlfriend Marilyn.

Robert (left) and Richard (right), thirty days later, after the battle along the Kum River and Taejon. In only a month, I lost 65 pounds of my former 225-pound frame thanks to dysentery.

"Dear Robert, I hope your tent is comfortable... and that you remember to go to church every day, etc., etc."

A familiar laugh turned me towards the soldier sitting nearby with his rifle slung Mongolian-style across his back. "Hey, Sieto, how in the hell did you get out in one piece?"

He turned in surprise. "You missed a good one, Robert-san. Six other stragglers joined us in that yard right after you left. Once we got down, grenades started popping in around us. Cronin caught a slug through his throat after he emptied a clip into a Gook who stuck his face through the fence. BB got nicked. Most of the others got it when we returned their fire. 'Killer' Gay got out without a scratch! I waddled low like a duck behind a link of paddy walls, and never stopped."

I asked if he'd passed a Korean with a .45 stuck in his belt as we thrust our mess kits into the steam vats. Nearby, jaundiced-eyed old men and young boys nervously picked through the garbage scraps. "No," he said.

Later, alone by a tree, I watched the company assemble on the sun-bleached road and dissolve like turpentine-splashed figures on a canvas. I vomited up clumps of blood.

Hungerford snorted as he passed, "What's wrong with you, Mercy."

I forced another up-chucked clot in his direction. "I'm sick, Sarge."

His mustache twitched. "Sick? You're a goddamn malingerer, Mercy, and that's a court martial offense!"

I trudged forlornly to the Aid Station, sensing the company was headed for a monumental firefight. I was seen by a doctor, a captain. "It's dysentery, sir."

His eyebrow arched. "You just need a little sleep. Grab a bunk, the corporal will get you some pills."

My body reeked. "Sir, any chance of getting some clean clothes?"

He nodded towards a pile of torn, insect-covered fatigues, taken from the dead and wounded, outside the rear door. I rummaged through it with my bayonet. The corporal woke me in the morning.

"It's time to move out. You're going back up."

I staggered out into the broiling noonday sun. I don't remember anything else until I came to in an ambulance, parked next to a steam-huffing relic of an engine at a rail siding. Raucous mothers and bewildered children peddled spoiled fruit to the dazed and wounded soldiers inside the stifling cars. Military trucks and Jeeps moved slowly between the arriving ambulances and the walking wounded. Korean MPs and soldiers were on the periphery to keep order. On the locomotive's iron fender sat two tawny Buddha-like guards, amid decorative national flags, who would scan the tracks ahead for signs of sabotage. Hours later the train whistle shrieked as we neared the mythical center of the universe, where the teeming embryonic waters of the Japan, Yellow and East China Seas converged: Pusan.

CHAPTER 15

Rear Echeloners

The three-ambulance convoy honked through the crowded city street. I shouted pidgin English out the open door to some passing teenagers. "Hey why you no in army?" Back came the learned reply, "No, you here, do for me!" The army of gritty kids caught in our wake crashed against the braced carbines of the hospital's Korean guards and roared, "Gum, gum, gum!"

Two medics led us through the stretcher-flooded compound. No concern was shown over my worn pistol inside the warehouse-like plaster chipped walls of the makeshift hospital. I was issued a thumbnail-sized bar of soap, some chalky pills and a cheap three-cent disposable plastic razor, thanks to the millions collected by the American Red Cross. Assigned a cot on the second floor I saw no ROKs among the seriously wounded G.I.s that a hospital ship would take to Japan in the morning; and wondered where the ROKs were sent.

The city lay quiet under martial law from dusk to dawn, save for the gunfire from the ever-nervous rear-echelon guards. In the hospital, rumors were plentiful. One of them touted that if the NKs broke through the Pusan perimeter a massive guerrilla uprising would follow, and they'd be led by the full NK division that's already in town posing as civilians. I heard a doctor say that there were nearly four million refugees in the city. Even without an uprising more than a third of them would die from starvation, jaundice, leprosy, plagues and a host of other unimaginable diseases, if humanitarian aid didn't arrive soon.

Next morning, with my pistol tucked safely under the pillow, I looked forward to my first shower in over a month. I walked downstairs and through the swinging doors of the latrine. There was something familiar in the haunted stare of the near-naked soldier I glimpsed in the wall mirror. Then, half-startled by a sudden comprehension, I crazily spun around thinking I'd see myself walking in somewhere behind me. The dark, listless eyes in the mirror acknowledged the sixty-five pounds of muscle I'd lost, and clarified why my brother and the others hadn't recognized me. The ingrained dirt on my face and limbs remained intact, no matter how hard I scrubbed. Strangely, I still longed for 'the line' and the prospect of killing NKs.

After three days of medication, food and sleep I began to appreciate the ward's curious Alabama father and son medical aid team duo. The younger, a private, listened as his corporal dad read aloud a letter from home, telling him that his Uncle Billie Bob had been killed on the Naktong. The private vowed a Hatfield and McCoy vendetta against the wounded NKs who arrived daily.

Although they were segregated the NKs managed to infect the medical staff with a pathogenic compassion and they leaped like stampeding gazelles over a seething savanna of wounded G.I.s, each to see who could treat the enemy first. I cynically looked for hidden Press Corps cameras while thinking about the fifty soldiers who were bayoneted on their litters up on the Kum River. I listened nightly to the mud-caked wounded in the congested corridors and heard our regiment was up at Chonon.

"Yeah," said a soldier, "they're tied in with that goddamned 24th Infantry Regiment, and taking a beating."

Another caustically added, "Yeah, their 2nd Battalion deserted *en masse*, left *all* their weapons, ammunitions, and rations and bugged out on hijacked trucks."

A G.I. with an arm wound spoke next. "One night it took a military police battalion and two rifle companies to get them back on line, but they were gone again by dawn."

Another said a captured NK regimental commander credited the 24th Regiment of the 25th Division with keeping his battalions alive for months with their discarded supplies of ammunition, food and weapons.

One morning, with sunlight pouring through the window I saw Richard standing beside my bunk, his right arm in a dust-covered sling. Over a shared canteen of warm water he told me about the firefight I'd missed when taken ill.

"It was one hell of a good shootout! It started out with the whole company strung out like a column of ants, climbing hand over hand up the side of a high rocky cliff near Yongsan. Given the shape Hungerford told me you were in, you never would have made it. My platoon, in the lead, cleared the top then fanned out on line across an open plateau, slowly advancing towards a crest fifty yards away.

Somewhere in there we heard the Gooks yelling on the other side. They were working their way up to the top, but I don't think they knew that 'bad G.I.' was coming up on the other side. Then, for a split second, we all came face-to-face, and before I could even think about drawing my .45, both sides jumped back and hit the dirt. Their *Kimche* breaths started to water my eyes, we were that close. This is where it gets unbelievable.

From inches below the crest, we launched what I would call 'the grenade battle of all time!' We threw first then they threw theirs. All sides took casualties. I yelled for everybody to throw over a barrage of rocks, counted to five, and then pitched over hot iron. I timed some good airbursts, but the rock thing only worked for a while.

You could hear more Gooks working their way up on the opposite side, even over their screams. Just then, somebody yelled, 'grenade, grenade!' I did a fast one blink check, then dove for the ground headfirst. Didn't see the goddamn thing lying between my shoulder muscle and head, not four inches away! Luckily I was facing out in the opposite direction when it blew. My helmet and rifle stock were splintered to smithereens. All I got was one little chunk of iron in my shoulder. According to the MD who operated it missed a neck artery by a millimeter. Amazing."

"What happened next?" I asked enviously.

"Well, not being able to throw or use my piece I fell back to find a medic, and who do you think I came across, in one hole?"

I smirked, "Herbert and Krocheck?"

He laughed. "Never did see them, but there was 'Combat Joe' Wylan, 'Bug-out' Wassick, 'Killer' Gay, Goodman and some other NCOs. I'm standing there dripping blood, and they tell me I can't jump in because it's already too crowded! I told 'em to go fuck themselves, and headed back to the rear.

Worse yet, there were no officers around and the highest ranks fighting were corporals. Unbelievable! I don't know how this fucking Army ever wins a war. Once I got to the aid station my hatred for the rear echelon increased." Richard's eyes turned to burning coals. "They pulled out a dime-size piece of shrapnel that was close to a major artery, powdered me with sulfur and ordered me back on line. Then this fat horn-rimmed glasses wearing rear-echelon MD tells me that even though I can't use my rifle, I could still throw grenades and fire a pistol—with my left hand! So I said, '*Oy vay*, like John Vayne, you mean already?'"

He threw me a double take, but like an obedient asshole, I went back up. Next morning the wound festered and I tossed a few 'lefty' grenades like that schmuck suggested. That kept everybody at a respectable distance in fear for their lives. So then I got back to the battalion aid station and while I'm conked out on a cot another rear-echelon son of a bitch steals my pistol! To make a long story short, I got it back."

Richard made a left hand lightning-fast draw, grinned and twirled the revolver back into its holster. "I should have shot the son of a bitch on general principle."

Our Alabama medical duo changed Richard's bandages and, while he slept on an adjoining cot, I ran a recon patrol into town to find a place for us to celebrate. Curiosity sidetracked me into the cool interior of a makeshift Episcopalian church. The pastor asked that I leave my pistol at the door. I refused. It was a lifetime first, being in a church other than that of "the true faith." *Wonder how many of these guys are hoping God sees them here and will issue them a safe conduct pass?* I fearfully downed the sacramental wafer the parson offered, not wanting to offend him, but wondered if I'd violated some Catholic canon law.

After chow Richard and I toured the town and passed one of the "Welcome G.I." posters that the local guerrilla underground had half torn down. I commented that they probably believed their own rumors about Taegu having fallen. A few days later ROK Intelligence had discovered a cache of weapons hidden under a pier just down the road.

Richard laughed. "Probably a lot of people hobbling around here now with fewer toes and fingers than they were originally issued. Come to think of it, maybe MP duty here wouldn't have been so bad after all."

We entered a smoky pier side bar and fueled our war remembrances with hot milk saké.

"Hey, Butterball, did you know the Gooks almost won the war on the first day?" He stared back at me blankly. "They might have, if a South Korean patrol boat hadn't spotted a blacked-out NK troop ship a few miles off the Pusan coast, just about the time their army was crossing the 38th. They sent her and a battalion of six hundred Gooks to the bottom."

Richard shouted, "*Banzai*! Hey, did you hear that we might use the atomic bomb?"

I smiled. "That would be a hard political call for 'Harry,' considering what Truman did to the Japs. He might get away with it again, *if* our whole goddamned Army got wiped out to the last man. Then, *maybe,* the public and even the liberals might demand it."

Richard trumped my flawless logic. "Yeah, unless it's baseball season, then all bets are off."

I saved the biggest news for last. "You know the North Koreans are giving an acre of land to any Gook who kills over fifty G.I.s?"

Richard smirked. "If we had something like that, I'd go back up with a BAR in each hand, especially if we're talking beach front property in Hawaii." We laughed and he asked, "Did you hear about the million troops the UN was going to send to help us hold the line?" That drew a blank stare.

We shared our mixed feelings about returning to George Company. "We could always jump ship and join up with a Marine detachment," I said. "If they carried us on their MR (morning report), we couldn't be charged with desertion or even being AWOL."

Richard broke the silent pause. "Barszcz put 'Combat Joe' in for a Silver Star, for leading the company crossing the Nam River while under fierce attack, which I don't recall."

I told him what really happened at that river on the run to Chinju, and hinted that his story pissed me off enough to join up with an NK rifle company and get in on the Pyongyang land grab.

He shouted to the bartender, "Two more drinks, *dozo!*"

We adjusted our holsters, staggered back through 'No Man's Land' and reached the hospital in one piece. Richard slept late and I went to the docks. The rumor I'd heard was true. Our former 17th Regiment had arrived and was preparing to unload while an NCO from the ship set up his miniature field desk to check off the names of the disembarking troops. I shouted up to the rows of familiar faces on the port side rail as a deep baritone voice called out from the shadows of a shed thirty yards behind.

A tall lean black MP stepped out into the light; his hand poised an inch above his un-flapped holster. The lip of his helmet liner rested on the bridge of his nose and masked his eyes. "If you ain't gone when I gets back, you be one dead motherfucker."

I tied the rawhide thongs of my holster to my thigh and voiced what I'd tell the court martial board if he drew. "I'm an American soldier making an authorized visit on a non-restricted pier in broad daylight."

He rendered a parting shot. "I be back in ten minutes, man." My gratitude was brief—he was punctual.

"I pretty fas' wit' a gun, man!"

The topside troops hooted and jeered "Ten bucks says Mercy gets the Spade before he clears his holster!" The only exit in the air's heavy curtain of expectation was through an irredeemable loss of face before my former regiment.

"Not fast enough," I said, "but if you were carrying a spear you might have had a chance." The gentle lap of water against the pier cut through the sudden silence.

"I gonna kil-l-l-l-l yo white ass!" With fingers spread wide I mimicked the stance of Gary Cooper in *The Plainsman,* and paraphrased a class B movie line. "If you're tired of living, shit-face, draw!"

A motionless minute passed. 'Johnny Ringo' wordlessly turned back and dissolved into the wharf's shadows. The NCO at the desk cried, "That ain't no way to be talkin' to a man on duty!"

Years of suppressed resentment exploded in his face. "You loudmouth rear-echelon son of a bitch, go for your gun so I can blow your stupid goddamn head off!"

His hands froze. "You're lucky you ain't goin' into the line with us, Mercy. You might wind up dead."

I fought down the impulse to pistol whip him down through the planks and into the deep six. "I doubt if a potbellied twenty-year drunk like you could do it!"

His impotent fist smashed onto the desk and blood drained from his face as the topside troops whistled, jeered and cheered. Departed, my bubbling bile steamed me through the hot city streets, until I found myself back in the tobacco-hazed bar of the previous night. Endless cups of saké brought back thoughts of the G.I. I'd left behind at Chinju. When I slipped out into the dark through the café's burlap strip door I saw the back of a boisterously drunk G.I. who stood a few feet away. He cursed and hip-fired his grease gun into the flank of a farmer's horse. The animal winnowed pitifully as the petrified owner stood nearby in fearful silence: *You might have to kill him...the blow you'll need to knock him out...could fracture his skull...which he deserves, but you could get some serious stockade time...if he shifts the weapon towards the farmer...kill him anyway.* I left there as a homicide waited to happen.

Richard slept away the next few days and I listened to the atrocity stories told by the incoming wounded. Up at Waegwan, a G.I. platoon that surrendered got tied up and machine-gunned by a grinning squad of encircling NKs. One G.I. got away, ran into a US combat patrol that returned to capture the NK officer and his squad. Incomprehensibly they were brought back alive! A crazed looking 8th Cavalry engineer added, "We hid three of our wounded officers, hoping to pick them up later with a Jeep, but the Gooks got to them first. They slow roasted one and ripped off his thumbs. Then they gouged out the eyes of another two with bayonets. They torched them all with gasoline." Another 8th Cavalry man said three ambushed G.I.s from the 35th Regiment had their tongues ripped out, hands cut off, and then were blinded by bayonets. Elsewhere, four other soldiers were thrown alive into a raging pit fire to the wild jeers of their captors. In another sector a wounded and out of ammo engineer killed eight NKs with his entrenching tool and was posthumously awarded a CMH.

That afternoon, I visited an airborne buddy named Lewis at the 536th MP Detachment's POW detention pen. Inside a guard left his loaded carbine lying behind him while he sawed wooden planks and his prisoner sat nearby scanning a Captain Marvel comic book.

I bellowed to Lewis, "Nice rest camp you're running here, when does the USO show start?"

He pointed his jaw toward my belt-worn bayonet. "Keep that in the scabbard, Mercy, or we're both in trouble." I nodded, with no mention of the pistol under my jacket.

We chatted beside some cowering NKs who survived yesterday's B-29 saturation bombing that allegedly killed fifteen thousand of them along the Naktong.

"I hear you've got that Gook who killed a platoon of G.I.s up on the river yesterday." Bill motioned to a row of tents.

"Yeah," he said. He called out Major Kwong Taek.

"Remember, Mercy," he added, "we're the good guys."

The sturdy arrogant shifty-eyed slime had the overconfident fast-talking demeanor of an Asian back alley pimp and an unconcealed threat in his voice. "I'm an officer and that warrants a salute, doesn't it?"

My eyes locked with his and my hand fused onto my bayonet. I inwardly cursed the discipline that had me give a gut retching salute that severely tested my belief in military customs and tradition, and knew I'd face murder charges if I didn't get out of Pusan soon. Later that afternoon I drew a carbine and ammo from the hospital's supply and went up into the surrounding hillside to vent my anger on tree stumps.

At nearby Yongsan heavy tank and infantry battles raged. Two hundred Navy planes filled the skies at all times to block the breaches the NKs made in the UN lines. That was where I wanted to be, wading ammo belt deep in slaughtered NKs.

Thoughts of death drew me into the night's shadows beside the hospital's morgue tent. A busy medical team sang *I've Been Working on the Railroad*, while they stacked up piles of G.I. corpses: *How different from the movies...would Taps ever sound the same again? Yet, it's worth the risk...why does nothing but war exist for me?*

Richard was well by the end of the second week and we had photos made at a local shop before he departed for the line at Changyong. Wanting to make phone contact with Robertson back in Sendai, I volunteered to serve as a stretcher bearer aboard the hospital ship U.S.S. *Mercy* that sailed to Kobe the next morning. Shipboard and weapon restrictions in Japan forced me to reluctantly entrust my .45 revolver to Private Cranston who I'd met on the S.S. *Brewster* three years before.

The ship docked in Japan, and the wounded were loaded into waiting ambulances. All onboard volunteers were free until 1700 hours when the ship sailed for Pusan. With the greatly improved phone service, Robertson was on the line within minutes and he carried his written transfer request to regimental headquarters that afternoon. The remaining hours were spent with a former Japanese soldier-turned-reporter. He recognized in my dirt-baked hands a potential infantry story and hissed approvingly over our shared rice cakes and tea at my negative assessments and embellished accounts of the personal carnage I'd inflicted upon his country's former vassals. He departed and I went on a frantic two hour search for a *Samurai* sword to fulfill my fantasy of leading Asian troops in battle. By occupational decree these were denied to all Japanese, causing the shopkeepers I visited to apologetically bow with deep regrets over failed accommodations.

Docking at dawn in Pusan I should not have been surprised to learn that Cranston was under arrest in quarters for having wounded a G.I. with my pistol in a barroom brawl the previous night.

"God damn it, Mercy, he drew on me first!"

The provost marshal wore my prized S&W. It was futile to try and get back the pistol that had unfailingly released the larcenous instincts in all ranks.

I bought a 24x18 inch South Korean flag from an old street vendor whose eyes glittered appreciatively when I chose his country's colors over my own. I visualized it fluttering from my rifle stock, Nipponese-style, as in the newsreel footage I remembered from vanquished China. I was back home in G Company two hours later.

CHAPTER 16

We're Breaking Out

I ran toward Richard standing beside the mess tent's cleaning vats. He wore, as did I, a camouflaged Marine Corps cover on his helmet and a standard issue automatic on his hip. We spoke simultaneously.

"Where's your revolver?"

He laughingly told me about selling his pistol to the G.I. truck driver who brought him up from Pusan and how that was better than having some officer or medic steal it. He sympathetically nodded when told how mine had been lost to the 'dust bin' of history then followed up with some G Company news. The daring duo of Herbert and Krocheck were still 'present and accounted for.' Barszcz still had the company, which had been pulled out of the line to rest up for tomorrow's big event. I asked what that might be. "We're breaking out," he gleefully answered, "crossing the Naktong! And I've saved you a squad leader spot in one of our new platoons, if you're interested?"

I wondered aloud why the captain would approve of that, but the riddle was partially demystified when Richard brought me to the edge of a precipice. Below in the gulch I saw the miraculously baffling workings of the gods in the eyes of one hundred South Korean soldiers that stared back up at us. My lifelong dream had come true! I raised my arms and shouted in jubilation. *"Banzai!"* I returned their silent bows, knowing that this was more than unintended chance.

Later Richard introduced me to our platoon leader, Lieutenant Bill Buckley. He smiled and with a firm handshake welcomed me aboard. The former Marine from Teaneck, New Jersey was a lean twenty-three year-old, with a quick wit and a dash of Irish melancholia about him. He also had a sense of humanity to his otherwise military veneer and looked forward to tomorrow's crossing.

"There's a shortage of G.I. replacements," Buckley said, "so battalion sent us 100 Koreans instead. They're cannon fodder meant to do all the dangerous jobs and save the lives of G.I.s." Half of them formed up our 5th ROK Platoon, and the other fifty made up the 6th Platoon. This gave the company an additional 100 men above the normal four platoon TO&E. "Our men will lead tomorrow's assault," Buckley said, "and probably every other one the company makes for the duration. They'll run most all of the patrols and we're going to kill a lot of Gooks, though preferably not our own."

Our Korean 'Katusas' (**K**orean **A**ugmentation **T**o the United States Army, a program still in effect) suffered from not having come from a longstanding gun culture such as our own, which made just loading a rifle difficult. Most had been inducted into the Army via some roadside checkpoint. Conscripted in the morning, by nightfall they were armed and in uniform, but few received any real training. Most were in their early twenties and a few in their mid-thirties. I hoped that some had at least fought as guerrillas against the Japanese.

Their poverty-stricken nation produced varying degrees of patriotism, but all held the mythic belief that Korea, was indeed the center of the universe. I would have to rely on my rough Japanese to communicate and the few words of English some of them knew. What I knew of the Koreans was that they had lived under conquering armies and warring regimes for millennia and had therefore developed an uncanny ability to easily size up authority figures. I was unsure as to what type of persona I should project: *Should I be a cold militaristic grunting type, like a cinematic Samurai? Or be more Western and reasonable?*

Inspecting the platoon proved disappointing. The eyes of my troops lacked those signs of Asiatic fanaticism and cruelty that I'd remembered from *The Mask of Fu Manchu* and *General Yang,* and which was so abundant in their northern brothers. They all seemed to lack a potential for violence, mayhem or murder, but hopefully war would 'bring out the best in them.' I smiled in recalling their similarity to the peaceful farmers in Korosawa's film, *The Seven Samurai.*

After chow Richard and I talked with Sergeant Jackson of the 3rd Platoon, a vet of WWII. I asked whether I should use a Thompson submachine gun or an M1 on tomorrow's river crossing. His mild manner and voice drew others in.

"Stick to whatever makes you comfortable. Well, you boy's better get some rest. You'll be busy tomorrow. And by the way, that's when I'll be checking out. So I'll just say good luck and goodbye to y'all now."

He seemed serenely indifferent to his fate as he left. A nearby soldier whispered that he'd earlier given his watch away to another NCO. I thought Jackson to be the perfect stoic soldier, unflinching in the face of death: *"If you have to die, better in a firefight than in bed. Besides, he's pretty old... almost forty."*

Near dawn, Richard and I watched from a distance the Chaplain praying with his mostly Mexican-American flock. An hour later our regimental truck convoy arrived at the Chang-dong assembly area and Buckley gave us the order of battle for the Naktong crossing. The 2nd Indianhead Division and General Keen's 25th would be at the extreme left flank of the Pusan Perimeter, at a place known as the Hook. Our 24th was next, with the 19th and 21st Regiments on line and the 34th in reserve. Our 2nd Battalion would be the first wave across, followed by the 1st with the 3rd Battalion held in reserve. On our right would be the 21st Regiment, then the 1st Cavalry Division and the 5th RCT. The extreme right of the line was the old port city of Pohang-dong, which was being covered by the ROK 3rd Division and supported by the big guns of the battleship *Missouri*.

A shot rang out as the company fanned through its assembly area and I dashed towards a group of seated ROKs. One who I didn't recognize stepped out of the circle with a smoking pistol and said, "Gun go off by accident." I overrode an impulse to bend the barrel of the piece across his nose.

"Learn how to handle that weapon or turn it in. Who the hell are you anyway?"

He paused dramatically. "I am… Han."

He was the captain's interpreter. The thirty-one year-old heavy-lidded and devious-eyed translator held an attitude that was common among favored indigenous personnel, who often believed they shared their patron's rank—and authority. I distrusted him at first sight.

For the next three days confusion reigned over the hourly changes in the Eighth Army's jump off time. Pontoon boats and required bridges were misplaced or never delivered. To the northeast, 108 air miles away, General MacArthur's X Corps was driving on Seoul. Marines had taken Wolmi-do Island as a prelude to the landing at Inchon. Next, they captured Kimpo Airbase on their way to the capital city.

Eighty-two B-29s were scheduled to carpet bomb the northern shores of the Naktong River and the impenetrable walled city of Waegwan. GHQ hoped the 500-pound bombs would demoralize and/or obliterate the North Korean army's resistance and psychologically reenergize our troops with new zeal and gusto. Unfortunately, high winds called off the raid and the enemy's resistance stiffened.

At 1530 hours, Buckley and I crawled to the edge of a clearing and scanned the wide motionless stretches of beach on each side of the river, but saw no signs of troops, guns or movement.

"Sure looks like they're out of artillery, doesn't it, sir? They have to know we're here."

Buckley nodded and pointed over our abutment's knee high grass to the fifteen yards of open beach we'd cross to reach the water. On the far side was a rocky, five-storied, dragon-shaped ridge that loomed up 200 weed-filled yards from the shoreline.

He handed me his field glasses and said, "That's our first objective." I could see no signs of life there either. He dipped his head towards the flanking shrubs and the dozens of olive drab aluminum boats that the 3rd Combat Engineers had secured there the previous night.

"I'm sure the Gooks saw those being delivered, Mercy. The Ol' Man told me this morning that the NKs have already launched a counterattack in four or five sectors and are actually holding some high ground on this side of the river!"

I was surprised. "Did he say anything else, sir?"

He smiled. "Yes, there'll be no artillery support. Almost every round was used up last month to keep those little bastards over there on the other side; and we damn near wiped out their whole goddamned army in the process."

"I hope not, sir," I said. Still smiling, he told me to bring the men up in ten minutes.

I could almost feel my facial features turn Asian as I ran headlong to the boats with the platoon and my rifle's Korean flag snapping in the wind. Halfway across the river low flying U.S. jets roared in with guns and cannons blazing. Rockets and *whooshing* napalm tanks erupted with searing artistry across random beachhead points and the ridgeline of our first objective. The intoxicating sounds of battle played inharmoniously to the ROKs who aimlessly shifted oars as our boat drifted towards shore. *They're having second thoughts about landing...*

Enemy fire raked the flotillas of small squad size assault boats on both our flanks in the winding river, but mysteriously disregarded us. I stood and fired my pistol under a squall of spent .50 caliber and 20mm cannon casings that dropped from the low zooming jets on their second run. My pistol rounds went unheard or noticed beside our boat's stilled portside paddles. My sights shifted between the backs of the two soldiers who rose from their seats as the others huddled together. I hesitated. *If I kill one, they might all panic and overturn the boat.*

Robert (left) and Richard (right) after crossing the Naktong River and on the road to Taejon.

I shouted. "*Kogu masu! Kogu* [Row it! Row]!" Their hesitant halfhearted pulls brought us nearer to the beach's grassy knoll and the burst of LMG fire I expected at any second. I leapt in and foot-paddled the stalled craft to shore then shoved, pulled and kicked the bug-eyed troops up to a low abutment wall. I saw no bloodlust in their eyes when I yelled, "*Tsuke-ken* [Fix bayonets]!"

Barszcz bellowed as he and Hungerford approached. "Get your men moving!"

I stammered. "Sir, I was waiting for the artillery support."

The captain fanned an impatient hand up into the sky, empty of planes. "You just had it, now move them out!"

The flutter of my rifle's flag pulled me onto the knoll and I sang out a long awaited call. "*Tatsuseki* [Charge]!"

Sporadic enemy mortar and machine gun rounds cracked around us.

We raced across the field with Richard's men almost abreast when a single shot rang out from the rear. Han, lagging behind brought down a concealed NK before he could shoot Buckley in the back. We reached the crest against light resistance and I hurled down grenades on the fleeing NKs while the ROKs secured the extreme left flank. The company arrived and an enemy 85mm tank shell sent two of my men screaming to their deaths onto the boulders below. I dug in beside a raised grave mound, knowing that the seated corpse inside faced east by custom. Two more tank rounds slammed in. Richard spotted the muzzle flashes 400 yards out. He fired two clips of tracers that at best only ricocheted off the turret. The gunner fired another round that shaved off the right half of the mound from where Richard was firing, an instant after he'd instinctively rolled to the left. That maneuver saved his life.

Below, on the east-west running roadway a near tragic-comedy drama was being played out. In the close to impenetrable darkness, two American recon patrols entered from opposite wings and clashed center stage in a forty-minute firefight. Then both withdrew in a haze of enshrouding cordite. Casualty count unknown.

I awoke to a macabre and gothic style dawn, and a strong premonition that Robertson was in the company area. It wasn't only the ROKs that sat staring at the F-80s, screaming in with banshee-like wails as they strafed and napalmed the valley. The cleft skeletal jaws and empty eye sockets of the dead that had been unearthed from the burial mound by the night's tank barrages shared the vista. The napalm left a heavy gasoline scent wafting along the Songu road where we later formed up. I nodded when Lieutenant Buckley asked if I knew Sergeant Jackson.

"He was our only KIA during the crossing. Sergeant Gay lost a leg when an artillery shell fell on the battalion's motor pool."

I shrugged. "That's a strange place to be while your platoon is making ready for a crossing. Well, that will slow up his bugging out considerably."

A familiar voice spun me around and Robertson leapt from the passing Jeep. With a grin he shouted, "Hi Boy-san! Where's Butterball?"

I laughed and pointed to the skyline. "He's bringing down the last squad. What time did you get here?"

He paused. "At 0300 hours, but the first sergeant wouldn't let me cross the river 'til daylight."

Buckley looked him up and down and immediately offered him a squad leader spot as Robertson went on talking about Camp Schimmelphenning.

"You wouldn't believe it, Boy-san! The post was overrun with cheating wives, black marketing, and rumors of a Third World War. Three

MPs from the 519th Group in Sendai committed suicide after they got orders for Korea. They probably didn't want to leave their Japanese wives, or their comfortable off-post housing."

Richard also offered some comic relief. He read aloud the NK surrender pamphlet he found, written in English and signed by the 'Dear Leader,' General Kim Il-sung:

> Do you miss your parents, wives, children and homes? Thanks to the kind care of the People's Army, war prisoners are treated by doctors at a moment's notice. Surely you have aged mothers at home who spend their days and nights sighing for you, and dear wives who fondle youngsters crying for their absent fathers. To those dear ones awaiting letters and your home coming, news informing them of your dog's death must prove not only a shock but also an arrow of keen pangs. What an unworthy death it is that you should be sacrificed on a battlefield that has no personal interest whatsoever for you and in a war that has been staged by Wall Street warmongers. For what infernal cause do you wander in this valley of death when you have your flowering youth shining before you in all the rays of hope? Cast aside anxieties! Do not hesitate to surrender to the People's Army! You will then be able to meet again your comrades who have come before you, soon to return to your sweet home. Wave this handbill high in the air and come over to us! This is the only way of saving your precious lives and of enabling you to return to your families. The Korean People's Army never shoots those who surrender. Come over to us in full confidence.

Richard added. "All that takes place, of course, before they roast you alive."

At point with the platoon as the company advanced, I inwardly looked at how we'd all been thrown together: *It was my phone call that brought Robertson to the platoon...what if he gets killed—or wounded?* He was an extension of our twin ship, and we'd all agreed long ago that a wartime line company was where we wanted to be, even before we knew each other. Sharing all this together though, only made it better, and similar to the three soldiers in *Gunga Din*, Ballentine, Cutter and McChesney.

125

CHAPTER 17

Back to Taejon

With the platoon a hundred yards behind, Buckley and I moved into a village, and leapt inside a roadside hut. We suddenly stood nervously laughing in a web of crisscrossed beams of light shining through holes made by the twenty rounds that ripped through the mud walls. Miraculously, we lived. *Maybe there's a God after all*! Though Robertson's squad, sheepishly grinning, mistook his sole shot as a signal for random fire; nothing was said that would dampen their spirits on the march north.

Later, with Robertson and Richard at point, Buckley's excited messenger quickly led me up from the rear to where they and some of the platoon stood over the dark green and bloated body of an NK.

Buckley somberly intoned, "Mercy, this man is dead" and I replied in kind, "Are you sure, sir?" I fired a round into the corpses' ballooned belly, which neither exploded nor deflated as expected, but added a gothic touch to the burning huts and charred black mosaic of other malodorous decomposed bodies and smoldering fields. Nearby, other jubilant ROKs swarmed, like victorious elephant-hunting pygmies, over the strafed and rocketed remains of a gutted Russian made T-34. A week of sporadic nighttime fighting followed.

GHQ assumed that the fleeing NK were defeated and would either surrender or quietly hide *en masse* in the mountains until the danger passed. They sent our army on what they thought would be a lackadaisical and bloodless pursuit, a long term mistake almost equal to Hitler's in letting the defeated British forces escape from Dunkirk.

The company mounted up on Sherman tanks and advanced on Obongni, until mortar and burp gun fire started raining in on us. Our tank's commander shouted from his open turret for everyone to get off. In the glare of a mortar round exploding among the trees I saw a ROK run through the branch-laced darkness to retrieve his helmet left on the tank; then shot dead by the startled sergeant as he sprang onboard.

Twins on Road Back

Associated Press Wirephoto

BRISK PACE is set by Corp. Richard J. Mercy (left), 19, and twin brother, Pfc. Robert W. Mercy, both of 82-61 166th St., Jamaica, Queens, on way to Taejon as 24th Division moves up to recapture town.

An Associated Press news clipping immortalized Richard (left) and me (right) on the road back to Taejon at age 19.

Our assault ended in a trophy hunt. Butterball collected C-rations from the enemy dead, as Robertson and I relieved them of their American-made watches.

At dawn we passed a few napalmed T-34s. We spent all day searching for the fleet-footed NKs until 2200 hours when Barszcz ordered the company to set up a roadside ambush.

The same shot as in the previous photo, but without the news copy. This photo appeared in the Journal American, the Daily News and other publications.

"Men, a cut off company of Gooks might be coming through here later tonight. If their hands aren't up, shoot to kill."

All night my fantasies went unrealized and Buckley's insights proved true, when he predicted that "those Gooks have already escaped into the countryside wearing their civvies."

Our roadblock before the shooting started when some NKs were spotted in civilian garb.

Our roadblock position after the shooting started.

The NKs were known to wear civilian clothes under their uniforms, which made possible their continual escapes. Our inability to track them down seemed to have dashed my hopes of at least one good firefight before the war ended.

At week's end a few determined enemy rear guard machine guns held up our battalion. Sherman tanks lashed out their fiery annoyance while 1st Battalion patrols flanked into a village a mile away. In the police compound there, they found the mutilated remains of nearly two dozen G.I.s. The 1st Battalion guys caught up with the executioners and—inexplicably, brought them back alive.

Later, I used my bayonet to assuage my curiosity with a mangled bundle of sopping wet rags that were embedded in the tread marks on the road. A bit of forced 'combat humor' and hatred loosened my moral anchor. I shouted to a nearby G.I. and urinated on what thirty tons of rolling steel had compressed. "It's a fucking Gook!"

He snorted back. "Fuck, if I weren't laughing so hard, I'd piss on him, too!"

So much for 'a little touch of Harry in the night...'

During our forty-eight hour pause we re-christened our squad leaders and machine gun crews with more manageable Americanized names. Hyun Sin Wo, Whang Bang Hyun and the like proved too difficult to remember under fire—or otherwise. Excluded from this was the unflappable "ROK One," whom the Koreans had personally picked as their titular platoon leader. This tall, muscular, mild-mannered thirty-something-year-old wore an air of intelligence and unassuming humility that was impressive and uplifting. He had the respect and allegiance of the entire platoon.

We named each of our four twelve-man squads after a major Korean city. Robertson's was Chin-ju, my brother's was Seoul and mine was Masan. The fourth squad, made up of two LMG sections, was called Taegu. Taegu was commanded by Passwater, an egocentric self-promoting corporal who recently transferred in from the company's disbanded 6th ROK Platoon. His only known talent was endearing himself to officers who could influence his career. We wondered how he wound up in the infantry. His two machine gun crews, the 'Ritz Brothers,' and the 'Three Stooges' often proved dangerously amusing.

Left to right: ROK One (who was later killed), ROK Tom (my squad leader), Kim (an LMG gunner) and the ever-loyal ROK "Toshi," who was wounded at the battle for Uijongbu.

I thought the wisest Korean was the broad-shouldered, forty-year-old farmer from Kwangyang who I named Tom, and made leader of my Masan squad. His rugged expansive smile, intelligence and acute sense of justice constantly reminded me of my much-admired uncle Mudge who'd served on the Yangtze River during American's gunboat diplomacy days

131

and in WWII.

Richard baptized his chosen Seoul squad leader with his own given name. ROK Richard was more of a soft spoken student than a soldier. His intellect and growing ability with English would prove helpful. He compensated for his lack of killer instincts with steadfast patriotism, loyalty and strong Buddhist beliefs.

Robertson's choice for an alter ego was perfectly placed in the imposing six-foot-one muscular Korean he'd named Ken. His tanned, chiseled face regularly ran the full gamut of undecipherable emotions. This sometimes made him appear guilty when he wasn't, which was quite rare. He was quick in sizing up situations and somehow reminded me of 'Big Stoop,' the comic book character in *Terry and the Pirates*. Good natured Ken was a skillfully disarming raconteur who'd served as one of Japan's infamous prison guards over captured G.I.s in World War II.

Those Koreans usually labored hard to win favor with their Japanese masters and could prove as sadistically cruel, a difficult feat to accomplish. Ken, stationed at the Hiroshima Prison, survived the atomic bombing by being in the lower dungeons guarding downed U.S. airmen when the bomb detonated. He would mime how he'd comforted the frightened women who sought safety in the bowels of the prison.

"Boooooooommmmmmm," he bellowed, with his broad hands parting the air into a mushroom cloud that turned and fell onto imaginary soft shoulders. His libidinous grin through a half-dozen gold capped teeth startlingly resembled the "Yellow Peril" propaganda posters of WWII. After the blast, he said, enraged civilians mobbed and murdered some of the American POWs. They had been waiting outside to be trucked to a different location, so that Japanese intelligence could re-interrogate them about the new awesome weapon. Perhaps it was this that prompted Ken's "caring" lieutenant to threaten a fear-maddened crowd with his half-drawn sword and saved the lives of those downed airmen.

Repatriated in 1946, Ken was transported back home aboard the ill-fated *Oki Jima Maru* along with three thousand other Koreans. Many were former "comfort girls" who'd been subjected to the sadistically lascivious whims of the Japanese infantry. In the predawn hours and miles from shore, a mysterious explosion sank the *Oki Jima*. Ken and a few hundred other potential hostile witnesses for the forthcoming Tokyo war trials were later pulled from the oil-slicked waters. Ken said, "Japanee no want see Korean in court."

A lesser star of the platoon was the reluctant soldier who cursed every order under his breath. Robertson dubbed him "Badass." Then we had the omnipresent smiling ROK whom I named "Toshi" in deference to the film actor Toshiro Mifune. His loyalty and quiet bravery were both welcomed and touching. Then there was "Kumasuri," meaning "medic" in Japanese, who carried a rifle despite his compassion. Last, but not least was "Our Man Friday," the platoon's runner. Though seventeen he looked to be an innocent twelve-year-old that seemed to transform every weapon he held into a misplaced toy. He never questioned any given mission or order.

We marched unopposed toward the nemesis city of Taejon, which General MacArthur had wanted captured by his old 1st Cavalry outfit, and which plan had fallen through. Following Mac Arthur's September landing in Seoul, the Chinese and Russians retreated north with a major portion of the NK army and four hundred U.S. POWs. Robertson, Richard and I talked about the expected house-to-house fighting and paid little attention to the Jeep with two correspondents that stopped nearby. Richard's seven-grenade necklace, six overlaying bandoleers and our twin-ship caught their eye. We happily posed for photos, which were to be run in our hometown papers, the *New York Daily News* and *Journal American*.

Jubilant crowds of flag waving children, matronly women and old men lined the banks of the railroad tracks and cheered the company on towards Taejon. "*Mansai, mansai, mansai* [Hurray, hurray, hurray]!" Private Copeland, the captain's nineteen-year-old black driver, was some yards ahead and responded most to the pomp and circumstance. Each time he raised both arms in the traditional responsive fashion the crowd enthusiastically cheered and roared. "*Mansai! Mansai! Mansai* "He laughed hysterically as I passed. "Man, I feels like a motherfuckin' king!"

We closed in on Taejon and were disappointed that the NKs left without firing a shot. One of our squads later spotted a hand breaking from the earth. The G.I. was barely breathing when pulled out; the other two American and ROK soldiers buried alive with him couldn't be revived. Fifty-three more G.I.s and scores of ROKs were entombed in a well behind police headquarters. That night, two other trenches give up four hundred additional executed political prisoners. By week's end over twelve hundred murdered civilians and 100 G.I.s had been found.

Twenty miles north, in a prison yard at Chungju, the NKs spaced sticks of dynamite beneath five hundred rope-bound ROKs and eighteen G.I.s. The survivors of the blast who weren't killed outright were buried alive. A pyromaniac commander of a retreating NK column nailed shut the local jail doors in the village of Sach'on. Three hundred officials and other suspects were burned alive. Their horror filled screams would be remembered forever by civilian witnesses. The NKs made no distinctions between northern and southern civilians and would kill either on a rule violation or whim. Yet, one incredible tale emerged from the recaptured city of Chinju.

A G.I., suffering from pneumonia and five battle wounds, had gone almost a week without food and water. He told an incredible story about an NK soldier who had courageously defied his officer's orders to kill him and the other soldiers and was pistol whipped then machine-gunned along with them. The South Korean State Police firing squads were busy, too, killing one hundred and twenty suspected saboteurs and communist sympathizers in a single mass execution outside Taegu. This, not surprisingly, received more press coverage than did the NK atrocities against our troops.

Richard and I searched out every house for any NK stragglers then returned to the company area where one hundred fearful POWs sat in an open field. Curiously benign G.I.s stood nearby to view them. I called out my dark intentions to the captain as he passed. "Sir, let me and my men take the prisoners back to the rear!" He wordlessly turned into the CP.

My brooding concentration was broken by a sudden and prolonged gasp from the kneeling prisoners who, like shafts of wheat caught in an artic blast, were reeled back on their haunches. Their terror-frozen stares remained on the shirtless Private Copeland who demonically leapt out from the shadows of a flanking hut. His eyes bulged, his head and lean ebony body swayed in the syncopated rhythm of an awe inspiring Watusi dance, topped off with quasi-Swahili wails, while making menacing spear-like thrust with the bayonets he held like spears in each hand. The only missing prop was a boiling kettle. Copeland may have been the first black many of the NK had seen, other than the ebony-hued images of the Buddhist pantheon. Copeland's ferocity echoed that of the local sprites as he loped off with his long Nubian strides, back into the shadows whence he came. I was tempted to applaud.

Three prisoner's hands rose to use the latrine. In a bit of trivial revenge, I barked in Japanese, "No."

The voice of Sergeant Goodman, the company's dewy-eyed would-be Chaplain's assistant called out from behind "Don't you threaten those men!" Those were astonishing words, given what we found just that day. "You are not to threaten those men, Mercy. It's God's will," he said.

I quelled my sudden impulse to strangle his nauseating evangelism. A wave of depression swept over me, knowing a summary field court martial had not been convened as in WWII, when captured enemy officers and ranking NCOs were executed for far less reason than the crimes we had discovered in Taejon. I wondered why this war was being fought so halfheartedly.

Angrily I left and took George Sieto along to run a patrol into the

134

surrounding hills. An hour later a flushed out NK dashed across our path a hundred yards ahead. The amused ROKs shouted reassuringly he'd not be harmed after my warning shot cracked across his bow.

A shrill cry rang out from behind. "Don't you hurt that man!" Goodman seemed to have followed our trail for indiscernible reasons. Sieto asked who he was. "God" I mockingly replied, hoping Goodman's deluded dream for everlasting salvation would move him to obstruct my sworn duty, so I could then personally introduce him to Jesus; and assumed, too, that I'd be exonerated by any court martial convened in Taejon that day. I hated him far more than the fleeing NK whose head was wedged in my sights. It wasn't Goodman, but some unfathomable thing inside that made me lower my sights to his waist, where the bullet exited above his hipbones and caused only minimal damage.

Sieto shouted. "Good shot, Mercy!"

Oozing blood, the panicked NK soldier ran and fell bowing at my feet. His fear-filled eyes snapped to my rifle fixed bayonet as I gave a *Samurai* bellow "*Oui, kunyaro, anata-no tamodachi-o, doko ka* [Hey, bastard, where are your friends]?" Long rivulets of sweat poured down his head, as his pleading eyes followed my yanked back rifle for its intended bayonet thrust. A convulsed cry stuck in his throat.

I mimicked the stance and pitiless expression of the Japanese soldier seen in my mind's eye, ready to bayonet his Chinese prisoner: *Do it! Kill off all weaknesses!* Then, just as suddenly, another inscrutable cry unraveled my fantasy: *Don't do this...live the meaning of our name...mercy. Funny, why would I think of something so ridiculous as that?* In spite of myself, my pose thawed, and I had the ashen NK taken back to the company enclosure. Goodman, nearby, ordered me to follow him to the CP. The crushed pebbles beneath my feet whispered up, "Kill him. Kill him. Kill him."

"Captain," said Goodman pompously, "I want this man charged with war crimes against humanity!"

Barszcz spun and snarled an inch from his face, "Get the fuck out of my sight, now!"

Together back outside, I wasn't sure if it was God, conscience, or fear of a court martial that kept me from killing him. I found a secluded spot to think and sharpened my bayonet under what warmth was left in the late September sun: *Goodman won't be missed...everyone knows he's never fired a single shot during the course of the entire campaign.* I rationalized wanting my yet-to-be offered sergeant stripes more than I wanted retribution on Goodman, Herbert, Krocheck or the Gook? Robertson's arrival broke my dark and all consuming spell.

135

"I just killed my first two NKs. Pumped three rounds into one's face and emptied the clip into the other guy's chest. Also ran across a squad of G.I.s out there too, and funny thing was that when the shooting started their lieutenant bugged out." Later, near the officer's mess, Robertson pointed to Herbert. "That's him."

At dusk Buckley ordered me to set up a guard perimeter around the company area with two squads.

"They've been running nonstop patrols since we crossed the Naktong, sir! Besides, this is supposed to be a rest area."

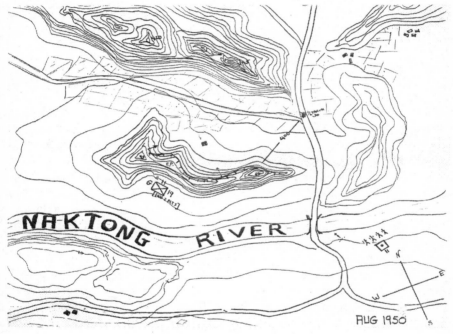

The Naktong River.

He smiled blankly. "Four hours on and four hours off."

I repeated this in labored Japanese to each of the ten guards I positioned at wide intervals across the pitch dark field and cautioned the accompanying squads to memorize the route they would take when it was time to relieve the others. Thirty minutes later we headed back and found the first guard I'd posted asleep. They all understood the penalty for this and from the squad's emanated searching gaze I knew they wondered if I were capable of dispensing their army's borrowed version of Japanese

Bushido, which required his instant death to avenge the insult to my authority. That God-like mantel sat uneasily on my untutored western shoulders, if only for lack of early inculcation and recognizing the improbability of applying conflicting cultural codes. Yet I admired Bushido's idealized moral and martial demands. My mind raced for a viable solution I suddenly recalled a scene from *The General Dies at Dawn: Yang's men smiled when he countermanded his own order that an offending soldier shoot himself...do I show mercy as he did...and gain their loyalty...or kill him...as they expect and win fearful obedience?*

I slammed the butt of my rifle into the sleeping soldier's chest, in lieu of a bullet. The tip of my bayonet beneath his chin lifted him to his feet. I told him that if he slept again, he would die. He grunted: *I should have killed him and relied more on fear.* During the silent march back I equated the night's event to my failure with the Pusan firing squad...

Regimental patrols had picked the area clean of any potential for combat. Surprisingly, battalion hadn't sent down directives for close order drill to break the growing monotony. Buckley changed this after morning chow when he told me we were moving out, and to "saddle up the men."

The perpetually starved ROKs wolfed down their folded pancakes that dripped with jelly. They fumbled with their shoulder-slung rifles and jiggling helmets while they and the rest of the company mounted up on a column of waiting Sherman tanks. We soon closed in on a large village with a small mountain range behind it. Richard and Robertson quickly deployed the platoon. I aimed the tank's .50-caliber at a battalion-sized column of NKs struggling up the distant slope and shouted down to the officer who peered up at me from the open hatch.

"Range, one thousand yards, sir."

He swiftly replied, "Don't fire!" I bolted a round into the chamber. "God damn it, don't fire, that's an order! The war's almost over, so why kill all those men?"

I paused in stunned disbelief. I'd been stopped by another dangerous religious freak from getting all five hundred Gooks in my sights. I quietly mumbled, "Wake me up when this ridiculous game is over!"

Two weeks later Buckley gave us a briefing. "Last night a guerrilla band penetrated the lines of our flanking ROK regiment and killed its entire headquarters command. They looted and burned a nearby town; murdered every man, woman and child in it."

We ran weeks of endless patrols across the scorched fields filled with pockets of napalm-blackened dead. I was mesmerized by the one that eerily died still standing, with a charred calcified arm pointing us up to the high ground where we searched for the elusive NKs. They had committed over 25,000 atrocities to date—that we knew about.

CHAPTER 18

Seoul

We didn't know our destination as our mud splattered trucks rolled by bullet-riddled decomposing bodies on the northbound road. Those scenes were reminiscent of a World War II *Movie-Tone* newsreel. ROK Richard's ecstatic cry startled me and awakened the drowsy troops in all the other trucks.

"Seoul! Seoul!" The platoon leapt, shouted and waved their rifles wildly in the air. "SEOUL! SEOUL!"

Tom slid to my side pointing to the capital's moon-drenched ancient Yi Gate. "Look, Sahji-san," he said, "Is Seoul!"

Buckley led us through the dawn tinged flat expanse of land bordered by dunes and paddy fields that became our bivouac area. He moaned, "No guards needed tonight...the army's in no hurry to catch up with the NKs"

His attitude and comment left me with the empty feeling that the war was all but over. Then, the next morning after he'd returned from the CP he confirmed our deepest suspicions: "We've been ordered to trim a little fat from the platoon, get rid of the less productive ROKs. It looks like the party's over, boys."

Seeing the disheartening glances that Robertson, Richard and I exchanged over our brewing coffee Buckley smiled, "That's the way the cookie crumbles." Near noon he took a bottle of Southern Comfort from his pack and headed towards the CP. Richard called after him, "Hope you can find out what's really up, sir?"

Buckley laughingly pitched back an imaginary grenade. "You can count on it."

We watched him walk away and Robertson sourly noted, "He should have offered us the first drink."

Richard disagreed. "No, he should have invited us along because there'll be other EMs there among the officers, so why not us?"

I chimed in. "Ah, how quickly he's forgotten how we covered his ass on patrols. I hate it when he acts like that, reminds me of my Mick father and his barroom buddies."

Richard groaned, "Well, he's a college boy, what can you expect? By the way, have you noticed how cool the weather's getting?"

With oiled pistols and freshly issued passes we three followed ROK Ken's direction to Seoul's legendary street of *Choon Mo Ra*, known to the Japanese as *Bonjong*, "The Market of Thieves." We found the five city block wide, U.S. Government sanctioned flea market stuffed with mountainous stacks of OD blankets, C-rations and wool sweaters. The Army's brand new issue heavily lined green overcoats, yet unseen by us, were sold at an inflated price beyond our reach. Two of the area's many assigned American MPs disrupted our "liberation" of three of those warm-as-toast and misappropriated items. When the conversation got 'testy' they wound up staring down the barrels of our drawn .45s before theirs could clear their holsters; then politely asked that we leave the overcoats.

Clumps of worn, weathered wooden houses, muddy streets and rows of shops with intact windows ringed the outskirts of an area that had escaped the recent fighting. A joyless blue mixture of potbellied stove smoke, the fragrances of *kimche*, sandalwood and tangy sauces filled the air. Sullen people scurried by to whatever hovel they might call home as we entered Mr. Kim's Watch Shop and earnestly examined the tray of assorted American timepieces he brought from his safe.

Robertson whispered, "They're probably stolen from the PX, or from dead G.I.s."

The impatient owner became rude. "You! Show money or get out!"

Richard's pistol swiped across his skull for that 'insubordination' and Robertson scooped up the watches for added punishment. We dashed between the street's parting crowds and smack into a startled Lieutenant Buckley, whose loyalty instantly transformed him into a chance accomplice. After signaling us into an alley he casually blocked the entrance with his body and pointed the jeweler's pursuing posse down into a long dead end street.

We made a clean getaway, except for the Korean in a ragged trench coat and slouched fedora that skulked behind us. Richard fired a warning shot close to the detective's head, which discouraged his pursuit, then laughed while baring his forearm.

"More watches, just what we needed. With a few more good firefights we might have to start carrying field packs!"

Robertson cynically replied, "We could always fence 'em back to Kim, Boy-san. How much should we charge?"

Back in the company area, Buckley sternly warned us against repeating the day's events just as Supply Sergeant Pollocheck arrived and angrily waved a Statement of Charges at my weaponless hip.

"This is for you to sign, Mercy, for the .45 automatic I see you lost!"

I refused and loudly listed all the artillery, tanks and assorted weapons the Army and G Company in particular had abandoned since Taejon.

He did his enraged bull routine and snorted, "God damn it, Mercy, I'm reporting you to the Ol' Man."

I shouted back, "Get out of my sight, you lowlife rear-echelon bastard! Tell Barszcz I'm never going to sign that, or any other scrap of paper, even if it means a general-fucking court martial!" I waved another red flag in his face. "While you're at it, ask him how much he thinks we owe for all the ammunition we expended taking those goddamn hills while most of you guys sat on your asses writing each other up for citations and promotions!" When he huffed away I pulled the 'missing' pistol from out of my blanket roll. "I hope I gave that bastard a serious case of ulcers." Buckley laughed.

That night, while we sat staring blankly into a small fire, I began to ruminate: "You know it's over when they start breaking out Statements of Charges. Why, in the end, did everything boil down to money, even in the Army where duty, loyalty and honor should reign supreme? That was a plot line they never showed in the movies.

ROK One, Tom, Ken, Richard and Toshi gathered around the fire with us to ward off the late October chill. Despite knowing the platoon would be overjoyed in hearing they might soon be going home I kept it secret. I suggested that each of us should pen our name to the platoon's battle flag, a time-honored Japanese custom. I used my bayonet to draw blood from my arm.

Tom whispered nostalgically, "You, Sahji, Japanese-ou same-same."

Then, out of the shadows stepped the thin and bespectacled Sergeant Winfield Black. He'd lost his WWII non-combat officer status during the 1948 military cutbacks then chose EM status over getting out. His greatest desire was to win the prized Combat Infantry Badge. As the company's PX-NCO he had carte blanche from the CP, so when a patrol or battle loomed he'd become part of the platoon. His spectacles won him the nickname of 'Granny,' which he didn't appreciate. When I placed our platoon flag over his knee and asked him to sign he struggled to conceal the tear that glistened in his eye.

Robertson flipped open the towel he was carrying, revealing the Spandex-banded watches from Kim's Shop. "What do you think of these, Granny?"

Black whispered, "Good Christ, did you guys rob the PX, or what?"

Robertson smirked. "They're tokens of appreciation from the grateful merchants of Seoul for their liberation."

Richard exhaled a cloud of cigar smoke. "Yeah, I thought I'd throw in a little something extra, too."

Robertson mocked, "You mean those boxes of one hundred won notes you and Cass robbed from that bank?"

Black and I muttered simultaneously, "Bank...bank?" What bank?!

Richard recalled a small firefight between some Gooks and G.I.s in a forgotten town weeks before. "This crazy fuck Cass comes running toward me, waving a bazooka round in one hand and pointing the launcher he held in the other at a bank some yards behind him. I threw a fresh clip of AP (armor-piercing) ammo in my piece thinking he'd come across a tank or something. He told me not to pay any attention to firing up front because they were just fuckin' around and that he's found a way to early retirement. We raced into the deserted bank and Cass yelled, 'Don't nobody move, this is a stick up!'

We shot up the counters and walls then he blew the Mickey Mouse lock off the vault with his bazooka. *Vaaaaa-boooommmm!* Suddenly it was raining smoldering money! Cass laughed while we loaded the loot into two empty LMG boxes and admitted he just wanted to rob a bank—any bank! Here's the best part though, we'd marked the boxes 5th ROK Ammo and stashed them in Pollocheck's truck. If the scrounge knew he was sitting on that much cash, he'd pull out what little hair he's got left!"

Next morning we unloaded the moneyboxes and the *Samurai* sword I'd left with Pollocheck weeks before. I smiled recalling how I'd come by it after we'd crossed the Naktong River. I was questioning a farmer, when, for no apparent reason, he began to dig up the battle-worn sword that he'd buried next to the well in his yard. Its timeworn chrysanthemum-dotted handle was nearly as neglected as its dark army scabbard. I tried to decipher the deeper meaning of the moment when he'd presented it to me on bended knees. I wondered if karma was at work and also how he'd came by it; and what about the Jap officer or NCO who carried it? I had no idea why he was giving it to me.

Later, with the sword imperially rested at shoulder, I drilled the platoon by Japanese commands. Barszcz shouted from at the edge of the field, "Get rid of that goddamn sword, Mercy!"

I considered this a blatantly ignorant order in light of what the sword personified in the eyes of my troops: the age old symbol of authority melded with the soul and essence of the warrior; and a thousand years of history. I pushed anger aside and instantly drove a foot-long length of legendary steel, and some measure of my own essence, into the ground. *That stupid bastard could ruin all my work in a second!* There was some comfort in knowing that the platoon couldn't understand the captain's rapid fire English. I halted the drill and saluted as the captain approached.

"Congratulations, that's impressive work, Mercy."

His appreciation paled beside the collective bow and shout of my ROKs as I dismissed them, *"Go Kurosama!"* That translated into "Thank you for all you have done and the lessons you've taught us!" I saluted them with my reclaimed sword and shifted my subtlety defying glance to the captain. He watched me over his shoulder as he walked away.

In the firelight that night we presented each of the astonished ROKs with five one-hundred-won notes, decoratively secured with a flex-band watch. It was an impressive sum for men who only earned fifty cents a month.

ROK Richard was near tears, possibly imagining all the books he'd buy when he got home. 'Big Stoop' Ken endlessly repeated, *"Ah, Sahji, Sahji,"* stuffing single notes into each of his pockets, contemplating God knows what.

For a comedic touch, I did my best Edward G. Robertson impression as I lighted my cigar with a hundred won note. "Say, listen you mugs, stick with me and you'll be eatin' *kimche* outta the swellest joints in Pyongyang, y-e-a-h." ROK Richard turned critic, objecting to the misuse of national currency as he politely bowed.

At dawn, Buckley happily approved our plan to exorcise the "fat demon" out of the lives of our food-binging troops. We ran frontal assaults across the damp fields and backland dunes. Robertson, Richard and I feigned simultaneous death at one point to see which ROK would take command. We would have ended up turning over in our graves had that been a reality! Robertson's mini carbine burst around their feet cut short their heated 'democratic' debate over who should do what next, as all fifty of them stood in a tight compact circle.

They were sopping wet by noon, but understood that an objective was to be taken at all cost. In the process the corpse of an NK was accidentally unearthed. Its bloated black body had a face near liquefying into decay, with spongy mustard colored brains brimming to the edge of a partially severed skull. Legions of maggots fed on what was a perfect prop for a dab of pre-lunch 'combat humor.'

I quickly improvised the witch scene in *Macbeth*, stirring up the putrid matter with my spoon then crackled as the raised ladle dribbled back its contents into eyeless sockets. *"Tabe masho, tabe masho* [Let's eat, let's eat]!"

I pressed the nauseating substance closer to my lips and pantomimed eating. "Mmmmmm, yummy-yummy, gooood!" They collectively cringed. I thought I'd found the ultimate appetite suppressant! For some reason, though, at chow time I couldn't even look at food, but they all went back for seconds.

CHAPTER 19

Kaesong

TWO days later, we happily left the boring bivouac area, with each ROK carrying multiple bandoleers and five grenades. George Company led the regimental column towards the 38th Parallel. We hoped the NKs would prove as fanatical as the Germans did at the Remagen Bridgehead in WWII. It was close to midnight when Buckley pointed to four deserted roadside huts, with an LMG-mounted Jeep parked nearby, and told me to put the platoon in there.

Robertson fell asleep on a corner shelf in the kitchen, nibbling Baby Ruth candy bars. Richard zonked out at the opposite end of the room. I dozed beside the partially opened door that allowed moonlight to fall across the tightly packed ROKs sleeping on the floor. Near dawn the faint sound of crawling and pungent smell of *kimche* startled me into an anxious wakefulness: *They're here...all around me...and outside, too...at least two squads...my M1 won't do it...where was that LMG? Think! Yes! Outside...on the Jeep!Run!*

My heart pounded as I leaped though the door in a do or die effort to reach the Jeep before they could shoot. I sprang up to the pedestal-mounted gun, double-bolted home a round and leveled it at the hut and began to squeeze: *what?!* My trigger finger froze in place by the startling shout that came out of the darkness. "Whaddya doing there!"

I squinted in bewilderment: *Why is he there...a G.I....and coming around that other hut? The Gooks would have killed all the guards...why is he... why am I...*

He called out again, "I said what are ya doin' there?" His voice chilled me as much as the sudden feel of the metallic coldness of the LMG.

In a flash I relived the whirl of images that had brought me to where I stood then whispered in disbelief, "Oh my God! It was a dream!" Dumbfounded I stuttered, "Nothing, I was... doing nothing... I'm okay." The guard stood at High Port and watched as I tiptoed back into the room to lie down again. I was alarmed at how far my dreams had taken me. It was more than a trillion to one chance for that guard to be there at that precise second, to keep me from firing into my own men in the hut. I kept the incident secret from Richard and Robertson.

Soon the regimental march stopped and we deployed throughout the ancient and one-time capital city of Kaesong. ROK Richard gave me a guided tour to where the Japanese had slaughtered the royal family on the eve of their annexation in the 19th century. I only saw it as another rest area far from the line. The 38th Parallel was an hour away, but circulating rumors hinted we'd never do battle with the disintegrating North Korean army that reeled back toward Pyongyang under nightly bomber raids. Behind us another five hundred murdered ROKs and G.I.s were dug up in the town of Yonghung.

The following morning, 15 October, Butterball, Robertson and I sat by a small fire and sharpened our oil-slicked bayonets. Sergeant 'Granny' Black arrived and called us out by our newly bestowed nicknames.

"'Combat' and 'Banzai', the Ol' Man wants you both to report to the CP."

Richard and I exchanged glances, and followed him to where Barszcz, Buckley, Hungerford, Pollecheck and a few others stood next to the field kitchen tent. Their unfamiliar smiles and grins were as surprising as the beaming captain's greeting.

"Happy Birthday, to the Mercy Brothers!" Mixed expressions surged across our faces as the mess sergeant and Rundell came out of the tent carrying a large vanilla iced cake. It was decorated with four erect grenade pins and a single candle lit the inscription: "HAPPY BIRTHDAY, COMBAT AND BANZAI." The Old Man of G Company had done something our own father never had. I felt sandpaper being pulled behind my eyes.

Hungerford quickly added. "I wanted to write 'Mercy' at the top and 'Have No' and 'Show No' around the bottom."

Barszcz laughed. "Before you blow out the candle, make a wish."

Then Pollocheck chimed in, "And whatever the hell it is, I hope it ain't in my truck!"

We spoke in twin-like unison. "That we'll be around for our twenty-first!" My well-honed brass-knuckled bayonet deftly sliced a piece of cake for everyone present and we saved one for our other brother Robertson:

God, I love the Army.

"YOU ARE NOW CROSSING THE 38th PARALLEL, COMPLIMENTS OF THE 1st U.S. CAVALRY DIVISION," read the sign when our trucks passed a blind turn along the twisting road. A blood-curdling cry suddenly rang out—"Mansai!" In a flash every weapon was instantly trained on a group of oddly dressed soldiers sitting beside a fire. They were partially obscured by rocks and I excitedly shouted to the ROKs, "*Utsu nei* [Don't shoot]!"

Robert (center) and part of Richard (right) in January 1951. The bayonet used to cut their birthday cake at Kaesong, which was eventually stolen by a new company commander.

Richard good-naturedly yelled back to the Brits who were enjoying their spot of morning tea and our startled response. "You stupid Limey fucks, you almost got a burst of six on lend-lease!"

A voice like David Niven's laughed back. "Oh! Jolly good, Yank!"

Richard pointed back through our dusty wake. "An ambulance will be heading that way any minute now. Herbert's in the next truck."

Unbeknown to us, China's ambassador had cautioned Washington to proceed no further. He and every communist down to the lowest coolie porter believed that "the foreign devils" were again intending to plunder China and overthrow their infant regime in favor of Chiang Kai-shek.

CHAPTER 20

On To Pyongyang

Ever-darkening clouds covered our long march across the rugged Chungch'on valley hills towards Pyongyang while somewhere ahead 8th Cavalry troops slaughtered hundreds of NKs at the Hamp'o-ri Bridge. Australians bayoneted their way through an apple orchard while on our right the British and ROK forces pressed on smartly. Enemy contact seemed imminent. We trudged shivering wet through two days of torrential rain. Along the way, we had looted some thatched mats and threadbare blankets from the burgeoning refugee caravans that passed on the southbound mud-clogged roads. These lined the interior of our CP foxhole on the ridge. When the company halted, Han's protests about the 'crime' fell on Buckley's deaf ears. Sitting in a foxhole flooded up to our necks we wondered if the ammo in our submerged and waterlogged cartridge belts & bandoleers would fire. Prudently, we each secured a clip of dry ammo under our helmet.

Our rot-smelling uniforms and warped boots didn't dry out on the bone-chilling windy march despite some momentary warmth from the many huts we torched over the next few days. At first sight I felt the rendition of a rolling T-34 tank atop the ten-foot-high obelisk in the next village should suffer the fate of the *Swartz-sticker* that adorned the Nuremberg Stadium. Sergeant Pollocheck thought otherwise.

"God damn it, Mercy I ain't issuing any goddamn explosives for you to go around blowing up monuments without permission."

"Listen," I replied, "this isn't Grant's Tomb we're talking about. I need some dynamite!"

Since I couldn't get any explosives, I returned to the shrine with my

LMG and peppered it with 150 rounds. It looked like the Brandenburg Gate after the fall of Berlin.

Buckley led our morning guerrilla patrol. Sergeant 'Granny' Black tagged along with his M1 on one shoulder and a captured burp gun on the other, wondering which he'd instinctively use under fire. Suddenly Robertson, twenty yards ahead and with my borrowed sword held high above his head, let out a *Samurai* shriek and charged towards a terrorized farmer standing beside his house. I held my breath. The glittering blade slashed to an abrupt stop a fraction short of the man's skull. The quivering farmer cried at his unexpected reprieve. Robertson walked off pacifying his exhausted adrenalin with Baby Ruth candy bars.

Further on a burp gun blast rang from the high ground. 'Granny' hit the dirt with a raised M1, which answered his question. We searched and found two-dozen spent cartridges on the woody hillside before we entered the next partially inhabited village. We depth-charged the hamlet's water well with grenades and, seeing no oil slicks from a destroyed cache of submerged weapons, returned to our CP.

Buckley briefed us on the metaphorical "restraining line" General MacArthur had reluctantly stretched across the peninsula, which Washington decreed only the South Korean army could cross.

"Mac should just keep right on going," he said. "Screw the spineless politicians."

Richard laughed. "Sounds like the State Department 'fellow travelers' are giving the NKs time to rest up, re-equip and dig in nice and deep."

Robertson snickered, "Maybe the R&R will pump some fight back into them?"

I shrugged. "If those gutless bastards in Washington hadn't backed down on the Berlin blockade and Mao running the Marines out of Tientsin, we wouldn't be here right now."

Robertson snorted a popular cliché. "Better to fight them here than in Burbank."

I argued the point. "How would *they* get there? Frankly, I'd rather fight them in Burbank where we could chow down on great milk shakes, hamburgers and watch the pretty little drive-in carhops roller skate by in their miniskirts. Maybe do some R&R at Santa Monica beach and get a suntan. Besides," I concluded, "what has Burbank ever done for you?"

He pondered. "Well, now that you mentioned it, Boy-san…"

Richard hit on the truth "Who cares who, when or where we fight. If the Army pointed us at Washington DC, we'd march, right?"

Robertson said, "I'll take point."

Days later the platoon swung into a compound of a half-a-dozen weathered gray huts. Freshly shaven Barszcz, and Hungerford in clean fatigues and Prussian haircut stood in a muddy yard amid some clucking chickens. After getting haircuts Richard and I patrolled the hamlet.

The suspicious-looking pint sized boy we stopped in tattered khaki trousers and grungy white jacket turned out to be a cut off NK. Dragged by his earlobe to our CP he stood petrified before the silent glare of Robertson, Ken, Our Man Friday and all the ROK squad leaders. I gave my best Toshiro Mifune impression.

"*Mizu cho-dai, samonai atama wa karui* [Bring water, or I'll chop off your head]!"

He shook so violently in going to and from the well that his jacket was thoroughly splashed with water; his hands trembled as they were secured behind him with telephone wire while Robertson sinisterly sharpened his bayonet. He answered all the questions ROK Richard put to him without one 'Pinko-commie' Freudian slip. Buckley christened him 'Chung-Boogie,' which literally translates into an amalgamated "Bad Man with Gun." Released from his night of isolated bondage, Chung-Boogie proved trustworthy. He happily cleaned the house, scraped mud from combat boots and oiled our weapons. He even polished my sword.

Domestic boredom sent me on a long range one-man patrol that found no NKs, but over a hundred piled up 120mm mortar rounds. With no detonator I took cover in a culvert a hundred yards away and fired eight rounds of ball ammo into the humungous stack. Fortunately it didn't ignite—everything within two hundred yards would have been destroyed. I backed away leaving it for some ordnance team to find. Later I spotted Johnny Murr, the CO's radioman, and his buddy in a shady ravine with a young NK nurse they captured in a bloodstained hut not five hundred yards away.

She threw me a hate-filled glare through a swatch of dust-streaked hair that sensuously clung to her sweaty face and damp full lips. Her open green tunic bore neither rank nor insignia. With defiant allure, she refused to reveal the number of, or in what direction her former patients had gone. I jerked back her head, with the barrel of my cocked pistol perched on her nether lip. "*O hanashi maus, ki kana eto utsu* [Talk, or I'll shoot]!"

Johnny winked and held her unresisting arm. "You just gave me a better idea." His green eyes leered as he led her deeper into the underbrush.

I laughed. "Check her out for concealed razor blades! Oh, and by the way, you could get ten years for this."

Stumbling into the bloodstained shelter I found a badly wounded NK hidden behind a fallen tree. He was thirty-something, hunger-thin and wore no rank insignia. His eyes stayed glued to the tip of my bayonet as his dirt-caked hands compressed a gangrenous thigh. I kicked over his water bowl and putrid puss-stained sleeping mat. He had no weapon: *Put him out of his misery...and get even for some of those murdered G.I.s.* He was surprised at my soothing Japanese and that I hadn't already shot him.

"Would you like a speedy and honorable death?" His widened eyes filled with panicky fear instead of the mythical Asiatic indifference to death.

"No, no, no," he pleaded.

I thought of the farmer I'd killed at the Nam River and surprisingly slid a half empty pack of cigarettes and tin of crackers towards him, and refilled his water bowl. I left overflowing with inwardly directed curses: *Christ...some 'combat soldier' you are...this fucking Gook would kill you if he had the chance.*

Buckley laughed over my near catastrophe with the mortar rounds. "Remember, Mercy, you're federal property and had you successfully vaporized yourself I would have had you tried in absentia for that destruction. Now, have the platoon on the road at 1030 tomorrow, we're moving out. MacArthur's ordered all UN troops to the banks of the Yalu River, pronto!"

All four of us shouted in unison, "*Mansai!*" Robertson threw a freshly oiled double banana clip into his carbine. Chung-Boogie nervously walked backward towards the door. After dawn I returned to the gangrenous NK. His grave illness left me unsure whether to kill or save him. My offer of the *coup de grace* was again declined with a terrified bow. Returning to the platoon I gave Chung-Boogie a swift boot to his butt and set him down the southbound road.

"Go home, you little bastard, and stay there!" He waved and we headed north to the bay of Chinnampo.

The company flanked west along a gray coastal inlet. We randomly fired on the scores of scattered boats and sampans trying to escape seaward. The gusting winds over the two-thousand-yard range cut down the effectiveness of my two expended bandoleers. Barszcz arrived and directed Buckley to move over the ridge and destroy the small village we'd find on the other side.

"Level it, Buck. Burn it down. Don't leave it standing!" The captain left.

Buckley ecstatically shouted, "They want us to burn everything, men, everything!" I wasn't sure if his ceremoniously offered up prayer was a joke or not. "Oh, Mars, great God of War, protect your loyal troops, who offer you this day's work."

The tightly packed houses were sprayed with rifle and BAR fire. Then I shouted the squads forward with lighted thatch torches. *"Tatsugeki!"*

The regimental commander in his L-5 spotter plane watched as we raced down the flame-licked streets. Buckley shouted over the blaze of weapons and exploding grenades, "Burn, burn, burn everything, men!" Robertson left two NKs dead in the street and ran on, laughing. I nailed another from behind the cover of a wall before he could bolt home his second round. My bayonet later popped out three of his gold-capped teeth as Robertson arrived. I mirrored the callous indifference I recalled from the newsreel clip of a Marine waving the severed skull of a Jap on a Pacific atoll. Trophy collecting was an ancient tradition and reinforced the sense that life was valueless. Later Buckley passed along Colonel Moor's congratulations to our soot-stained platoon, but seeing added dead NKs in the smoldering ruin would have been more gratifying.

Pyongyang fell. Thirty-two miles north at Sukchon, F-80 jets strafed the drop zone where 150 cargo planes dropped the 187th Airborne Regimental Combat Team. Rain and bad timing kept them from cutting off the bulk of the 30,000 fleeing NKs and rescuing two trainloads of captured G.I.s. Seventy-three of these prisoners were later found murdered outside the Sukchon railway tunnel. Elsewhere twenty-nine more G.I. victims of bayonets, torches and burp guns were discovered, then thirty more in Kujang. After they landed northeast of us in Hungam, the Marines found 700 slaughtered civilians buried in wells and tunnels.

Behind us full-scale guerrilla armies rampaged through the south, but the slim pickings in the bleak northern hills offered little in the way of revenge. The G.I. troops heard General MacArthur's hint that they might be home for Christmas and became even more attentive and overly relaxed.

Butterball and Robertson's mission was to find some NKs for G-2 to interrogate, but they only succeeded in capturing a cow that was destined to be the company's dinner.

Richard told his story: "We hit a place that had two cows, and not wanting to come back empty handed, I had ROK Richard lead away the meatier of the two. Then Han shows up waving his hand under his nose, like he smells dead fish. 'No, no, you no can take cow.' I asked why. 'Because,' he said, 'is friendly cow.'

Then he points to a stumbling dilapidated old fleabag with hoof-and-mouth disease, and says, 'is communist cow, enemy, you must take him.' If I hadn't been laughing so hard, I would've put a round right between his conniving eyes."

Me [center] holding Thompson Submachine gun with Robertson and the cow that Butterball had brought back while on patrol.

As Thanksgiving neared, small Chinese units clashed with U.S. patrols along the Yalu River, some miles away. GHQ classified these incidents as "not serious." The ROK 2nd Corps, on our immediate right sent long range patrols up to the base of the Taebaek Mountains, and into the town of Unsan, forty-five miles from the Chinese border. Ten miles southwest, near the village of Onjong, other patrols found an abandoned freight train filled with tanks, weapons and ammunition.

The local civilians who voluntarily told of large concentrations of Chinese troops hiding in the mountains weren't believed. Neither was the Chinese officer who defected with his army's entire battle plan! Aerial reconnaissance found no signs of troop concentrations or movements at the Sinuiju bridgehead, or on any road that led down from the Chinese border.

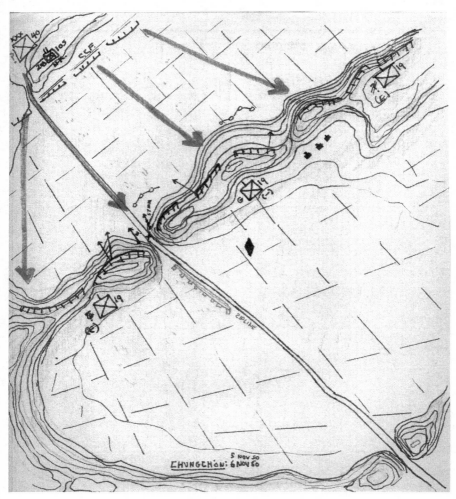

Tactical situation on Chungchon River.

Intelligence showed little concern over the scattered and insignificant number of captured Chinese 'volunteers.' Interrogators never learned that they were part of a tough 250-thousand strong peasant army that was waiting in the misty, formidable and near impenetrable Taebeak Mountains to greet the unsuspecting U.S. Army; nor had they an inkling as to the mythical and sacred significance of that locale, which both the Confusion Chinese and Koreans believed to be the birthplace of "Hwanung," the son of God, as well as the cradle of their own national origins. On 26 October in the northern Chosen and Fusen Reservoir areas, a daylong Chinese attack nearly destroyed the entire ROK 3rd Division. At about the same time, the Chinese smashed a ROK battalion of 1,000 men from the 6th Division below the Yalu. Then on 29 October two more ROK regiments, 3,000 men each, were crushed in the vicinity of Huichon. The ROK 7th Division's 10,000 men fell back to blocking positions in the Chungchon River Valley, where the British 27th Regiment ran into small detachments of NKs making their way north. On 30 October General Walker pulled his 8th Cavalry Regiment out of reserve in Pyongyang to assess the situation in the town of Unsan and to shield his temporarily halted army on the extreme west coast of Korea.

Walker's Eighth Army Headquarters was deluged for two days with communiqués of destruction by divisional formations of bugle-blowing Chinese. These were dismissed as signs of "ROK hysteria." This reflected the unfortunate and general contempt UN forces had for the South Korean military. There were exceptions made, though, for the Marine and those army divisions that had proven themselves on line. Overall, it was an unfair assessment. ROK divisions, compared to U.S. units, were minimally supplied, received lower air support priority and traveled mostly by foot.

As for poverty-racked China, "they would never dare challenge the unquestionable might of the United States military." General MacArthur's promise to President Truman was that if China were to attack, they would experience a bloody defeat unlike any the world had ever previously seen. Truman failed to inform him that the political Council on Foreign Relations wouldn't allow such a victory under any circumstances.

CHAPTER 21

The Sleeping Dragon

Near noon I told the captain, "Villagers reported seeing some NK troops just ahead, sir." He handed me a map and told me to check it out then report back. Castelluci bribed me with two pepperoni sticks he got from home to join our two-squad patrol. We followed railroad tracks and passed hamlets not shown on the map. Halting at a deserted rail station we spied a small 4'x4' iron safe in the far corner, which withstood the impact of three clips of armor-piercing ammo. Then we turned it around and found it backless and empty. "*Marone*," shouted Cass, "some fuckin' thieves got here first!"

Entering the last hamlet on our wide loop back to the company, we met a reception committee of five gray-bearded old men in black stove pipe hats. Following ancient custom, they drank first from their offered wooden bowl of water then presented it to us. I bowed, drank and listened to their genuine thanks that our Army had arrived. Our presence seemed to give them some hope.

As we headed back towards the CP, Cass held out a battered copy of *Time Magazine.* "Did ya' read where the Chinks might be comin' into the war, Merc?" I shrugged and asked what it said. His lips pursed and his hand gestured broadly. "Oh, nothin', except dat dey are threatenin' to kick our ass if we get any closer to dere turf."

I paused. "What's the bad news?"

He chuckled. "Dat if dey *don't* do it, we might all be home fer Christmas!"

I smirked, "I can hardly wait to see a million Chinks coming over these hills. This war could last another five years. I jokingly added my true sentiments: Who knows, I might get a battlefield commission and become company commander."

He smiled, "Hey, Merc, I'm wit you."

Thirty miles north in the primitive little town of Unsan, the 8th Cavalry Regiment staff officers set guards around their CP. Their 1st and 2nd battalions were five miles forward, while their 3rd battalion and supporting field artillery were five miles to the rear. They were tied in on their right flank with General Paik Sun-yup's ROK 1st Division. General Paik was a former lieutenant in the Japanese war against China who still maintained the *Bushido* code of discipline. He was reported to have shot a battalion commander at a staff meeting who'd failed in his duty.

That night the god's of searing winter struck Korea. Blustering icy winds and freezing sub-zero temperatures hit the 8th Cavalry. They had not yet received their cumbersome snow pack shoes, heavy parkas, gloves, long underwear—items that were often filched in the rear areas and sold into Seoul's flea market.

Soldiers on outpost duty burrowed deep into anything that would ward off the numbing winds, while dreaming perhaps of Christmas at home. Security around regimental headquarters and forward positions were weak. Some troops believed the war to be already over, and carried less than a minimal supply of ammo and grenades. Tanks were not deployed. No interlocking fields of fire had been set up at bridge crossing points or roadways into town. The troops of the flanking ROK division acted no better, building large warming fires on the freezing forward slope. The undetected Chinese were able to pinpoint their positions with ease.

Radio communications between the 8th Cavalry's regimental CP and its three deployed battalions was sparse and faulty. Not much thought was given to the night's widely dispersed fires a few miles ahead that swept across entire mountain ranges of spruce and pine. Smoke and sparking embers near blanketed out the silvery mammoth moon. The cavalry had long ago lost its edge in deciphering signal fires after the Apache Wars. They couldn't have guessed that the gigantic blaze was a message sent by the hidden Chinese 39th Field Army back to group headquarters in Manchuria: "Three full armies and sixteen accompanying divisions [250,000 men] are going into the attack." They avoided radio contact for fear of detection by roving aircraft. Their disciplined troops, under threat of execution, remained camouflaged and motionless for many weeks of daytime hiding within the thick overlapping primeval forest that crept up the 8,222 feet volcanic slopes of what the ancient Chinese named "Shanshan Daling [Big-big Brother Mountain];" known to us as the Taebaek mountain range .

Before dawn on 1 November, Chinese Special Forces dressed in captured ROK uniforms went right past unsuspecting G.I.s guarding the perimeter and reached the town's center. Satchel charges detonated around the U.S. headquarters and tanks in motor pools. A shrill bugle call rang out as rifles, bayonets and trench knives killed the confused and bewildered G.I.s.

Two Chinese divisions of 20,000 troops simultaneously attacked the forward U.S. battalions that totaled 2,000 men. At ten-to-one odds they were quickly overwhelmed. Hundreds of G.I.s and ROKs fled into the barren western hills to escape the carnage. Flares and tracers from the embattled forward battalions streaked across the moon tinged Prussian blue sky, but little concern was shown back at the regimental CP. It wasn't unusual for rifle companies to fire away throughout an entire night, only to find a dead stray cow at dawn—and ammo expended didn't have to be carried.

The Chinese nearly annihilated the regiment's rearmost 3rd Battalion and captured thirteen Patton tanks with their full ammo racks intact. Startled line officers in Unsan called in artillery barrages that fell on battalion-sized formations of attacking Chinese, and watched in shock as they held their ranks despite heavy casualties and kept on advancing. Encircled G.I.s held and fought as best they could, hoping their brothers in the 5th Cavalry Regiment would break through the enemy's roadblock on the mountain pass six miles back.

Well dug in, the Chinese remained impervious to multiple bomber strikes and artillery barrages. Heavy smoke over the almost hand-to-hand combat severely restricted the pilots' effectiveness. Still, they managed to deliver their payloads, terrifying the Chinese with a weapon they'd never seen before. The "long-nosed devils" called it "napalm."

American units dissolved in panic. An escaping truck towing a howitzer overturned and blocked the major artery out of Unsan. Most of the men in the backed up column died in the fusillade from a roadside ambush. Surprisingly the trapped and wounded were treated humanely—until they reached the POW camps; as every soldier knew, "the further back you go the worse it gets."

U.S. firepower raked devastation over the Chinese troops, tanks and artillery, but the combat-hardened ROK 1st Division on their flank suffered even more. A tidal wave of literally tens of thousands of screaming Chinese blowing whistles, blaring bugles and beating gongs spread terror throughout the surrounding hills. Their sword and torch brandishing cavalry slashed through the ROK lines, slaying them by the thousands as did the Mongol hordes in their ancient past.

Returning to the company, Cass and I heard rumors of "more Chinks being captured" and goose bumps rippled across my shoulders. I asked ROKs Tom, Ken and Richard how they felt about fighting the Chinese. They sighed, "Oh, Sahji," with enough elongated teeth sucking sounds to pass for an afternoon sipping-soiree at a Tokyo Teahouse.

Buckley ordered me to run a patrol to where Butterball and Robertson were reconnoitering a village. Two hundred yards beyond that point, a pair of burp guns opened up from somewhere behind the hillock to our front. The squad advanced over the skyline and I spotted Richard and Robertson standing over a dozen smoldering NK bodies lying elbow-to-elbow in the muddy farmyard below.

"What happened?" I asked.

Robertson smirked, ejecting an empty 71-round drum magazine from his smoking burp gun, as did Richard.

"They tried ambushing us."

I sighed. "It must be a new Commie tactic, ambushing from an open yard in a close interval dress left formation?"

Richard shrugged. "Fanatics."

Having been treated cruelly by the North Koreans, the locals gave up the soldiers who Robertson talked into coming out of the house. "I frisked them," Robertson said, "and was starting to take 'em back when something happened."

I replied, "Ah, then they'd marched out of step?"

Robertson snapped a new drum into the gun, nodding to a near jawless corpse. "He wouldn't tell where his buddies were, so I clipped him," he said holding up his spike-knuckled bayonet. "We decided to give 'em all a summary court martial for what they've been doing to our guys since day one." His logic seemed faultless. He and Richard joined the ROKs searching the houses while I investigated the dilated eyes of the dead for clues of what they might have felt at the moment of death.

As we waited in the CP, Han arrogantly entered, spewing indignation over the executions. I wondered which of the ROKs had carried him the tale and if it had gotten to the captain; what repercussions might follow? Concern for the platoon's morale and for things to run smoothly kept my impulse to pistol whip him in check. Han glimpsed Richard and Robertson entering the compound and quickly left. I questioned his compassion for the murderous NKs and wondered, too, what the ROKs might do in a real firefight. Stories of how ROKs with the 2nd Division threw grenades into the open turrets of our tanks came to mind. Buckley's shout broke my contemplation.

"Mercy, saddle up the men, we've got a patrol to run."

Robertson and 'Big Stoop' Ken took point. Butterball and I followed with the squads in column, and Buckley brought up the rear. We trekked for three hours before stopping at a deserted hilltop house. As I scanned the terrain, Buckley closed in on me with an angry hiss.

"What the hell do you think you are doing, Mercy? You didn't put out flank security!"

It was a stupid mistake. "Sorry, sir. I'll fix it now." Suddenly we heard the unmistakable thump sound of mortar rounds being dropped into their tubes and firing somewhere below in the woods. I went to a flanking crest then reported back.

"Sir, there's a camouflaged battery of 120mm mortars down there. The crews look Chinese." Buckley grunted as I continued. "Sir, maybe we didn't make it in here by accident."

His eyes sparkled. "I know. We might have to fight our way out."

Robertson hissed, "*Mansai.*"

Butterball added, "I think we just got lucky and slipped in unseen, or their infantry would be all over us by now."

Buckley nodded, "If there's infantry around we'll soon find out. Keep your bandits quiet and follow me." I didn't remind Buckley that we were lucky there were no flank guards to trip over those mortars, or we'd have been cut off for sure.

We moved silently through covering woods until we reached the hilltop path that led back to our lines. Robertson pointed out a low cruising blue Navy F-4U Corsair, over a thousand yards away. All of a sudden, it banked and fishtailed towards us for a strafing run. I shouted in Japanese to our ROKs. "Don't move! He'll think we're Gooks!"

The platoon held fast beneath the .50-caliber bursts the Corsair spat out from a hundred yards ahead. The ship roared overhead, almost within arm's reach, to rake some unseen threat to our rear. It came back in on a second run. Swirls of dust rose from gullies beside the path. We must have been followed out. We gave awestruck cheers and waves. Those pilots could probably kill more troops in one pass than an infantryman could in a year. I was filled with admiration.

Buckley beamed, "Barszcz will be surprised when he hears about the Chinks." We turned in a report to G-2, but were never questioned further.

Knowing the platoon had been ordered to full alert I checked the line in the predawn darkness and crept from hole to hole and found every last one of them asleep. Stealthily I removed all their weapons, except the Ritz Brother's LMG as they snored in unison. Suddenly there were giggles and sheepish bleats. "Oh, *Sahji*, is you."

I wracked my brain trying to think what forms of punishment to inflict for their lack of concern, or even panic that I might have been an NK. I cursed and threatened death for anyone found asleep in the coming nights. In either of the Korean armies, North or South, they would have been beaten unconsciousness with their own rifles then shot dead, but my mind burned with hollow rationales for not following the custom. I knew they were not full-fledged soldiers, nor even properly trained. I'd been four months in the line with them, but I wouldn't hesitate to shoot them for mutiny or treason. I wanted obedience from loyalty not fear and loathed anew those periodic inclinations towards humanitarianism. I called for Han who translated as I spoke.

"I did not come all the way to Korea to kill you, only your enemies. I want each and every one of you to live through this war. But that will be impossible if all soldiers are asleep on the front line at the same time. The enemy will not be as forgiving as I. They will happily cut your throats for that violation. I expect each man to fight for Korea, as I willingly do."

Their faces lit up like Christmas trees, but their thunderous shouts of new dedication didn't wash away my gnawing doubts as I dismissed them. Fifteen minutes later I unexpectedly found the entire platoon in the mess area. Kneeling face to face, in two rows of twenty-five men each, they patiently waited over their untouched food until I knelt at the head of the long open corridor. In a gesture pulled from a *Samurai* film, I placed my sword with its handle backwards and slightly to my right rear in a sign of respectful trust. I returned the deep collective bow of my Asian brothers. I felt greatly honored and raised my brimming cup in a heartfelt salute.

"*Domo arigato, watakushi-no hatietati, tabe-tai masho* [Thank you, my soldiers, let us eat]." *It's just like General Yang's personal guard...aboard his junk... "My troop's faithful."*

The cheerful look on Butterball and Robertson's approaching faces told me something was up. "Buckley wants to get the platoon ready and run an ammo check," said Richard. "Some cavalry outfit is getting its ass kicked further north and we'll be moving out tonight."

CHAPTER 22

Seven Days at the Chungchon

The regiment's motor column pulled out of Pakchon with Robertson and I on opposite fenders of the lead truck from where we could more easily give counter fire if we ran into an ambush. Green bath towels worn around our face and neck warded off the night's icy winds. When we finally disembarked near dawn, Buckley signaled that I should punch out the insubordinate driver who had stuffed so many draft blocking blankets and rags in the cabin there was little room left for anything or anyone else. He even told Buckley to "ride in the back," but I was too numbed by the blustery journey to exact revenge for the lieutenant, or for the pentagon's misadventure in democratizing the Army.

The expansive Chungchon River ran from the Yellow Sea in the west to well past the middle of the peninsula, forward of the U.S. lines. The terrain consisted of flat marshy land, shallow rivers, streams and low-lying scrub sprouting hillocks, all of which we'd searched until dusk for the elusive Chinese.

Our platoon dug in on a twenty-foot high hillock, just above a dirt road and a Patton tank took up a firing position on the crest directly behind us. That road was our left boundary. To our front was a set of frozen rice paddies, four hundred feet wide and equally as deep. On my far right, some 120 yards away, a long finger stretched down from a higher elevation. This was our tight field of fire. The left boundary road, two hundred yards south of us, cut between two other hillocks that were our fallback positions if needed.

Easy Company, on our left, set a 57mm recoilless rifle right on the road. Their hill, like ours, rolled back at its height like a curved scimitar for nearly a mile, ringing in the seven hundred yard valley behind us. Tom and I dug in together, with the squads deployed on line. Buckley jumped into our foxhole and pointed up to the high ground.

The Chungchon, 19th Infantry Sector, 5th ROK Platoon tactical position, 5-6 November 1950.

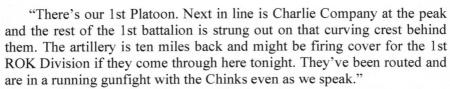

"There's our 1st Platoon. Next in line is Charlie Company at the peak and the rest of the 1st battalion is strung out on that curving crest behind them. The artillery is ten miles back and might be firing cover for the 1st ROK Division if they come through here tonight. They've been routed and are in a running gunfight with the Chinks even as we speak."

I scanned the narrow road they might follow. "That could get tricky, sir."

Buckley snapped back, "Think positively, Sergeant, and be sure you identify what you shoot at. I&R (Intelligence & Reconnaissance) will be out there making certain it's only ROKs who'll be coming through."

I nodded. "Sir, about that sergeant thing, I wanted—"

He cut me off: "Not now, Mercy."

Then we noted the oddity of an unexpected major from battalion, dug in behind Robertson down near the road. It was a rarity to see anything above the rank of lieutenant on the forward slope. Something was definitely up.

The Mongolian artillery fire, barely audible to us, rumbled through the predawn sky as their miles away cavalry attacked our 3rd Battalion's forward positions; and the Chinese lost 250 men and mounts to napalming jets as the sun rose. On the western flank both the 5th RCT and some ROK units were pushed back under the full fury of the Red assault.

"Have you made an ammo check of the platoon, Mercy?"

I nodded up towards the ridgeline. "Yes, sir, and stashed extra ammo boxes and grenades on the reverse slope."

He clasped my shoulder and smiled. "Good, I think we'll need them."

I beamed. "Sure hope so, sir."

Buckley smirked. "Stay alert, a couple of Gook patrols infiltrated the line last night and shot up the rear."

I feigned shock. "Oh no, I hope Herbert and Krocheck made it out okay, sir?"

Our eyes were suddenly drawn to the major's rapid departure, "Time to lock and load, sir." Buckley winked and dashed to Butterball's position where G.I.s busily planted landmines down near the road.

I was hurled from sleep up to Tom's side against the parapet wall when there was a sudden eruption of rifle, machine gun and 57mm recoilless fire around midnight. The victors over our cavalry at Unsan had arrived! Mortars exploded and the spectral glare of oscillating flares illuminated a floodtide of zigzagging troops moving through flash-pulsing patches of otherwise windswept darkness. As the tank's 90mm cannon fired, it bathed the forward slope with a silvery hue and shredded the nearing ranks of the Chinese assault like a string of paper dolls. Screams and dismembered body parts flew in every direction.

Silhouetted figures crumbled in the blinding flashes of my bucking M1, to reappear again, and again, and again. The sudden and heretofore unheard clarion call of four mournful notes from a Chinese bugle immediately silenced the guns of both sides. Tom and I peered through the wind swept swirls of vaporous cordite to glimpse an army straight off the pages of *Terry and the Pirates.* Strangely no thoughts of death entered my mind, only an excited sense of the familiar. Tom seemed amused at finding that we still lived.

The Chinese battalion crumbled and limped back to firing positions across the field: *How many more of them are there...beyond those low-lying hills?* A sudden barrage of 120mm mortars covered their recon platoon as they probed to see if we'd fled as expected. The official Chinese combat assessment of the U.S. ground troops following their encounter with the 8th Cavalry at Unsan was less than glowing:

> The American soldier is fearful of death and lacks the courage to either defend or attack. They are overly dependent on artillery, tanks and airplanes to do all the fighting for them. They can only move fast when the terrain is flat and the weather is good, ideal conditions for their trucks and the movement of troops and cumbersome supplies and equipment. When their fast transportation is cut off, they lose the will to fight. They have some ability in daytime fighting, but lack experience and are very fearful of night fighting and will avoid hand-to-hand combat whenever possible. They panic easily, particularly if surrounded. They are fearful of our grenades, firepower, knives and courageous infantry attacks. If routed they have no organized formations and tend more to hide rather than fight. At Unsan, when surrounded for three days, they were demoralized, lost their will and did nothing; and if they believe that they are surrounded, they would rather surrender than fight. They are truly a paper-tiger army.

Rifles and machine guns from both sides raked each other's positions as their dauntless infantry advanced behind concealing shields of dust churned up by their supporting mortars. Tom and I sprayed endless clips down to silence the moans and cries that rose from the kaleidoscopic fury of the exploding minefield. My respect swelled for the bravery of the Chinese soldiers who unerringly attacked and were blown away like so many autumn leaves. A second bugle sounded across the smoke-filled field: *They're calling retreat...*

Near dawn unseen knife-wielding Chinese commandos silenced Charlie Company's outpost on our right flank and followed its telephone wires up to the crest. There they met a Sioux warrior; a corporal named 'Chief' Mitchell Red Cloud who launched a one-man counterattack that killed seventeen with his BAR. He kept firing right down to his last breath and was awarded the Medal of Honor, posthumously.

Whatever mythical Valkyrie-like maidens Asia's Valhalla has, they swept the killing fields clean by dawn and wrought the Chinese battle doctrine to cause the enemy to doubt the prowess of their own weapons. Still, G-2 estimated that a questionable one hundred enemy dead were left in our platoon sector alone. That night Sgt. 'Granny' Black left the relative safety of the CP and helped us stave off another attack and as dawn rose on his birthday he fired into the new waves of Chinese that broke across the fields.

I bellowed out, "Here come your presents, Granny!"

He cried back through a gusting gale of incoming fire, "Thanks, Mercy!"

I called out again as the probe fell back. "Is there anything else you'd like for your birthday? Black?" He was dead, with a bullet between his eyes.

Tom cheered my less-than-well placed round into the determined solitary soldier who fell at 150 yards. "*Mansai!*" I emptied my clip into his flinching dead body with admiration, wishing I had a platoon, or even myself, that could be as fearless as he'd been. On the flank I glimpsed Private Pierce—he'd somehow tied in with us during the night, bring down a Chinese stretcher team with his BAR. Their Red Cross armbands didn't save them after they tilted ammunitions and grenades off their blanket-covered stretchers to those who feigned death across the field. I leapt into Pierce's foxhole as another medical team arrived and he repeated the same drill.

I gave an impression of the classic Prussian Eric Von Stroheim. "*Ach zooo, dees svines haf fiolated ze code of var. Kill zem!*" He did.

Later a sustained burst of LMG fire that sparked at my heels catapulted me into the foxhole where Buckley waited.

"Mercy, the captain said we can't get artillery, and now that tank doesn't want to silhouette itself on the skyline. Stand by to pull 'em back when I give the word!"

I emptied three more clips into the fresh wave of blue coated Chinese that skirmished across the field and shouted down to Passwater, "Have your men fall back now!"

The reply was astonishing. "Don't tell *me* what to do!"

I couldn't believe our *Prima Donna* was doing *The Lament of the Slighted Corporal*. My piece lay restlessly across my knee, with him in its line of fire and only a murderous whim away from showing up on the morning report as KIA: *Who would ever know? Or care?*

"Great, you stupid son of a bitch, tell it to the Chinks. They'll be here in five minutes."

Chinju and Mason squads. Han is in the front row, on the left, while Richard is fifth from the left in the back row, next to ROK Tom.

Robertson led the Mason, Seoul and Chinju squads across and marched them in column back to where the company had redeployed across the road. Weaponless, which was a cardinal sin, Passwater darted across and raced behind me as the Chinese neared the skyline. He called out in a more conciliatory tone, "Hey, Mercy, how about throwing me your pistol?"

I pitched it to him. "Don't drop that like you did your rifle."

Richard crossed the skyline and was surprised when he stumbled over the bullet-riddled bodies of our 60mm mortar section on the reverse slope. Some Chinese had gotten behind us during the night. We two headed straight for the Patton tank, whose 90mm gun traversed the ominous skyline.

Mason Squad. I'm in the back row, fifth from the left, with Richard and ROK Tom on my left. In the first row, the last soldier on the right is machine gunner Lee.

I shouted, "I'm going to dust off the ridges with its .50." Richard's objections were lost in the 120mm mortar explosion just inches forward of the bow and the dust-laced gale of steel that ricocheted from the hull. We wordlessly sensed, as did the driver, where the next round would land and made a nanosecond dash from behind the tank.

The M-4 fifty ton behemoth lurched back full-throttled and we barely escaped being ground into the dust, and on the very spot where the expected round exploded seconds later. Shockwaves and shards of steel pursued our zigzag dash to where the company was peering over a drainage ditch. The tank circled back to position itself between the Chinese and us. Their 120mm mortars crumbled our battalion' front and unerringly fell on the pockets of retreating G.I.s. Barszcz shouted for us to get on the tank and fall back 200 yards to our second defense line.

Minutes later two mortar rounds registered in the "V" cut pass fifty yards ahead and the troop-laden tank jolted to a halt. Its sergeant shouted down from the unbuttoned turret.

"Everybody, off this goddamned tank, now!"

He couldn't see me forward and below, hugging the 90mm gun from the underside while the troops scrambled off and ran *en masse* for the fall back position on the ridge. An incoming 120mm WP shell fell among them and spewed out thick white smoke and glowing pellets that could burn through steel: *I hope Richard and Robertson aren't out there with them.* Machine gun fire flayed the impervious back of the lumbering tank as I clung hard to the slippery surface of the barrel. When two more 120mm mortar rounds simultaneously slammed in just forward of the looming breach, I questioned the sanity of my staying onboard.

The tank plunged and pitched heading for the immutable wall of exploding flame ahead and I remembered the flattened bleeding bundle of rags I'd desecrated along the Taejon road. Then it crested between the swells of erupting earth and squalls of splintered steel that rained against the hull before it imperviously veered from the road and stopped below in an open field. I knew I had just used up another of my nine lives.

I raced up the slope to where Barszcz directed the fire of the gathered ROKs and G.I. stragglers, but Butterball and Robertson were not among them. I ran towards the road that was covered with shredded equipment and broken bodies. Buckley's voice called out from behind me.

"Stay put, Mercy—that's an order. I'm going."

I covered him and a nearby ROK asked if he too could search for "*ototo Sahji-san* [young-brother sergeant]." Twenty minutes later, Buckley appeared with Richard.

"Instinct pulled me away from that crowd," he told me, "and halfway up the crest I thought I'd soon be knee deep in picked-off Chinks, but

China-boy never showed."

Robertson arrived soon after that, and credited his survival to the same impulse. We lost three ROKs. Passwater yelled so loud from the bullet he caught in his foot that the captain ordered him to shut up. A flight of F-80 jets zoomed in with rockets and guns ripping up our old position.

Barszcz ordered us across the field. "We'll follow up if a second wave is needed."

I shouted through the wind that rippled my rifle's bloodstained flag and had the ROKs sing their army's favorite battle hymn, *Insang eh Mokseum*. Richard and Robertson were at the flanks and Buckley, five paces behind our horizontal line, offered up another prayer to Mars. The Chinese fell back without firing a shot. We took the ridge and found our three dead ROKs close to Sergeant Black and the dozen six-foot tall Mongolians killed in the air strike. I examined the .30-caliber pinwheel marking of the sniper's bullet between Black's eyes and the ravages of the jet's two .50-caliber rounds in his chest. He was otherwise fully intact.

The Mongolians were fresh, well-groomed troops in new quilted blue uniforms. They carried light khaki packs, which held toothbrushes, small bags of rice and often a picture of a girlfriend standing beside a mud hut. Others had extra submachine gun magazines, but none had more than two crisp one hundred won North Korean notes, valued at twenty-five cents, and some small Chinese coins. Their American cigarettes and watches probably came from the 8th Cavalry dead at Unson. Their mint-condition Thompson submachine guns were marked "Made in the USA." I slung one across my back. The U.S. had armed the Nationalist Chinese, who were regularly routed by the communist Chinese. That left the Chicoms with a lot of brand new U.S. material when the Nationalist Forces were driven off onto Formosa.

Shots suddenly rang out and kicked up three dust-geysers around my feet. I led two squads up to Charlie Company's former position but found no signs of the shooter among the dead. The company crossed the road and passed Easy Company's patrol as we headed towards their old positions. No reconnaissance was sent to the abutment 400 yards to our front, where the Chinese would logically be.

Robertson and I returned to the hill and discovered 'Granny' Black's ring finger had been hacked off and the PX money we knew had been in his pockets was gone. It had to have been done by someone in the E Company patrol.

Robertson mumbled, "I wish I'd walked in on this."

I wondered about the old Articles of War that allowed for battlefield ghouls to be shot and whether it was still in effect. I would expect this sort of thing from North Koreans, but not for G.I.s to rob fallen Americans. Would a Chinese or even an NK rob their own dead? I personally didn't think so. What was it in our national character that allowed some "apple-pie Americans" to rob the dead, and their wounded in hospitals?

Robertson broke the silence as we sat on the reverse slope. "Ah well, Grandma picked a good way to go, in a firefight."

I nodded. "He lived a pretty long time. He just turned thirty-four today, and dying in a battle is better than in bed."

Richard laughed. "Yeah, it was a great fight and those support mortars were coming in pretty close!"

Robertson and I exchanged patient glances. "I hate to pop your bubble, *Boy-san*, but those weren't our mortars." I smiled at his blank stare, cleaning my sword. "Remember, we had no FO or radioman with us?"

Robertson continued. "The Chinks will probably hit us again tonight, but we could spook them off with a couple of warning signs."

Richard bolted up like a prairie dog. "Warning signs?"

Robertson lit a cigar. "Yeah, like putting a couple of chopped-off heads on stakes, right in front of our position, with a sign under them, "G Company hill, keep the fuck off!"

I droned out an impression of W.C. Fields. "Ah, yes, chop off a couple of heads..."

Butterball's eyebrow arched. "Sure, then all we need is for that nosey newspaper broad, what's her name, Maggie Higgins, to drop in with General MacArthur and his platoon of cameramen. I can just see the N.Y. *Daily News* headlines now: "Mac busts psycho headhunting G.I. trio!"

Robertson tried logic. "Come on, *Boy-san*, you know those people never get that close to the line. Besides, going from PFC to private isn't much of a bust in rank."

Richard pondered the point. "Aw, I don't know... Why don't we just go on killing the Gooks in our same old fashioned, good natured way and not piss them off any more than we have to?"

Robertson's words came through a perfectly blown ring of smoke. "Fuck, you guys don't have any imagination!" The rumble of the returning Patton tank muffled our laughter.

I stood under its cannon some time later talking with our new company officer, Lieutenant Walters. A thirty-five year-old RA (Regular Army) veteran of WWII, he was lean, mustachioed and of medium height, with a dry sense of humor. His wife waited for him back in New Jersey.

A sudden deafening explosion of combusting gas and flame buckled us to our knees. The cannon had fired at a distant motorcycle courier without warning. We rose with ruptured ears and beat our rifles against the hull. Walters, with half his mustache vaporized, screamed vengeful threats at the tankers. They wisely remained buttoned up for the rest of the day. I was tempted to drop a WP grenade down the barrel, knowing the Statement of Charges would keep me bankrupted for life.

An hour later the platoon took company point and moved westward to where Buckley said there was 'some kind of breakthrough.' He read the puzzled expression on my face.

"I thought you knew, Mercy. We've been surrounded for two days!"

We passed the notch in the road between the hillocks of the secondary fallback position and saw E Company clustered up on its knoll. Five minutes later the deafening roar of a full-throttled Saber jet skimming in just thirty feet above us nearly exploded my skull and I tried to squeeze into a rabbit hole. The jet's purple-tinted heat trail brushed across our backs as it shot up ninety degrees to rejoin its wing formation at eight thousand feet. Somewhere in between I heard the sustained bursts of its cannons, machine guns and exploding rockets that hit Easy Company in its scrambled panic down the slope to our rear.

Above and behind the sky-tossed bodies that were careened from the precipice was another napalm-carrying jet streaking in. I watched two brave G.I.s from an overturned Jeep race against time to place their red ID panel on the crest and pull the plane out of its supersonic dive. The pilot apologetically wiggled his wings as he left. Someone forgot to check for the day's color code. I couldn't imagine what it was like for 'Joe Chink' to go through this every day.

After a night sweep through the peripheral hills we rested and talked beside a small fire in the morning. Richard commented on some G.I.s who'd been captured and escaped. "You see, I told you, the Chinks weren't as bad as those fucking NKs."

Robertson yawned and relighted his two-day-old cigar butt. "Those guys were just lucky, *Boy-san.*"

Butterball persisted. "Well, the Chinks got my vote. Anybody who would hide you from air strikes, bandage you, and then lead you back to our lines in the morning can't be all bad."

Buckley sensed a sympathetic drift. "Let's not go planning any picnics with these guys just yet, okay. Here's the straight scoop on that captured E Company patrol up on the Chongch'on-bang River. They didn't want to fight and let themselves be captured and I'm sure they probably believed that the Chinese would treat them okay. Well, imagine their surprise when the Gook patrol hogtied them up and dragged them back to their angry captain who was waiting with a blood dripping ax."

I spoke impulsively. "Sure sounds like NKs to me, sir."

172

Buckley glared. "And on the ground next to him were the headless bodies of three other propagandized G.I.s who'd also surrendered. Ordered to kneel, the bastards trusted their luck and ran. They dove headlong into the river under a hail of rifle fire and foot paddled their sorry asses back to safety on the other side." He looked into our silent faces. "Think about it men—these Chinks are no better than the NKs."

Robertson spoke up. "There's no way I'll ever surrender to any goddamned Gook, sir."

Richard and I jiggled our bayonet-affixed rifles. "We feel the same way, sir."

Buckley gave a grim clenched-jaw smile. "Excellent, men, excellent. We'll fight those bastards right down to the last round and then it's 'fix bayonets!'"

We shouted back as one, "To the death, sir!"

He smiled and asked, "And what's the spirit of the bayonet, men?"

We dutifully replied, "To kill, to kill, to kill!"

At nightfall the platoon dug in on a low westward facing hill. Sixty yards below, the smoldering remnant of a hut threw its glow across the dried up wash of stone that stretched towards an elevated foothill two hundred yards ahead. Butterball's squad was on the right flank and Robertson's on the left, with the weapons squad and mine centered below the slope's raised rock formation behind me. Buckley called down from above, reminding us that if anyone showed up during the night, we were to shoot first and ask questions later. There were no friendlies beyond this point.

An hour passed and those dying house embers cast their amber tint on the shadowy phalanx of troops that were advancing up from the base of the hill. The safety on my Thompson was frozen tight and I grabbed the M1 and called out to the figure held in its sights. "Who's there?"

A voice from the stilled line echoed back, "Who are *you*?"

Easy Company's patrol had taken a different route back and I wondered as they passed why the ROKs didn't fire, or at least call out? It was too quiet! I ran down the line and bit my tongue hoping to awake from the nightmare. All our troops were gone! My panicked brain sizzled, but I didn't think to run and tell Butterball or Robertson. Acid ate at the lining of my stomach and rage numbed my fingers white. Only spilling Han's blood could cool my own. I knew it had to be him. I considered Han to be traitorously sympathetic in wanting to save any and all Korean lives. Being overly disciplined—and fearful of punishment—I didn't kill him previously, which I probably could have gotten away with. My MP experience, though, told me not to trust military logic or justice.

I stammered on reaching Buckley's position. "Sir... I don't know how to tell you this but... the platoon, sir, it's, it's... gone!"

Buckley's head tilted quizzically, as though examining an alien creature under a microscope. "Gone? *Gone*? What the *fuck* do you mean, *gone*?"

My reply didn't lessen his shock. "I mean just that, sir. Gone, as in *Gone With the Wind*."

Fury filled his eyes and he smashed the heel of his carbine into the ground. "How... When?"

I caught my breath. "I'm not sure, sir, but I know it has everything to do with Han. The men would never pull back on their own."

He grunted and I drew closer. "Sir, I want permission to kill Han. It's just between us, sir. I'm not going to post this on the goddamned company bulletin board." He just sat there, staring motionlessly, a bewildered look in his eyes. I continued, "Sir, please, let me kill that fucking conniving Gook son of a bitch! Please, sir, just nod or wink but let me know that it's okay with you.

This silence from an officer and a former Marine seemed illogical when he should have handed me his own cocked pistol, with blessings and a clip of dum-dum rounds. I suspected he either felt some sense of indebtedness to Han for having saved his life back at the Naktong, or feared the unknown aftermath of taking any action. Either way, I wanted Han dead: *Why didn't I kill him when I had the chance?*

Buckley snapped out of it and we hurried to find the troops, gambling that Butterball and Robertson could hold out alone if they were attacked. We commandeered a slow crawling Jeep in case we needed rapid transport back. Buckley ordered me to kill the driver if he moved. I kept my Thompson pointed at the back of his head until Buckley returned. We set him free and jogged towards a nearby concealed tank. Its commander hadn't seen our platoon, and hadn't heard of any Chink breakthroughs.

Suddenly, we stumbled on our ROKs, silently huddled together inside the battalion perimeter. ROK One said Han had ordered him to keep the platoon out of sight and stay close to the battalion CP until he arrived. Bile-laced images of pumping endless pistol rounds into Han's head filled my shattered mind as we double-timed the platoon back to the hill. Han was nowhere to be found.

After a fitful sleep I awoke at dawn and spotted Han. He stood just behind the captain with fearful eyes as I approached with an impulse to rip out his throat with my teeth: *Should I use a knife...the pistol...or the Thompson?*

Barszcz, either psychic or complicit, quickly placed himself between us as I neared. "Mercy, get back to your platoon!"

My suspicions grew in knowing that he'd used Han to spy on us before and then protected him at every turn. I gritted my teeth. "Sir, the platoon can get along without me, I have something important to report." *What if he reaches for his pistol when I kill Han? Do I shoot him too...in self-defense...everybody else around might think I've flipped...murdered the captain...and if they move...do I fire?*

He bellowed the ultimate command. "This is a direct order: Get back to your platoon, now!"

I turned and cursed the discipline that made me impotent even in the face of treason. I felt like a coward, not risking everything on my convictions as I'd often seen done in the movies, but never in the reality of the Army. I returned to the hill and sat in a foxhole with a dead Mongolian and faced his fixed open-eyed stare: *Strange...I feel far less hate and dislike for you...than I do for people on this side.* Struck by a sense of déjà vu, I recalled the classic scene in *All Quiet On the Western Front.*

Actor Lew Ayres, as a compassionate German soldier, shared a shell hole with an open-eyed dead Frenchman whose family he promised to visit after the war, and apologize for their son's death. Then I crazily imagined how Humphrey Bogart might reenact that scene in a Yak tent in Manchuria. I lisped out his remembered line when he 'plugged' Bob Steel in *The Big Sleep:* "Sssso-long, Canino;" and sank three .45 slugs into the Mongolian's chest.

Robertson called out from the next hole. "What's up, Boy-san?"

I slid my index finger slowly across my lip. "Nothin' kid. I'm just ... closin' out a case."

Barszcz gave me a bizarre order over the walkie-talkie "Have your platoon police up the area and then report to me."

We picked up all the expended brass and grenade pins along the slope where I glimpsed the captain standing proudly below in the swirls of dust made by the three M26 tanks that halted beside our company's fourteen poncho-wrapped dead. I reported to him as ordered. Barszcz stood beside the tank's second lieutenant boy commander who sat resting against its muddy treads. The lieutenant's hand rose to grab the barrel of the Thompson balanced on my hip. I stiffened.

"Better let me have that before you hurt yourself," he said.

My finger was on the trigger and the safety off when he tugged the muzzle down towards his chest. I knew the arrogant bastard's death would look like an accident, with Barszcz as a witness to his violating the cardinal military rule of never to pull a weapon from a soldier's hands! My mind churned, but I couldn't trip the trigger...

175

The captain, true to the Officer's Code, said nothing: *And we're supposed to be loyal and willingly give up our lives to protect these arrogant bastards?*

CHAPTER 23

North to Sinuiju

General 'Bull' Walker's assessment of the Chinese encounter differed from Tokyo's. He knew his troops needed winterized clothing, weapons and ammunition if they were to conquer the last frozen vestiges of North Korea, which General MacArthur had impatiently ordered him to do the previous week. Instead Walker moved his divisions cautiously after the morning of 6 November when the bulk of the Chinese Field Armies mysteriously disappeared from all of Korea. They left a smattering of dead behind as a warning that the U.S. Army was to proceed no further.

Walker's command was reduced to patrols and occasional skirmishes against roving bands of guerrillas. MacArthur's GHQ believed the Chinese had been defeated and had no capabilities for a renewed offensive. Nevertheless the State Department and the Council on Foreign Relations wouldn't allow MacArthur to bomb the Chinese supply bridge at Sinuiju, only the southern end of it, which would look less 'provocative' in the eyes of the One World they envisioned. It eliminated any impression that America was fighting a war it intended to win.

Stripped to the waist we sat near a small fire. Close by lay a half-dozen dead Chinese. We watched, long pale gray columns of lice irresistibly march from our stretched out shirts to the greater warmth of the flames. Butterball 'napalmed' them with burning twigs and all survivors were buried alive in crevices. We picked them from each other's bodies and heads, wondering if we'd ever be clean again. Robertson nodded towards a column of troops with chalk-marked helmets that moved towards us along the ridge.

"Ah, brand new stateside replacements!" said Butterball in a tone that cued us for some combat humor.

"The least we could do is roll out the welcome wagon," I suggested. "Lunch then, with our Chinese friends?" Robertson winked in agreement.

Korea as seen from a hilltop as we marched north to Sinuiju in 1951.

The eyes of the nearest Chinese corpse were dilated and his mouth agape from the three rounds I'd earlier pumped into his chest as he dashed from his bunker. He was a tall, powerfully built Mongol with strong rugged features and a face that showed much character. He made a perfect table. Robertson plunged a bayonet into his chest, just above the fruit cocktail, cookie tins, and canteen cups that rested on his abdomen.

Butterball moaned ruefully, "No candles or Gallo wine?"

The startled replacements watched as Robertson extracted the blade and lathered gobs of marmalade over the biscuits we pretended to ravenously eat; they strained their necks backwards to see, tripping and stumbling their way up towards the company CP. A little while later, Hungerford shouted for the company to 'saddle up.' I lingered behind and watched the fading sunlight glitter in the Mongolian's distantly searching eye: *Could he ever...in his wildest dreams...imagine ending up like this...or me, here with him...maybe it's his Karma...for cruelty in another life? Then what's mine for what I've done in this one?*

Barszcz's radio blared out battalion's warning of an approaching enemy MIG fighter. He ordered the company onto the rear slope, and me to remain forward with an LMG. The gun was suspended by rope between two sapling trees. The ammo belt was draped over my shoulder. I figured I was a perfect target, knowing that the gun would be totally ineffectual against an armor plated fuselage. The gods smiled however, and the MIGs, immune even to countless 20mm cannon hits, didn't arrive.

I had the platoon skirmish onto the next high ground and found 'Bug-out' Wassick's outfit pinned down by ineffectual incoming fire. We pressed on through to the summit and counted the enemy dead. Ordered back on the trucks, we headed north. The increasingly cold winds cut through our lightweight field jacket as we rode on opposite fenders again and pressed our hands onto the hood for warmth. Snow pelted the road ahead and by 0400 hours. it had blanketed the small hamlet where we stopped.

Three G.I.s who exited the last truck were surprised to see that two other vehicles had somehow tied into our column during the night. They went to tell them we'd halted for a 'piss call' but were gunned down when they stopped at the door of the first Russian-designed vehicle. The NKs inside started a panicky gunfight and men and trucks vainly tried to escape into nonexistent alleyways.

Buckley pointed up from the gridlock to a flanking ten-foot-high ridge, and ordered us up there. The shooting slowed to a dribble and I requested permission to run a recon, which Buckley denied, fearing that we'd draw fire from both sides. When dawn arrived, I cried, "*Tsuke ken* [Fix bayonets]!"

Bleary eyed, the ROKs moved down past the scores of dead and lifeless limbs that hung from the truck's shattered doors and windows. They went past the mangled body of a teenaged mother with a dead baby strapped to her back. Robertson's and Richard's squads advanced thirty yards ahead into town.

Cassiluci tagged along with Buckley at the rear of my squad and Barszcz was further behind bringing up another platoon. Butterball, ahead, shattered the eerie silence with five rounds and a grenade he threw through a plate glass window. Cass and I moved into the dust-filled room. The eyes Richard had seen staring back at him belonged to a jumbled pile of children, lying there like discarded dolls. I dashed out to catch up with the squads that neared the end of the truck column. A nearby door flew open and my instinctual bayonet thrust pierced but a fraction of an inch into an alarmed trucker's jacket.

He screamed. "G.I., G.I.! Don't shoot! I've been hiding out all night in here."

I showered him with curses, and watched Butterball approach the last bullet riddled Russian truck and the wounded NK who'd been left behind on a blanket-covered stretcher. He leaned up in a gestured surrender as Butterball's level bayonet approached.

Cass excitedly called out, "Bayonet that fuckin' Gook, Merc, bayonet 'em!"

The Korean's eyes filled with terror as he parried off two of Richard's lunges. Then he stepped back and coolly fired a round through the NK's head. It splattered his brains and recalled my thoughts back to a time when we were eleven. Richard had stood tearfully over the dead bird he'd shot from a tree in our yard.

"I killed it," he had cried and ran back into the house where he stayed for the rest of the day. He wouldn't come back out, even to play war. Seared by the image, I couldn't describe my thoughts and feelings, but wished I hadn't seen it.

Moving up to an intersection, I motioned the ROKs to continue on as a group of elderly civilians ran toward me. Their hands were held high and Barszcz frantically shouted for me not to kill them.

I turned to him in surprise. "I wasn't going to, sir!"

I could see that he thought I was my brother. "Then why did you shoot that wounded soldier back there?"

I obeyed the unwritten law of the 'Sibling Code' and lied. "I don't know, sir." He dismissed me, telling me to catch up with the platoon.

Later, on exiting an alleyway onto the main road, I saw Buckley. He had found a chair, and he had it leaning back against the bow of a Patton tank, nonchalantly reading *Stars and Stripes*. The eternally famished platoon sat indifferently a few feet away beneath an enflamed sagging roof gulping down fistfuls of sticky rice. Nearby Richard and Robertson emerged through a veil of sooty smoke with the captain. He pointed to a large building 150 yards off.

"Take your squads over to that hospital and check it out." He shouted as they left, "Remember men, no goddamned firing in or around that hospital!"

Cass trailed behind them as I had my squad set up a roadblock. The patrol burst through the hospital doors with weapons raised and silence fell over the ward's thirty patients as their doctors and nurses fled. Cass reached the first bed and studiously read the hieroglyphic chart then solemnly fired a round into the patient's chest. Richard turned in shock.

"Why did you do that?"

Cass morphed into Dr. Kildare. "It was a mercy killin'. Da poor devil woulda limped fer da rest of his life." They were surprised that the ROKs didn't get the joke.

At the far end of the smoldering and near deserted town, Hungerford sounded mail call. Richard laughed and waved his girlfriend's letter.

"Joan said some company down in Florida is selling Bibles with 1/16 of an inch bulletproof jackets and that it saved the life of one 'God-fearing' 1st Cavalry man down at the Naktong."

Robertson snickered. "Yeah, well, a beer can opener could get through one-sixteenth of an inch of tin with no trouble at all."

Richard dryly continued. "Anyway, Joan's having one blessed and sent to me."

Robertson squinted. "Might help if you're planning to surrender, you could chuck the M1 and pass yourself off as a Chaplain's assistant."

Richard read her footnote "A Democratic congressmen proposed that frontline G.I.s get an issue of free beers, but some irate moms thought that might turn their sons into 'crazed drunken killers.'"

I laughed. "That would be quite an accomplishment on 3.2 beers."

Richard held up his next letter. This one was from the parents of that lieutenant outside of Taejon, who wanted to be called "Joe" by the truckload of guys he disappeared with when they tried to escape to Pusan. He read aloud. "We saw the photo of you and your brother in the paper. It said you boys were in G Company, the same as our son Joey, and we were hoping and praying that you might be able to tell us something about our only boy. The Army says he's 'missing in action' and we're worried sick. We love him so very much and need to really know what happened to him. So please, if you get this letter, please, write and let us know whatever you can. God bless all you young men out there. Our prayers are with you."

Later Richard showed Barszcz the letter and he snapped, "He and the others were deserters who got what they deserved and his parents shouldn't be shown any sympathy, either."

Butterball followed his advice and I thought about that obligatory war movie scene that shows a choked-up commander dutifully writing to the parents of fallen sons.

Next morning Robertson and I took our squad patrol into a nearby village and captured two NK deserters dressed in bug-out whites. The teenager shivered with fear and the stoic middle-aged man all but sneered as I questioned him. Robertson knocked the younger one unconscious with a blow from the linked .30-caliber ammo belt wrapped around his wrist.

"*Antano kaikyu no rentai desu ka* [What is your rank and regiment]?"

His unblinking eyes stared icily as I pressed the muzzle of my .45 to his forehead and pulled the trigger. Click. He didn't even flinch and he couldn't have seen that I'd silently unloaded the chamber behind his back. I wasn't sure whether to reward his bravery...or kill him? Things would have been different were our situations reversed. Both prisoners lived.

We were on a platoon patrol when ROK Richard's hand motioned to a crest northeast of us, as we examined a small mound of pebbles beside a mountain trail. "Ah, *Sahji*, stones say on other side more village." I asked how he knew. "At mountain pass, where foot trail cross another, pebble say, two village is nearby. People pay spirit with pebble, when cross mountain to other side."

The hamlets were empty and we returned to the CP. I found Buckley propped up against a wall. He was reading an article he'd written that his New Jersey College had returned published.

"Sir, it looks like the Chinks bugged out."

He glanced up at me. "I thought as much, Sergeant."

I seized the opportunity. "Sir, perhaps it's slipped the lieutenant's mind, but I'm still only a corporal."

He gazed and mumbled at the magazine. "We'll have to see about correcting that, Mercy."

I struck, while the proverbial iron was hot. "Sir, my brother's still a corporal and Robertson's only a PFC."

Buckley flashed a proud grin and handed me the fanned open pages of his magnum opus, entitled *A Line Officer Compares Fighting in WWII to Korea*. I masked my disappointment in not finding a single mention of his three faithful NCOs.

"A nicely written piece, sir."

He smiled. "There're rumors we'll be home for Christmas."

I grinned. "I am at home, sir."

I left the rain-drenched fender of the convoy's lead truck and sat a silent hour in the cab. The driver finally spoke. "You don't remember me, do you, Mercy?"

My thumb slyly rested on my pistol's hammer. "Hard to tell who you are in this light."

His eyes remained on the rain-soaked road. "I was at Schimmelpfenning, in Baker Company. You arrested me in that Christmas beer hall riot back in '48 and shot my buddy's ear lobe off." He smiled and confessed. "I was the one who crashed a case of beer over your head. That was a great fight."

We bellowed together. "Airborne! All the way!" We had reached our ice-encrusted destination.

"If I'd known I'd run into you, Mercy, I'd of put a pint of something nice in the glove compartment."

I smiled and shook his hand then he double-clutched away in low gear. Near noon the company followed our platoon into an almost deserted town and a massive souvenir hunt soon followed. Only one shot was fired, mine, into a small Chinese flag that was posted on the wall. I wanted to give it a touch of 'authenticity.' I stuffed that and the 7x5 foot flag I took from a deserted Chinese CP under my jacket. The whole platoon then crammed into an old red hook-and-ladder fire engine truck. Butterball drove, careening wildly through the streets as Robertson clanged the bell. The ROKs hung on for dear life. Barszcz noticed the flags spilling from under my jacket as we passed. Thirty minutes later he presented the larger one to the regimental commander in front of a battery of flashing *Stars and Stripes* cameras.

The platoon rendezvoused with Buckley on a hillock just outside of town, at a straggler collection point. There were about a hundred men and a Patton tank lazily lounging beside the refugee-clogged road. Suddenly shouts and shots rang out near the tank and all around me. I held a fleeing civilian in my pistol sights.

Lt. Walters frantically cried out to the action-starved troops, "God damn it, men, cease fire!!"

Richard mumbled. "Fucking embarrassing! Fifty guys shooting at him and the son of a bitch still made twenty-five yards!"

We boarded the awaiting trucks and I asked the captain our destination. We were headed to Sinuiju. Barszcz's gaze fell back onto the rotund driver seated up against a wheel, wolfing down gluttonous spoonful's of chow from his brimming mess kit.

Barszcz barked, "Get on your feet and into that truck!"

The stuffed-mouth driver's chin dripped gravy as he lazily looked up and said, "I ain't finished chowin' down yet!"

Barszcz disappointingly didn't kick in his face and I didn't vent a powerful urge to empty my .45 clip into the mess kit nestled in his crotch, less for insubordination than his grotesque table manners. Eventually he burped and waddled up into the cab. I laughed with Butterball, wondering if this could happen in any other wartime army in the world.

Halted at a junction, we saw the scholarly artwork of some G.I. by the side of the road. Three dead Chinese, in full rigor-mortis, were sitting in a rendition of the enigmatic Monkey Soul trio of the East: Hear, See and Speak No Evil. They, too, warned of what lay ahead. Patrolling jets had surprised their convoy and littered the charred landscape with twisted truck frames and the smoldering bodies of eight hundred dead—a full battalion.

By dusk we had stopped. It had grown increasingly cold, and I noticed Buckley massaging his bluing hands and cursing the sky's threat of snow. "Sir, why haven't you drawn one of those new issue overcoats?"

He shivered. "Don't want one, or the snow boots, or the heavy gloves. Can't fight with all that on and..."

He stopped as we noticed two Chinese soldiers serenely emerging from the wood line thirty yards down the road. Our weapons came up instantly. They wore submachine guns, pistols and freshly inked armbands in English: "FRIENDLY UN POLICE."

I whispered to Buckley, "They probably got those from our State Department." They ignored my Chinese shout. "*Qui qui lai* [Come here]!"

I set my sights between the eyes of the more arrogant looking of the two and suddenly sensed others were covering them in the woods. Ours seemed to be the only raised weapons in the otherwise indifferent company, ironic proof that the pen is mightier than the sword.

I lowered my rifle in concern for the column that had halted bumper-to-bumper; not knowing how many Chinese were in the wood line, I looked at Buckley. "How do we ever win wars, sir?"

He paused. "With a few good men."

Richard slung his weapon and cursed. "The next thing you know, those fucking Chinks will be falling in at the end of our chow line."

Robertson shouldered his BAR and hissed. "Maybe at the head of it, *Boy-san.*"

The convoy continued until nightfall when we stopped and dug in.

We skirmished through the dawn across an open field and secured a flanking ridge. Suddenly, a soldier I hadn't seen since the Nam River near Chinju approached. "Hey, BB, I heard you were dead."

He gave a hound dog sniff in my direction. "Nah, just got nicked, Mercy, and I'm glad to see that you're still here, too."

The skirling bagpipes of the Canadian Princess Pat Regiment (Princess Patricia's Canadian Light Infantry Regiment headquartered in Edmonton, Alberta) marching on an adjacent road cut short our two hour long conversation. The next morning they occupied our very positions and our regiment moved out. Shortly after we left, the Canadians were strafed and napalmed by U.S. jets when the wrong air identification panels were put out. They suffered heavy casualties.

As we marched, I felt the fear the people had of their own regime in each northern hamlet we passed, so I was surprised by the makeshift welcome banners and U.S. flags suspended across the main street of the next town we entered. Cautious villagers shouted "*Mansai!*" We marched another mile and the company halted. Barszcz gave a rare pep talk.

"Some of you men are slackers, but others of you fight day and night."
He nodded subtly in our direction. "Hopefully, everyone will now copy
their example."

I would have felt more satisfied had he given us our elusive
promotions, as was the case with Herbert who was pinned with the silver
bars of a first lieutenant.

Impulsively I went back into town alone. Not a half hour passed before
I was shouting to one of the terror-stricken civilians within the deluge that
swirled through the village pulling down flags and hospitable banners.
"*Doy stano* [What is the matter]?" He replied. "*Chosen-jin haytie o kaeru
desu* [Korean soldiers are coming back]!"

The people quickly dissolved into scattered nooks and crannies. I took
up a firing position and waited: *My shots should alert and bring the
company...I hope.* A full hour passed and nothing was seen on the deserted
streets. Some irate party member must have objected to the town's warm
reception and took revenge with a false alarm. Had the NKs actually
returned, their murderous revenge on the villagers would have been
indescribable.

Back with the company and at the end of the day's march, we stopped
in some distant hamlet. The ROKs snacked on chicken and rice, watching
in amusement as I practiced my quick draw and shot a few balanced water
jugs from off the heads of passing women. Robertson and I lounged on the
porch of our occupied house as sundown came. Over and over we played a
particular Japanese record we had found, on an old Edison Victrola.
Though I didn't understand the words to *Kojo no Tsuke* [*Moon over the
Ruined Castle*], its melody transported me back to a particularly snowy
night in Sendai.

My saké-fumed brain had then labored hard to decipher a half-torn
scroll on a Buddhist temple wall while I wondered if I'd been a Japanese
soldier in my former life. That memory came into sharper focus later when
ROK Richard explained it was a song about reincarnation. He said it told
of a centuries-old moon-drenched castle—in Sendai, and the cry of wild
geese as they flew over rows of glimmering planted swords that marked
life's passage through a thousand ages. My flesh tingled. I believe the
music I heard was of the spheres of life, and that it had played in my heart
since childhood: *It was fate then...and not chance...that stationed me in...
Sendai then here...with Asian troops...to war on the Chinese border.*
Buckley broke my reverie with the news that we would be spending
Thanksgiving in reserve.

Richard told us of his day's patrol: "I actually let the Gook go, but
ROK Richard and the squad convinced me that he was an out-of-uniform

hard-nosed commie. He got about four hundred yards before I nailed him with one round, which pleased everybody—but the NK."

Next morning, I broke the boredom by draping a blanket roll across my shoulder and wore my helmet backwards to look like a Russian soldier. I stepped out of the shadows and gave a passing woman a clenched fist salute and sputtered some Bolshevik gibberish. She nearly fainted. Giving aid or comfort to the enemy in North Korea meant instant death. Not able to leave well enough alone, a little later I put on some indigenous white clothes and strolled beyond the company area to experience how it felt to walk unarmed, dispossessed and powerless between two warring armies. My all too convincing farmer shuffle suddenly made me nervous: *There could be someone drawing a bead on me right now...like I did with that farmer at the Nam River.*

Thanksgiving turkey and all the trimmings were beyond the ever-hungry ROKs wildest dreams, but they didn't understand why soup and coffee couldn't be mixed in the same cup. The only pall in the clear, 15° weather was the mess sergeant's bigotry. He didn't dish out cigars to the ROKs as he had to the G.I.s because he knew they'd be given to us. Buckley made up for the loss later that night around our fire.

Richard and Eugene "Johnny" Murr on OP.

"The captain sends his compliments along with these stogies. He wants you guys to go out and capture him a Chink so he can make him his personal cook." We waited for the punch line... "It's true," Buckley persisted. "Barszcz got the idea from General Church of the 1st Cavalry. A Chink soldier found a wounded U.S. officer and two EMs, and protected them from his own patrols for sixteen days. Then, in broad daylight he carried them across our lines."

Butterball laughed. "They should give him a chop-suey joint down on Canal Street."

The next village we entered had a few cows. So, believing the war was near over, Richard and I decided to throw a dinner party for Barszcz and Tubbs, the new supply sergeant. Although not part of the captain's inner clique we still respected his soldiering. We scrubbed and polished the hut into a poor man's film version of *The Prisoner of Zenda*. We made place cards, and set them in lustrously polished clips of M1 ammo on the white-cloth covered bench that served as our table. Masan and Seoul squads stood as an Honor Guard with fixed bayonets along a thatched carpet that stretched from the rickety gateway right up to the door of the candle-lighted room. Barszcz and Tubbs beamingly returned their salutes. Sgt. Tubbs, humbled by the makeshift opulence apologetically contributed his 'Pot Luck' can of tamales.

"The ROKs might enjoy this," I said, "over their ice cream."

We laughed and smiled with delight over the trays heaped with thick steaks, rice and *kim-chee* that Our Man Friday and Slick ceremoniously carried in. I rose and they lifted cups of piping hot milk saké to the toast I made in the voice of Ronald Coleman.

"Gentlemen, I give you George Company and the regiment—forever!"

Johnny Murr's head excitedly popped through the door just as I took my first bite. "Captain, you're wanted on the radio."

Barszcz returned and grimly waved at the table. "We'll have to take a rain check, Mercy, we're moving out."

Looking around, I suddenly recalled my grandmother's old edict: "never leave food on the table when there are people starving in China." I stuffed juicy steaks in my field jacket pockets. Unfortunately, that drew in every starving dog within a mile to the tail of the company column. They wildly leapt, growled and barked all around me, as Barszcz did the same from up ahead.

"Get rid of those goddamn dogs, now!"

I ate as voraciously as my furry friends who only left after I turned out my empty pockets to prove the food was gone.

CHAPTER 24

Back!

A squadron of jets thundered in low over the smoking ruin of earlier strikes and columns of frightened refugees fleeing north to the imagined safety of China's border. The platoon flanked from the carnage littered road and fanned through the ramshackle huts on the far side of the town where I entered a yard. I didn't fire at the Chinese quilted jacket I glimpsed moving behind a small trash fire. Next to it were two bodies, a man and woman. Each had been shot in the back of the head. I was somewhat mesmerized by the bullet in the man's skull which hadn't exited, but protruded his forehead out six inches like a breaching rhino horn. I approached what I thought was the blood stained face of a wounded Chinese soldier, which actually was a seated infant who'd been partially covered with the coat. The clenched fist of the blood spattered infant tapped on the probing blade of my bayonet: *.surprised they didn't kill him, too… but protected him from cold…?*

When a sudden shot rang out I swept the infant up and dashed for the cover of a crumbled wall and returned the sniper's fire. The babe mutely smiled and gurgled throughout the explosive exchange and my flesh tingled in recognition of the blinding quirk of fate that made me the wooden soldier of *Babes in Toyland!* It was as if I had reached back in time and rescued my former infant self.

The shooting stopped and the puzzled ROKs wondered why I couldn't put the tot down. Reluctantly, I surrendered him some time later to an aged villager along with all the money I had.

The ROKs followed rapidly through the back alleyways echoing with sporadic fire. I had them hold fast as I ran ahead to the outer wall of a Buddhist temple where I heard the sounds of skittish NK cavalry horses on the other side. The three grenades I threw over in hopes of getting whatever troops were beside them echoed back the whinnied cries of pain and panic from the horses. Their anguish filled me with sorrow. I peered through a fissure at the dark wood temple fifty yards ahead. I knew Gooks were inside, but to get them out I'd have to level the 'church.' Early Catholic influences or pure superstition made me fearful of retribution if I did. I let the impulse pass to leap on one of the horses and charge through the temple doors with both guns blazing, á la John Wayne.

Buckley shouted, "Burn everything right up to the riverbed and then set up an LMG." I bypassed the temple and ran through billows of smoke and licking flames where I fired a WP rifle grenade into the back of a fleeing NK. At the far end of town, in a wide dried out riverbed below a precipice, two hundred frightened 'civilians' swayed to and fro. The urge to fire into them was overpowering, knowing the majority of them were NKs in their bug-out-whites, which is what they would do in my place.

Headed back towards the road, I was struck by a religion invoking vision of a tearful kneeling and deeply distraught woman raising aloft her dead infant with both hands; as Christ's Holy Grail is depicted in the painting of *The Last Supper*. A dozen emotionally touched ROKs slowly reached towards her from each side with outstretched apostolic hands as the jets that had taken her son's life streaked away low across the soot-stained sky. Next I stumbled upon an unarmed uniformed NK with a woman in an alley who arrogantly gestured for me to wait until he completed his talk. I took the slack off my trigger wondering why I hadn't killed him already and prodded him out into the column of passing prisoners.

Somewhere on the flank an NK ran into a cave and Richard threw in two grenades. They were hurled back out and exploded by his feet. Miraculously he was only pelted with dust. He then fired sixteen rounds into the cave and was astonished when a terror-stricken family of six emerged unscathed with their hands held high. Richard departed and soon dashed up the stairs in a nearby two-story house where he found a withered old man beyond medical help on his deathbed. Richard studied him then tapped his rifle, offering him a compassionate quick release from his misery. When the watery-eyed octogenarian nodded back with a grateful smile and closed his eyes, Richard fired an instant death round into his head; and to pay genuine homage to his courage he carried out the rituals of a Viking funeral. He torched the bed, as the ancient Norsemen had those ships that they'd set adrift as flaming pyres. Then, in lieu of the prerequisite volley of flaming arrows that denoted a farewell salute, he fired instead a clip of eight tracer rounds into his smoldering body then briefly stood in contemplative silence as the cremation started. After leaving the murky village Richard told us the story aboard our northbound trucks and Robertson smiled. "Butterball, I had no idea you were such a sentimentalist."

At nightfall we sat below the snowy mountain peaks near Chong-ju and listened to the howling wintry winds. Richard stared out gloomily over the ice-caked barrel of our LMG.

"Just as I figured, it's another false alarm."

I nodded. "Yeah, I think we've seen our last fire fight."

Robertson offered a ray of hope. "There's still China, Boy-san, just over those hills."

We argued and wondered if China was too large for any army to occupy, much less conquer, even with the A-bomb. Richard made a sage observation. "If we killed half the world's population, there'd still be over a billion Chinks left, and all of them in the Airborne!"

I was swiftly absorbed by the thought that if, or rather when, we crossed into China, some of them would join up with us.

Buckley's sudden shout turned despair into exhilaration. "Get the platoon down on the trucks we're moving up to Sinuiju!"

The convoy cut through hours of gusting winds and swirls of snow then stopped abruptly in an ominous silence. We three leapt from the truck, sensing 'something,' but not knowing what. The only movement on the silent zinc-white hills was the moon cast shadows of shivering pines.

Buckley shouted over the noise of trucks stripping their gears to turn rapidly round on the narrow snow-banked road. "Get your asses back here, we're leaving!"

The convoy roared down the coastal highway. Not twenty miles from the sea and ten miles forward of where we'd just stopped, the advanced guard of our 21st Regiment had skirmished with a Mongolian cavalry unit. The Chinese suffered heavy air attacks, but still pushed back the regiment. Their commander reported that for as far as the eye could see, there were divisions of Chinese avalanching down the hills all around. As it turned out, he only saw three of the Chinese undetected divisions. On our immediate left flank, as we headed south, five more full strength Chinese armies sprang out of the mysteriously dense Taebaek Mountains.

Lackadaisical discipline had allowed G.I.s to advance carrying no more than sixteen rounds [two clips] of ammunition apiece. Many wore warm pile caps in lieu of cold helmets, and most were without grenades or bayonets.

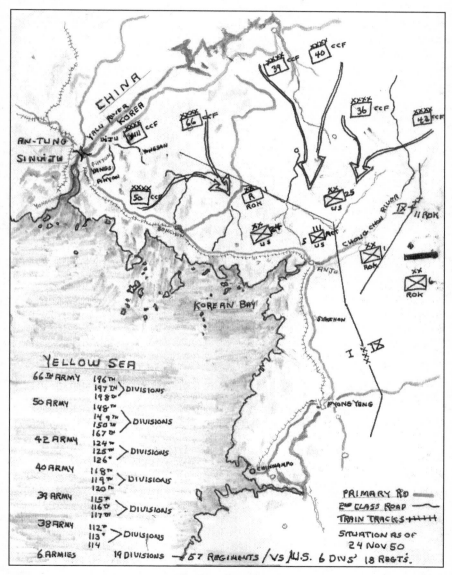

The lay of the land.

Cumbersome boxes of machine gun ammo remained in company supply trucks rather than be carried in the frostbitten hands of the crews who desperately would need them. Gross neglect of their individual and crew-served weapons also contributed to the panicky psychological shock that our Army felt when they clashed head on with the combat-tested Chinese mandate of *San Meung Kung Tsu:* Fierce fire, fierce assault and fierce pursuit! Already suffering from low morale, the dispirited U.S. Army was in full retreat. Many hoped it was headed for distant Pusan where imagined ships would carry them home for Christmas.

Over the next four consecutive days, forty thousand guerrillas simultaneously terrorized the rear-echelon areas. Doubtless, many still wore their FRIENDLY UN POLICE armbands. They blew up ammunition and fuel dumps, hospitals, command posts, and motor pools while cutting off supply routes. The 187th Airborne Regimental Combat Team, in reserve twenty miles north of Pyongyang, was under attack. The ROK 1st Division, the U.S. 1st Cavalry, 2nd Indianhead and 25th Divisions, 5th Regimental Combat Team and the newly arrived Turkish and English Brigades, which comprised the U.S. IX Corps central front area, were all in serious trouble.

Shamefully, an entire company from the 24th Regiment of the U.S. 25th Division had "gotten lost" during this engagement, and found their way into history by surrendering en-masse without having fired a single shot. That must have made great reading in Peking's daily press. General Almond's X Corps fought heroically in the far north around Hamhung, where General 'Chesty' Puller's Marines and the U.S. 7th Division suffered many casualties. The fanatical Chinese machine-gunned, burned, bayoneted and threw under the treads of half-tracks any American who surrendered or was taken captive. An Army captain at the Chosen Reservoir was stripped naked and had his rank insignia pinned into the skin of his forehead. He died spread-eagled in the snow, whipped by nightmarish arctic winds that often froze the dead standing upright in place. The cruel elements and the need for a punishing victory made the Chinese more vicious in the second phase of their battle. Strangely, they escaped being strafed by U.S. pilots who were reluctant to attack what they thought might be refugees, which had happened in the past.

The Eighth Army's narrowly averted catastrophe filled the southbound Pyongyang road with a truck convoy fifty miles long. They couldn't use the countries many other major roadways because powerful guerrilla forces roamed and operated with near impunity. As we raced south the ROK 2nd Corps twenty miles off on our left made chaotic contact with the Chinese. Hours prior to the major assault fifteen hundred guerrillas staged a coordinated attack against the ROK Corps' rear areas. Eight of its regiments were then simultaneously assaulted from their front, rear and flanks by three Chinese bugle-blowing divisions.

Three more Chinese divisions attacked the 1st ROK Division and cut off two of its forward regiments. They were leaderless and low on ammunition. Their tenacious General Paik Sun-yup, who'd served with distinction in the Japanese Imperial army of Manchukuo, and in Special Forces operations against Chinese communist guerrillas, again displayed his unique courage. He regrouped each of his dazed units and personally led them in successful counterattacks against staggering odds. They recaptured the lost critical ground over which our division was to escape. Had the Chinese broken through this sector, while all of I Corps traveled south in trucks edged against the inaccessible rocky beaches of the surging Yellow Sea, the American Army would surely have been totally obliterated. The hard-pressed and ill-fated 2nd ROK Corps suffered further injury when some of their escaping forces clashed with the Turkish Brigade. This brigade was made up of five thousand men who spoke neither English nor Korean, and couldn't yet distinguish South Korean from Chinese uniforms.

The ensuing carnage, which took place just beyond our hearing and sight, was reminiscent of the ruthless Tartar hordes that showed no mercy or took prisoners when they'd swept through Asia in ancient times. Fierce blood lusting screams reverberated from the surrounding hillsides where the primeval clamor of cymbals, gongs, whistles and drums terrorized the opposing forces. This noise had the added effect of driving away whatever demon spirits the ever-superstitious Chinese peasant soldiers felt lurked in the throbbing darkness.

Machine guns, rifles and dismembering barrages of heavy mortars lashed and crumbled the horror-stricken South Korean lines. Again there were *tsunami*-like waves of torch and sword-flashing cavalry, flaying bayonets, knives and axes. The battle raged as between wild cats locked in a burning cage. The four-day mêlée inflicted a near fatal blow against the American Army and the collective occidental psyche.

While we continued south, the U.S. Infantry 2nd Division on our far left flank lost five thousand men to the two full Chinese Field Armies that blocked their narrow escape route out of the lumber village of Kunu-ri. This was in spite of the Navy's gull-winged Corsairs and jets sweeping down throughout the day to bathe the hapless Chinese with fourteen liquid tons of scorching napalm. The blistering cold, combined with the sound and fury of constant shelling, diving planes, cries, screams of scared and wounded men, and the uninterrupted fire of every caliber weapon known

193

to man defied description.

The Chinese tenaciously attacked tanks and vehicles with satchel charges and stick grenades. They fought hand-to-hand with the Americans they pulled from passing vehicles. Smoldering and disabled trucks with cargoes of dead and wounded were crushed or pushed aside by the panicked tanks that tried to escape. In many cases, the tankers had deserted the infantrymen who'd deployed from their backs to engage the enemy.

Shamefully, some desperate G.I.s tried to flee in place of the wounded they pulled from passing vehicles. There was bravery, too, and many fought down to their last round. Most extraordinary amidst the raging savagery, and so different from what the Marines experienced in Hamhung, were the unexpected mercies shown to the seriously wounded and exhausted G.I.s found lying in the roadside gullies; all assuming they'd be murdered. Their Chinese captors administered first aid to many of these men, despite their habitual shortages of medicine. It was assumed they had been former Nationalist army troops who remembered with kindness the help America rendered their nation before and after Pearl Harbor.

Robertson, Butterball and I maintained our tail gunner vigils through flurries of snow driven by bitterly cold winds as we rolled past scattered huts and small villages. The night sky was inky black when we stopped, save for a few widely diffused stars and we braced against the gusting icy winds. We complied with the tactical scorched earth order and the ensuing yellow and orange tongued flames from burning houses licked away large swatches of the darkness. Not forty yards away an octogenarian Korean couple stood straight and motionless, silhouetted against the conflagration of their disintegrating home. They exchanged no words, but the resolute grip of the farmer's hand on her visibly shivering shoulder signified more of a shared love than any utterance could say. Their thin cotton garments, the low threatening howl of the Siberian driven winds and the destruction of their small rice granary all heralded what fate had in store for them; the image warmed my near frozen heart, I never knew why or who threw the grenade that instantly swept them away in an exploding swirl of fiery fragments, but I heard my whisper: *They'll suffer less this way.* I wondered next about all those Koreans wearing only light summer-weight cotton garments and open rubber slippers throughout the year; withstanding the elements and unimaginable hardship without a whimper, or even a cough or sneeze as I could remember.

The bitter temperatures and lack of food worked differently on us during the following night's march through a howling blizzard. At dawn we mounted the backs of passing tanks and gripped the rings of their icy steel turrets to brace against the blinding Siberian winds. My field jacket, pants and skimpy gloves stiffened into ice. I thought of other frigid battles from history: the Germans at Stalingrad, Napoleon's retreat from Moscow, and Washington at Valley Forge.

We dismounted and the tanks continued south. I posted guards around our roadside compound where the others slept, then thawed out over a small fire next to Buckley.

"I don't know why we just can't stand and fight, sir. The only thing we do with any regularity is bug-out."

His reply ripped into my stomach. "That's what they said about you and your brother before we crossed the Naktong." His gaze remained fixed on the fire.

"Who said that?"

He replied smugly. "The CP."

I stammered, "That's a goddamned lie and you—of all people, should fucking know it!"

I left and, secluded in my commandeered mud hut room, roundly cursed the Army, the captain, Buckley and the ceaseless crying of the baby in the adjoining room. I sprayed a string of Thompson-sub rounds high across the wall "*Yakamashi. Yakamashi* [Shut up. Shut up]!"

I stood veiled in cordite vapors and self-disgust: *God, we take over a man's house in the middle of the night...shoot it up...drive him and his sick kid out into the freezing cold...what the fuck are we doing!?* Irrationally my throbbing brain even had thoughts of killing Barszcz and Buckley mingled in with my own painfully remembered failures: The guerrillas at Taejon, the train engineer, and that surrendering NCO on the hill at Chinju. There was the NK major at the POW pen in Pusan, the arrogant US tank lieutenant up on the Chungch'on, and then God's apostle on earth, Sergeant Goodman. If I could at that moment have turned back the hands of time, I would have killed them all! *Maybe I'm losing my mind?*

Those thoughts kept churning through my head on our march to the roadblock at dawn. I exceeded my order to not let retreating ROKs through. I pressed my bayonet tip into the side of the soldier calmly seated in the passenger seat of a Jeep we had stopped. He dispassionately pointed to the single star on his collar. "I am general. I must get through!"

Anger fueled my disrespectful reply. "No one gets through!"

Barszcz chance arrival broke the impasse, and he waved the general's Jeep on. I grew angrier through the morning. I was becoming alien even to myself.

Our truck stopped beside a two-story high mound of C-rations on the Pyongyang road that was surprisingly guarded by a small baby-faced

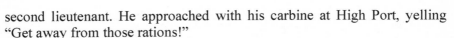

second lieutenant. He approached with his carbine at High Port, yelling "Get away from those rations!"

I stammered. "Sir, we haven't even seen a frozen can of beans for two days. My men are hungry."

He was smugly unmoved. "These are not for unauthorized personnel, they're to be burned!"

Our convoy skirted Pyongyang and the panicky service troops who busily torched vast stocks of critical supplies, tons of ammunition as well as the new tanks and trucks lashed down on railroad cars that could have easily been sent south. On a nearby airstrip, A-26 bombers that could have been flown to Japan had the rear echelon 'risked' the few hours needed to fly in parts, were being destroyed. Cells of local NK saboteurs helped in the destructive orgy and ignited whatever caches of fuel and ammunition the Eighth Army had not gotten to first. The freezing winds carried the stinging soot down to the muddy Taedong River where five million desperate civilians tried to cross on anything that would float. Who knows how many swimmers died of hypothermia?

Buckley's depression grew more worrisome by the day. He rarely spoke during or after a patrol and even cocked his fist in my face for having, out of necessity, eaten before our troops were fed. He was in dire need of R&R, but probably would have refused the offer. Like us, he felt there was no life beyond the platoon. Yet we were dismayed to learn that Barszcz had never submitted our names to regiment for that consideration, but many of his most undeserving NCOs returned to Japan multiple times on the nauseating premise of their being married! We rationalized his actions, deciding he didn't want to weaken his most reliable platoon.

The battalion halted for the night and the nearby strains of music from the bivouac area of the 6th ROK Division lured Robertson and I into what was their makeshift bar. A glaringly cold reception from a table full of Tong-warrior types dashed my hopes of recruiting some fresh troops. One heatedly shouted a phrase I easily recognized to his friends: "Give me gun, give me gun!"

To his surprise I defiantly slid my M1 across the table. Robertson and I stood with hands poised above our holsters. We waited in the deathly silence, but nobody 'drew on us.' After I retrieved the untouched rifle we exited backwards through the rear door. MGM would have been proud of us. Robertson made sure we weren't followed.

"I don't know, *Boy-san*, maybe he was strafed by one of our jets or some G.I. screwed his girl?"

I pondered that. "They must have seen a few cowboy movies and thought you were John Wayne."

He arched his eyebrow. "He was a 4-F, wasn't he?"

The battalion halted the following night with our platoon deployed as roadway security for the convoys. Alone on a hillcrest with my LMG, I watched the approaching running lights of an L-5 reconnaissance plane and clearly glimpsed the pilot in the glow of his cabin's red panel light as he skimmed by almost at eye level. A minute later he bombed a convoy that was stalled along the road. It was the infamous icon of NK resistance, "Bed Check Charlie," who only ventured out after dark and flew extremely low to avoid our B-26 night interceptors. I fumed: *I could have brought him down with a hip shot from my .45...been decorated... maybe even promoted. He was so goddamn close*! I was still cursing as Buckley arrived with new orders, that we were running a patrol.

We searched the nearby hamlet for prisoners that G-2 could interrogate, or weapons stashed behind walls but found only the sick and those too feeble to flee. Buckley's mood grew darker. A young woman down the road crouched behind her front door and lashed out with a gleaming white-hot poker as Butterball and Robertson entered the house; missing Richard's startled face by an inch. Robertson uncharacteristically shouted not to shoot her, freezing Richard's half drawn pistol. Robertson parried her second swipe and locked her throat in his arm. Dragging her to a corner brazier he plunged her limb bicep-deep into a bed of red-hot coals. Richard smiled and noted when she screamed and fainted that she was lucky they weren't Japs or NKs, or it would have been her ugly face.

Back at our roadside hill Buckley stood engulfed in exhaust fumes from the idling trucks and asked if we'd gotten the platoon's sleeping bags loaded up.

Richard nodded. "Yes, sir, got them on the truck last, just like you said."

An anger laced depression swept across Buckley's face. "Christ, that means we won't be moving up with the company!"

Richard apologized, not knowing the captain ordered whichever platoon loaded up last to remain behind and keep the escape route open.

Buckley moaned. "Think about it, men, our company is going into a blocking position and could be gloriously annihilated while we're back here sitting on our butts!"

He turned and stalked off into the night. Two days later the company returned from the Taedong River bridge where an entire NK regiment was reportedly killed in heavy fighting. Buckley was fit to be tied.

A day or so later our truck convoy stopped at daylight and I coaxed Han to follow me out to the isolated hut on the far side of an open field. I planned to shoot him for his treason up on the Chungch'on. I knew he'd give me legal grounds by his anticipated failure to carry out the standing "scorched earth" policy order. I handed him the matches as a bedraggled middle-aged woman stepped from the house.

"Burn it down, Han." *Kill him, and set a standard to command by.*

The woman's hysterical eyes brimmed with tears as she fell begging at my feet. I momentarily weakened in sensing the incredible cold, but reiterated the order. Some loathsome thing within wouldn't let me kill Han, even as he preened in the belief that it was his adamancy that won. Back in the truck my stomach churned as we passed endless columns of disheartened troops in the falling snow and I cursed my inability to carry out military justice—*or was it murder?*

CHAPTER 25

Happy Valley

It was 11 December, and the regimental convoy, with our battalion in reserve, rolled down the winding windswept road into a three-mile-wide pocket of the Imjin Valley that was flanked on three sides by serpentine ridges. As usual, Richard and I were riding on opposite front fenders of the truck.

Using my best Walter Brennan impression, I called out, "Looks real nice down there. Let's call it Happy Valley."

The company got off the trucks in the center of the basin near the dozen huts we would occupy. The vehicles continued on for half a mile and deployed our 1st and 3rd battalions along the banks of the shallow Yangpyong'chon River. The 105mm howitzers of the 13th Field Artillery were stretched out on the right side of the north road and I was enjoying the rhythmical cadence of their drumbeat fire as Barszcz approached.

"Welcome to the village of Chongsong-san," he said, as he pointed down the narrow frost-tinted path to the cluster of large houses the ROKs would occupy. We took one for our CP and I decorated the walls with our battle flag and a calligraphy scroll I had found.

I mused about a reality that would have disappointed the ROKs, who thought all Americans were rich, as I studied the compound's wide yard and sturdy adjoining hut. This was better than most places we'd lived in when we were kids. That night I sensed Buckley's growing sourness as he ordered Richard to set up an OP in the notch of the hill we had just come down. Two ROK squads were to be stationed up there every night. It was the only entrance in or out of the valley and therefore a prime target for guerrillas. This road had to be kept open at all costs. As usual, no G.I.

platoons shared this duty and our 'rest area' wasn't going to be restful.

The following night, Buckley briefed me for my tour of OP duty. "General Chang's 7th Regiment, of the ROK 6th Division, is our left flank tie-in. On the right, across the three miles of valley, is his 19th ROK Regiment. Both are out of visual range from here in the valley and on the OP."

Hours later a few ill-aimed rifle rounds from somewhere cut harmlessly through the unexpected six-inch snowfall that obscured the road and ridge approaches. Returning at dawn I avoided Buckley whose depression had grown worse over the week and joined Richard and Robertson's self-appointed guerrilla patrol.

Out post position in Happy Valley after snowfall.

An hour later we entered a small village behind our lines and discovered it was occupied by a platoon of the dreaded South Korean National Police. Its one stunning member, a raven-haired beauty of about nineteen, languidly leaned against an open doorframe and blew streams of blue-tinted smoke toward us as though they were poison darts. Her languorous sullen black eyes focused unblinkingly on mine while I surveyed her khaki uniform that was two sizes too small for her taut voluptuous frame. Aphrodite was draped with a banana-clipped carbine, a sheathed dagger and two grenades attached to her low-slung .45 pistol belt. Even the sweat rings at her armpits and the dust on her combat boots looked exotic. I thought I was in love. Her boyish-faced commander slithered to her side with an expression fit only for a wanted poster. They looked like something out of a would-be Dorothy Lamour film—'*The Last Train from Madrid.*'

Robertson murmured appreciatively, "They really know how to fight a goddamned war."

I spoke in rough Japanese. "*Anatawo dari ga* [Who are you]?"

The lieutenant puffed up into an arrogant fist-on-hips stance and a few shadowy faces peered out from behind the surrounding partially opening doors.

ROK Tom whispered, "*Kio tsukete kudasai, Gunsho-san, junsa o desu* [Please be careful, Sergeant, they are police]."

Butterball and Robertson, mesmerized by the bewitching ROKette's heaving breasts, paid little attention to the officer's anxious fingers strumming his holster. I lifted the walkie-talkie and loudly told Tom in Japanese that I'd call an air strike if there were trouble. The lieutenant stepped forward, enjoying the latent nervousness he sensed from our ROKs.

"I am Lieutenant Yim Yu Son, National Police, who are you?" After I told him, he stepped forward again. "Why you are here in village?"

I answered, "We hunt guerrillas."

He droned condescendingly, "Oh, well, we have killed already all guerrilla in area."

I fixed a surprised expression on my face. "*A soka* [Is that so]?"

He matched my sarcasm in English. "Yes, that *is* so."

We left without the courtesy of salutes and pressed eastward to the next hamlet.

I spun my rifle from the hip and shouted to the white-clad figures scurrying beneath the floorboards of the first hut we reached. "*Tomari* [Stop]!" Three very tense and quite pretty teenagers arose with their hands held high. I quickly brought them into focus on my recently liberated camera.

ROK Richard assured them they weren't going to be raped, which calmed the gathered octogenarians who obviously imagined us as the vanguard of a Cossack pogrom. They warded off their worst fears by bribing us with a cow that I later shot by the mess tent. Four indigenous KPs rushed out with a large pan and cut its throat. They ravenously drank in a millennium-old belief that the blood would give them the animal's strength, while ROK Richard looked on with embarrassment. Then the

201

mess sergeant validated the old maxim of "no good deed goes unpunished," when he told us that our men weren't going to eat until all the G.I.s had eaten first. The military can inure one to stupidity...

Two of three teenage Korean girls we found on patrol in Happy Valley.

At dusk the squad's entrenching tools bounced off the ice-encrusted crest of the OP and threw sparks against the gusting sky and the only warmth I found was in ROK Tom's gesture that I occupy the small trailside burrow he'd found. It wasn't long after I crawled in and balled up that Buckley arrived.

"Mercy, regimental orders are that no Korean units or stragglers be allowed to enter the valley through this position. Is that clear?" When I had responded in the affirmative, he paused, and then asked if I had any good dreams lately.

The only road in and out of Happy Valley. Note the brass-knuckled bayonet. This was our ROK outpost.

The image was fresh in my mind. "Yes, sir. I dreamed about a dam breaking and a lot of debris floating around. It startled me awake."

He stepped closer to my face. "What do you think it meant?"

I hesitated. "That we're going to get hit soon, sir."

He turned to leave. "I trust your instincts and I'm telling the guys to sleep with their boots on."

ROK Tom and I spent a trilingual hour, piecing together words of three languages. I got some inkling of how a turbulent history had fissured his craggy face and knew he'd make a great drinking buddy. He reminded me of Uncle Mudge, and I wondered if he could have been up on the Yangtze River while Mudge was there on his gunboat? I felt funny giving an older experienced guy like him orders, and wondered what he did during the Jap occupation and what differences he saw between this war and the last? I asked what he and the other ROKs honestly thought about us.

Tom smiled broadly. "Seoul *Sahji*, you brother, him number one. You, Masan *Sahji*, you number ten. Chinju *Sahji*, him number have-a-no!"

Toshi arrived and cut short our laughter and pointed to a barely visible column of troops making their way up to the OP from the outside perimeter. "*Sahji*, soldier come!"

I spent the ten minutes reviewing Buckley's orders before I called out. "*Tomari. Dari desu ka* [Stop. Who's there]?"

The four-man point stood motionless five yards ahead of the shadowy fifty soldiers behind. Two ROKs inched forward and literally sniffed them out as their lieutenant stepped forward from his three-man guard and accepted my salute. He paid no attention to the pistol in my hand and jutted his jaw toward the northeast corner of the valley and spoke in fractured English.

"We 19 ROK Regiment. Very tired, have all day march, hmmm, save many hour if can here go through."

I responded with regret in his second language. "*Chui-san, sumi masen, watakushi-wa dekimasen, ii tsuke desu* [Lieutenant, I am sorry, but I cannot. I have orders]."

He blinked snow from his dark intense eyes and his voice rumbled with emotion. "My men cold. We go through!"

I took a quick step back with a half-raised pistol. "*Matte* [Wait]!" I pressed down the button on my walkie-talkie. "ROK FIVE, this is ROK OP, do you read me, over."

What should I do if he moves...fucking orders...can't blame him for wanting to take a shortcut...they have no heavy weapons...not carrying boxes...no extra bandoliers of ammo...Tom and Toshi both nodded they're okay...what to do?

With no reply from the CP, the lieutenant grunted and stepped forward. Our eyes locked and I pressed my pistol into his stomach. It was the 'moment of truth.' I willingly would have died at my post, as expected, if I'd thought for an instant they were Gooks. It was a dumb order that would needlessly take many lives. I nodded permission to pass and he curtly bowed. I scrutinized every face, weapon, and uniform that passed, hoping not to spot anything regrettable. I resolved to kill myself, if I'd been wrong and felt the heavy tick of each anxious second through the next three interminable hours of unbroken area silence. My judgment was vindicated but my self-held soldier image was tarnished by not having carried out my explicit orders. At dawn I avoided Buckley's debriefing and talked with Richard in our room. We heard a nearby shot then Our Man Friday was pounding at the door.

"*Sahji, Sahji*, you come, *hayaku*! Hurry! Lieutenant, boom, boom!"

Robertson knelt over an ashen-faced Buckley lying in a pool of blood on the CP floor. A bullet fired from the adjoining room had ripped through the wall and lodged in his abdomen. Buckley clutched my hand as though it were life itself and moaned.

"Mercy, you are not to punish the ROK...that's an order. It was an accident. Understand?" I was deeply touched by his sense of compassion and forgiveness.

"I promise you, sir, he won't be harmed."

His lip curled into a grin as he passed out. *I've seen things like this in movies...but I never quite believed it.* Richard rode with Buckley's stretcher on the Aid Station Jeep and I ordered the men to fall in. "*Utsumari!*"

The squad leaders stood with bowed heads and the men stared unblinkingly ahead, knowing in their army the penalty for this was death. My softly spoken Japanese broke the pensive silence.

"Who shot Lieutenant?"

The least familiar ROK in the Taegu squad spoke up. "*Watakushi wa desu* [It is me]."

ROK Richard interpreted for me. "The merciful American lieutenant has ordered that the life of the man who accidentally shot him is to be spared. No harm will come to him."

They all sighed with relief: *Just like Yang's men had when he spared the life of that one soldier.*

Tom whispered approvingly: "*Jota, jota* [Okay, Okay]."

Yet my eyes remained unthreateningly locked into those of the remorseful soldier. Robertson and I returned to our hut and reminisced over some of Buckley's exploits. A strained chuckle broke from my throat a second before Barszcz called from the yard. I stepped out and faced his curious stare: *He's misread my laugh.*

Line-crossing patrol, with all troops in civilian clothing. Our interpreter, Han, is in the front row, center. Rear, left to right: ROK One, ROK Tom, machine gunner Lee, Toshi and an unidentified soldier.

The captain paused. "Everything okay, Mercy? I don't want any more 'accidents' around here."

I cleared my throat. "There won't be any, sir. I'd given Lieutenant Buckley my word."

He returned my salute. "That's good enough for me."

Two days later Lieutenant Walters arrived at our CP. "Lieutenant Buckley died, men. I know I can't really take his place, but I will have to lead the platoon on some occasions."

Four nights later, on Christmas Eve, he ordered a patrol. G-2 had reports that some Chinese troops had been spotted moving south. We were to check out the neighborhood and get a prisoner if possible. We formed up by the mess tent's urns to fortify ourselves with boiling black coffee against the biting winds that swirled up forty-foot high columns of ghostly white steam into the night's glacial sky; and so cold that any spilt drops instantly froze solid on the frosted faces of our field-jackets.

Robertson wrapped his hands around his blistering cup for warmth and muttered, "it's one hell of a cold night."

I shivered and stomped my numbed feet. "Maybe we should fill our canteens with this stuff in case the LMG ices up."

Robertson laughed. "It would eat the goddamned bluing right off the barrel."

In a casual turn we spotted the brass crosses on the regimental chaplain's collar ten yards away. He rocked on his heels in a gesture of hope that we'd invite him to bless the platoon before it went into battle. I winked at Robertson.

"Go check the goddamned fuckin' troops, shit-head!"

Ten more minutes of blasphemy unnerved the chaplain and he yelled and waved his fist as we moved towards the river line. "I hope you all die, damn you! I hope you all get killed!"

Warmed with laughter we met Walters at the LD [line of departure], and then splashed across the icy river as the moon tore like a jealous knife through sheets of tumbling black clouds. We were across the river and into the covering trees of no-man's land when Walters whispered to us.

"Remember, guys, this is a recon patrol, so don't go trying to win any CMHs. We *only* fire if there is no other way out. Understood?" We nodded and he checked the luminous dials on his watch. "Okay, 'simonize' your watches. It's now twenty-two hundred hours. Move out."

Robertson and I were on point. We halted at the crest of a commanding hill and listened to the faint clinking of the platoon's ammo clips and their canteens sloshing up through the rustling pines behind us. Butterball's binoculars skimmed the terrain while Robertson unearthed telltale clues from the rock fissures, cold ashes that someone had taken pains to hide.

Richard whispered, "They're here."

Robertson replied, "Let's throw out a few rounds... that should draw their fire."

He snickered at our blank stares just as Walters snaked in beside us. We followed him down to the floor of the narrow basin. Walters hissed. "Remember, men, no firing."

A tumbling rock from a flanking crest sent us into a wordless headlong dive behind a pile of snow-blanketed forest debris. Snapping off our rifle safeties sounded like crickets over Robertson's whisper. "Why aren't they firing?"

Butterball answered. "Maybe they know I'm carrying a bullet-proof Bible, or, maybe they've also got orders not to let anybody know that they're here!"

Stealthily we followed Walters through the winding draw towards the road where two furtive figures darted for the distant wood line. I instantly shed my rifle, ammo and helmet then gave chase with a .45 thrust in my belt and bayonets I commandeered from the ROKs held in each hand. The fleet-footed phantoms dissolved into the forest and Walters croaked out from behind, "No shooting!" Ten minutes into the woods I aimed both bayonets ahead at the sounds of snapping twigs. They missed and I zigzagged back to report to Walters.

Robertson shrugged. "You're getting rusty, Boy-san."

We reached the point where we'd forded the river earlier, when a shot rang out from a startled BAR gunner on the 1st Battalion's OP. He nicked a ROK. We cursed the shooter as we passed his position and headed for the Aid Station. Back in our hut we heated coffee and lighted cigars. I wondered aloud why the Chinese had let us escape and hoped no one noticed the peculiar and sudden dizziness that was overtaking me. I felt both 'in and outside of myself' and the voices of Richard and Robertson became my only anchor to reality: *Something in me...is leaving...yes...I'm...somewhere else...but where? Am I dreaming...that's it! I'm back in the woods...asleep...but...why do I feel I'm inside a room?* I barely heard Robertson's voice.

"Christ, he's at it again."

His playful tug at my rifle hurled me back into the night that I stood in the Jeep ready to machine gun the sleeping platoon. I leapt up with a start. "I'm...I'm awake, I'm awake! It only looks like I'm sleeping!" I heard distant laughter as I sank back deeper into sleep.

The next night Barszcz gave me an order too good to be true. "Get two of your squads dressed up as civilians. They'll be running a special patrol."

I smiled. "What time should we be ready, sir? What's the mission?"

He remained expressionless. "All you have to know is that they'll be escorting some civilian agents across the lines into Gook territory."

I stammered, "But, if they're caught in civvies, sir, they'll be shot as spies."

The captain answered impatiently. "For Christ's sake, Mercy, there are NKs out there! They'll be shot no matter what they're wearing. Have 'em ready to move at twenty three hundred hours."

I wondered what weapon I should carry. "I hope I can find a pair of whites to fit me, sir."

The captain drew closer. "You, Robertson and your brother aren't going anywhere. This is strictly a ROK operation. That's an order." He turned to leave.

"But sir, who'll lead them?" I shouldn't have asked.

"Han. Should they be stopped by Gooks they might be able to convince them they're deserting."

I felt like Cassandra at the gates of Troy foreseeing tragedy: *He knows Han did something up at the Chungch'on...yet...he protected him...but...if he really didn't know...and I tell him now...then Buckley is going to be remembered in a bad light...and me too.*

I photographed the platoon in their civilian clothes and fantasized how to circumvent the captain's orders, knowing I'd be in big trouble if I got caught: *But...if I don't go...?* My compliance proved prudent. The unsleeping captain checked on me in the predawn hours and found me awake and awaiting for some word from the patrol.

When the men returned at first light, ROK Richard told me Han had feared an ambush, so they skirted the objective hamlet of Uisauni. They had gone no further than the woods of no man's land and the two people they were escorting went on alone. I knew I should have killed him back on the Chungch'on.

We were lucky to get a hot breakfast of powdered eggs, shriveled bacon and burnt toast instead of cold C-ration beans. We sat semi-circled in our hut. We drank coffee and smoked cigars around the pile of delivered mail. Richard tried to out-bellow the nearby artillery, shouting "Merry Christmas!"

Robertson coyly asked, "Did Santa bring anything for me?"

Richard laughed. "Ho-ho-ho, let's see what Santa has for 'Number Have-a-No.'" Robertson caught the package that was intended for Sergeant 'Granny' Black.

"Remember," Butterball said, "anything of real value gets sent back, with a letter."

Robertson beamingly held up four pairs of white knee high cushion-soled socks, a penlight, soap and two crumpled boxes of fruit-filled cookies. The vibrations from the nearby artillery eerily pulsated Buckley's unopened package across the floor to the very spot where he'd been mortally wounded. I felt it an omen of his presence, and a symbol of his once expressed wish that if killed he wanted muffled drums and a horse-drawn caisson to carry his body down the cobblestone streets in New Brunswick, New Jersey, with all the disheveled ROKs in their oversized helmets as his escort. We divided up the box of socks, cookies and handkerchiefs, and swore an oath to visit his folks and tell of his bravery.

Robertson passed around family pictures of his brother Robert and his wife Fay then read his father's letter aloud. "A lot of big newspapers have reported that over five hundred "Aryan-type" men had been spotted around the railway stations in Shanghai and Tientsin. You boys haven't run into any of those German soldiers the Russians allegedly liberated to fight in Korea, have you?"

Richard laughed, "Christ, as if the Chinks weren't bad enough, now we've got the *Wehrmacht* to worry about."

I chuckled. "They've got great uniforms. Maybe we could join up with them."

The moment suddenly turned solemn and we reviewed our agreed to pact about the *coup de grace,* and how it would be wordlessly dispensed should any of us sustain wounds that would decidedly make life not worth living. Robertson feared blindness and/or the loss of two or more limbs. Richard wasn't sure. I spoke in a halting voice and gave a glassy stare while pointing to the cleft in my chin: "Should anything happen to this…"

After dinner we sat around a roaring fire on the patio of the CP, and 'Big Stoop' Ken produced a gallon bottle of milk saké. I shouted, "Let the games begin!"

Toshi did a ritualistic sword dance. The jug made its way around and gave vent to some of the platoon's more melodic voices. Robertson and Richard cheered through a veil of cigar smoke and all overflowing cups were raised in salute. Later, one inhibition-purged ROK portrayed a bound captive POW. His eyes darted fearfully from side to side and bayonets and raucous curses nudged him along on his dragon-like dance down toward the road. A curious Easy Company officer, thinking him a genuine prisoner, asked as he passed, "Are you guys going to shoot him now, or what?"

When we marched back to our compound the ecstatic ROKs glided into a wild and widening ring of euphoric leaps and bounds. Our Man

Friday stood in its center with one hand delicately raised beneath an ear in the fashion of a female vocalist. His angelic tenor voice was spellbinding. I joined the platoon's tribal circle and we flapped our allegorical wings and gave melodious squawks that Snow Cranes do when they alight upon the mountaintops. "*Jota, jota, jota!*"

I was caught in the melancholy cross currents of the happiest and saddest day I'd ever known as I walked alone to a nearby hill. Below, the campfire's shadows danced to the thunderous accompaniment of the outgoing artillery that sent recurring waves of silvery iridescence billowing into the outer darkness: *I don't want the war...or any of this...to end...ever.*

Three days later George Company set up an ambush in the crying winds and knee-deep snow just forward of the 1st Battalion's line. The stretching flames from a nearby burning hamlet lessened any chance of a surprise attack. My thumb and trigger finger remained operable against the bitter sub-zero winds by keeping them warmed in my mouth. The bitter cold made me actually wonder if death by napalming was really all that bad. The welcomed gray light of dawn ushered us back to our huts.

We later heard that General 'Bull' Walker had died in a Jeep accident and a former Airborne general named Matthew Ridgeway was taking his command. His first official act was to turn back a column of fleeing South Korean trucks at pistol point. Things were looking up.

CHAPTER 26

Battle for Uijongbu

On the dark night of 31 December, six Chinese field armies accompanied by whistles, gongs and blaring bugles attacked across the breadth of Korea. The mastermind for the Chinese winter offensive was the Soviet marshal whose headquarters was in Mukden, China.

According to operatives of the newly formed CIA he was Georgy K. Zhukov, former commander of the 1st Soviet Mongolian army that annihilated Japanese forces at Lake Khasan in 1939 and then victor in the major winter campaigns against the Germans at Stalingrad and Kursk in 1942. Now his surrogate Chinese forces suffered staggering losses in some fortified American sectors that included a thousand rolls of barbed wire, flares and an overabundance of heavy machine guns. To our front the Chinese 38th Field Army rolled in like an angry storm whose artillery barrages splintered the ramparts of our 1st and 3rd Battalion's Yangpyong'chon River line. Their infantry surged through minefields that left five hundred dead in front of Able Company alone.

George Company raced up to block the ever-widening breach made under a hundred strings of red and green tracers that ricocheted into the rumbling blood-red sky. A stick grenade sandwiched beneath a dead Chinese soldier's ammo belt ignited and wounded the three 2nd Platoon G.I.s who jokingly fired into his carcass. The line gave way under the weight of the second bugle-blaring assault. The heavy weapons companies couldn't stop the onslaught and Barszcz shouted for us to fall back as the regiment withdrew.

The trucks we boarded roared south and stopped at a dawn beneath the towering mythical mountain the ROKs called *Surak-san*, on the ancient

Uijongbu invasion road to Seoul. There we heated our coffee alongside the road and watched dozens of conscripted laborers load on their backs our heavy 57mm recoilless rifles, machine guns, ammo and boxes of rations. Bearers beyond their prime expertly navigated these up the rear slope of the devil-sculptured promontory we would defend, which was to be the battalion's extreme right flank.

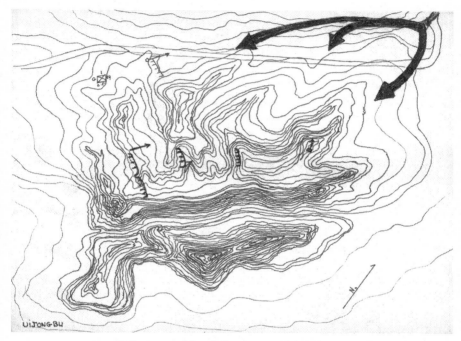

Hill occupied by G Company, 19th Infantry.

From its heights, looking down the forward slope, the mountain's narrow spine-like path snaked down and forward for a thousand yards; then melded into the wide open vale that stretched as far back as the low mountains we'd passed through the previous night. To the right and a few feet off from this path sank an extremely deep and narrow smooth-faced gorge that ran the full length of the hill. On our left was a fanned-out array of endless spill-offs, chiseled boulders, rocks, protruding mounds, pits and continuous shallows. These were devoid of vegetation, save for patches of the sickly weed-grass, thistle sprouts and a few stunted trees.

Below, on the opposite side of the road where we'd traveled in, was a raised a mountain of slightly less elevation. Its foremost point extended

150 yards further out than our own; and, unlike ours, ended in a blunt-faced one hundred-foot high wall. This served as the OP for Fox Company and had an unobstructed view for miles in all directions. Another difference on that seven hundred yard, smooth-surfaced hill was the three small huts that were centered between the OP and the rearmost summit.

The narrowness of our own mountain peak denied the company a normal horizontal perimeter and dictated using an in-depth defense we'd never employed before. Three of the company's platoons dug in on a string-like vertical line directly behind each other to theoretically fire down their left flanks toward the road, the point where we assumed the Chinese would attack. The abundant undulations of the terrain also limited the killing radius of any heavy weapons support fire.

Another Chinese attack option was to advance straight up from the base of the mountain and then along the spine of the ridge to the summit—a daunting fete at best. Our ROKs were the most forward unit and would be between the Chinese and the collective return fire from our entire company—nor was that a comforting prospect. 'Bug-out' Wassick's 3rd Platoon was directly behind us with 'Combat Joe's' 2nd next. In theory each platoon would hold its positions until the forward one exited under covering fire; then follow in turn in an orderly manner. The captain's CP was in a roadside hut and was covered by the 1st Platoon and part of the 4th heavy weapons section.

We dispersed the ROKs along a thirty-yard perpendicular ridge of rock-hard soil that defied digging. The men were lucky to scrape out shallow pits for cover. Richard put out the company's orange air ground control marker a few yards ahead. From certain sections of our positions we could see, over a cascade of lowering ridges with pockets and blinds, minimal swatches of the main road where a small quarter-ton truck was parked. The rumor was that this customized private "sleep-mobile" was used by Fox Company's commanding officer, Lieutenant Shea, as his rather unorthodox CP. It allegedly had all the creature comforts of home and proved a quite 'comfy' little command post from where he maintained radio contact with his under-fire line platoons.

Richard's binoculars bridged the eight hundred yards between our positions and Fox Company's high ground and said, "It looks like they're moving right into those three huts. Nobody's digging in, and only three guys are going up to the OP."

Robertson laughed. "Yeah, just look at the size of those camp fires, they're sure not expecting China-boy any time soon."

We estimated they'd arrive in two days, dogged by air attacks each step of the way.

At 1600 hours half our platoon had climbed back up to the 2nd Platoon's area for hot chow which the *chikes* (native porters) had brought up in thermo canisters. The night's menu was chicken, rice, bread and hot coffee. This was an unfailing omen for an impending firefight, especially if it arrived with mail, as it did. Equally ominous was Hungerford's cheery greeting as we reached the chow line.

Sketch of the Uijongbu locale.

"You boys got all the ammunition and things you'll need?"

Richard replied. "We could use a phone and a .50 caliber, Sarge."

Hungerford joggled his mustache. "I'll see that you get the wire and maybe, the fifty."

It quickly grew dark, but Fox Company campfires illuminated their ridge positions and stretched across to 'Bug-out' Wassick's platoon, who cursed and hacked their shovels against the frozen earth. Robertson and 'Big Stoop' set up an OP beneath a huge boulder a hundred yards down the slope, which couldn't be seen from our position. Near dawn Toshi's voice insinuated itself into my dreams. "*Sahji, Sahji*, enemy come!"

Bolting upright I followed the trace of his finger to the mist-shrouded column of murky silhouettes that emerged across the dark cobalt blue plain a thousand yards out. *"Moto Shinajin asoko desu, Sahji-san* [More Chinese are there, Sergeant]!" he said, pointing up to Fox Company's OP.

They were squads of the Chinese Special Force "Sharp Swords" that had infiltrated Fox's undefended night perimeter and captured its surrendered OP without firing a shot. Their commandeered LMGs rained fire down along our ridge, as did another captured Fox Company gun that fired on the scores of G.I.s that fled the hill. A dozen of them made their way up to our position an hour later and most just continued on towards the summit. .

One of them calmly shouted, "We've only got carbines so there's no use in hanging around." It was easy to see why they lost their hill.

Their company commander left his 'sleep-mobile,' after getting word the company had been infiltrated and gave an amazing report when he reached battalion later in the day. "I battled off four Chinese soldiers with my bare fists and suffered a grazing head wound from a rifle butt. They left me for dead. Later I made it down the road to Mike Barszcz's CP."

Robertson's silent BAR meant the Chinese weren't yet on our ridge. I continued a happy exchange of fire with the enemy gunner in the Fox Company OP until a sudden impulse pulled me to my feet. I frantically waved my towel and shouted, "You dumb Chink-son of a bitch! Drop your fucking sight fifteen clicks!"

Toshi gave a 'thumbs up' salute and some G.I.s cheered. The next incoming string of tracers singed my bravado. A Fox Company G.I. next to me stared blankly then left his 57mm Recoilless Rifle with four rounds and calmly headed for the high ground. My telescopic sight brought down two Chinese from the squads that were evicting the G.I.s hiding in huts on Fox Company's hill.

Robertson & ROK Ken, out at the OP were securely positioned inside a naturally formed convex chamber cut into the base of the huge commanding boulder that sat on the downward side of the ridgeline. Entry was through a long horizontal slit at the boulder's base, which also served as a firing port and only one man at a time could horizontally slide through. The chamber was large enough to accommodate three stooping men.

Robertson spotted large Chinese cavalry and infantry units maneuvering at the base of the hill and readied his BAR. Then an unsuspecting Chinese platoon emerged from out of the multiple dips and spill-offs less than a hundred yards below. They were using some fifteen captured G.I.s as tightly held shields along the full breadth of their thirty yards wide 'wedge' formation that headed directly towards them.

216

Robertson, an excellent shot, debated as he took critical aim: *If I don't shoot they'll overrun us...then our platoon...then knock the company off the hill...a lot of casualties....I can't let them break through...*

The tenacious Chinese exposed as little of their face and bodies as possible behind their human shields, whose terror charged eyes could have been those of men surrounded by scores of circling tiger sharks. Robertson fired single rounds when possible, and then unrelenting bursts as the melee grew wilder. Only five G.I.s escaped from where thirty of the enemy mingled their spilled blood with that of the ten American dead. Robertson, perhaps like no other, held the line.

I looked through a squall of Chinese mortars and machine gun fire raining in and saw Richard race back from Robertson's OP. His face was aglow.

"That goddamned Robertson, I'm putting him in for the Silver Star. He must have killed twenty Gooks!" I was envious. Richard related the events and added that four or five lucky G.I.s played dead under the fallen bodies and crawled out when the shooting and bayoneting stopped. They gave Robertson a funny look when they passed us. Richard answered my unspoken question. "Robertson will know when to pull back."

I laughed. "Glad he's on our side!" *I wonder if I would have done what he did...knowing they were all going to die. Yes...no...maybe.*

I watched seventy rounded up Fox Company G.I.s being herded up the crest by twenty evenly spaced guards on either side. A perfect target for a 57mm recoilless rifle I'd never fired before: *What if the rounds fall short and hit the G.I.s...they're prisoners...their lives are up for grabs.*

A lucky round took out the advance guard and my last one totally missed the OP gunner. After the ammo was gone I unpinned a thermite grenade and placed it down the bore then dropped the weapon into the deep ravine behind us. During a sudden pause I reluctantly followed the dictates of my inner voice, not knowing why it told me to 'go check out the left flank' and knowing that nothing would be there. I returned the salute of a nearby ROK and ordered him to guard my jacket and scope-mounted rifle while I slid down a flanking draw with pistol in hand. Finding nothing I quickly returned and saw the ROK sprawled across my jacket, with a bullet between the eyes; and felt a sudden guilt: *He was a nice guy...always grinning...why did I put him there? That could—should, have been me.* With his limp body propped against my raised knee I stared into his unfocused eyes and fastened a useless bandage around his brow. I mumbled reassuringly to a dead man. "You'll be alright... you'll be alright..."

A wounded G.I. straggler was suddenly at my side and echoed my chant. "He'll be alright, he'll be alright." Timeless minutes ticked away before reality set in. I reexamined the wound hoping to determine the bullet's trajectory, which came from the knoll forty yards ahead. I called out to Toshi. *"Eki masho* [Let's go]!"

We raced to the flank and slid fifty yards down into a draw and knelt motionless in the shadow of a scrub of pine. Ten yards ahead Asian voices rose from behind the crest. Toshi whispered. *"Ano katatachi Shinajin desu, Sahji* [They're Chinese, Sergeant]!"

I hurriedly scanned down the ravine thinking I'd see a platoon of Chinese rushing us with fixed bayonets. My focus switched to the crest and the sound of footsteps crunching on the snow and some faint laughter. The pair of vintage WWII grenades I skimmed over the top didn't explode and must have been seen but no response was raised. Then I uneasily watched the red star on a Chinese soldier's pile cap slowly break over our shared horizon: *He's about seventeen...and so close...doesn't know I'm here...his Thompson's not at the ready...a clean-cut face... looks like a good soldier...wait...see how many more might pop up with him.*

His concerned gaze was fixed on the distant summit where he perhaps imagined that fate awaited him there, when three armor-piercing rounds punctured his chest. He gurgled out a shout: *Maybe he gave his squad my position...what's holding him up...why doesn't he fall? Die!*

The next round stabbed through his eye and exited his skull: *Goddamn that armor piercing stuff...doesn't splinter, nor do enough damage...its ball ammo only from here on in!* My whisper to Toshi pierced the deathly silence. *"Eki masho* [Let's go]!"

We reached Richard's foxhole and shouted warnings to the platoon: *If they pin us down, we're all dead.* A ROK sprang up nearby and asked what to do about the three Chinese he was pointing to on a knoll thirty yards ahead. I shouted, *"Bakayaro, utsu desu* [Crazy-one, you shoot]!"

Richard and I exchanged quizzical grins between snapped off rounds and I wondered if he too was thinking of our seventh birthday and those *Dick Tracy* toy machine guns; and imagining the day we'd be 'killing real Chinese.' The metallic sounds of ejecting clips amid the buzz and whiz of impacting rounds had its own music, as did the hurled grenades we timed for airbursts above the building Chinese line. We both knew we had to hold until Robertson and 'Big Stoop' got back.

Richard noted that the Chinks might be working out a pincer move on our open left flank and wondered where our artillery was. I shrugged, knowing we might have to depend on 'Bug-out' Wassick and his platoon to get us and the casualties we'd be carrying out alive; and they hadn't fired a shot all morning! Robertson's BAR opened up again and Richard raced back across the shell-pocked field to help him withdraw; and drew fire from the LMG on Fox Company's lost OP. I covered him then scooped up some discarded bandoliers and was startled to glimpse what had to be a full Chinese division advancing a mile away across the vast open terrain. Their supporting artillery hit our summit, but high off to the peak's right flew a vision straight out of a World War II MGM movie. We all cheered the approaching winged armada that droned through the smoke-filled sky. "*Mansai! Mansai! Mansai!*"

Squadrons of blue Corsairs hummed in wing to wing. Above them flights of P-51 Mustangs whistled beneath higher-flying B-26s. Distant black dots swiftly grew to silver Sabers, Shooting Stars and Thunder jets that streaked past our snow-capped hills to strike at distant troop concentrations, convoys and supply targets. In an instant I recalled the P-38 fighters that had whistled in low over the Santa Monica beach in 1943 and shouted, "Come back you sons of bitches and strafe everything in sight!"

The gods heard.

A formation of gull-winged Corsairs swooped in and scorched the densely packed advancing columns with napalm; then barrel rolled back in again to rocket and strafe. The Chinese formations didn't break, but continued on through a field of bodies. 155mm howitzer fire rained in after the planes left. I didn't want to imagine what would happen to us if the Chinks had that firepower!

Minutes later, just beyond Fox Company's lost position, plumes of oily black napalm smoke rose where jets mistakenly attacked Easy Company trying to retake the lost hill. On their far left 1st Battalion was pushed back and to our far right the engaged 21st Regiment suffered additional heavy casualties from another misdirected air strike. And just beyond them the ROK 2nd Division was nearly destroyed in the same way. General Church held his uncommitted 5th RCT in reserve and ordered our division to fall back to positions south of the Han River.

Richard zigzagged and breathlessly leapt into our foxhole. "I'm putting Robertson in for *another* Silver Star."

I smirked, "Did he kill Lieutenant Herbert?"

He laughed. "Better yet, he knocked off two more squads of Gooks! When I crawled into their position 'Big Stoop' flashed all his gold teeth thinking I'd come to bring them back. The Chinks were all around, bullets zinging in and smashing everywhere, and Robertson popped up and let them have it! I've never seen anything like it."

I silently marveled, and asked, "Where's Robertson now?"

Richard gulped. "He's having a great time he'll know when to pull back." I wasn't too sure about that.

A 120mm mortar round, in a million-to-one shot, landed squarely on the helmet of a nearby ROK and all that was left was a smoldering shinbone in a bleeding boot.

Robertson and 'Big Stoop' returned with empty ammo pouches and reloaded their magazines with scrounged up ammo. Robertson tilted his head down the ridge.

"There's a company of Chinks right behind us. I'm surprised we haven't been overrun yet, Boy-san! The bastards even have some cavalry maneuvering around the base of the hill."

Richard looked up to the summit. "No fire coming from the G.I. platoons. Maybe that's a good sign?" I was silently less optimistic behind my stoic smile. We could already be cut off and not even know it.

"Think about this, the ammo is getting seriously low. We've got three KIA and five WIA, not counting those from Fox. The WE-8 line's dead, ditto the walkie-talkie and we have no idea of the tactical situation. So we must decide—do we give up now, or later?"

The laughs were cut short by a sudden wave of stick grenades that came from behind the knoll to our immediate front. Richard wrapped his arm in a hasty sling, announcing needlessly that they'd be coming any minute now. I gathered up grenades from the ROKs, and asked for covering fire.

Taut-lipped Robertson squinted out a smile. "*Banzai*, Boy-san."

I catapulted myself over the crest with the grenades stuffed in my shirt and a .45 in hand. I crossed thirty yards of the draw below and as stealthily as possible crawled up to within inches of the Chinese crest. I heard whispers and wondered if they knew I was there.

I could have grabbed the arm in its heavily quilted sleeve as it spiraled over a grenade that exploded harmlessly below in the draw: *They're not sure where I am...* A burst from Robertson's BAR severed the next arm that pitched a grenade, which also went off well below me. Holding my breath I clearly heard the scrape of bodies that crawled on pebbles just a few feet away. It sounded to be at least four, and close together. To muffle the sounds of the grenades popped spoons, I held them beneath my body then arched them into detonating airburst seconds apart. The screams and whimpers that quickly filled the air was followed by a retaliatory wave of grenades that arched high overhead and whipped up dust in the draw below: *They'll figure it out any minute now...and maybe get a sniper around to the open end of this draw...get moving!* Two more grenades tossed over the crest covered my return to our ridge.

When I rolled over the crest, I saw Lieutenant Pierce lying face up a few feet away, paralyzed by the bullet in his spine. His dead radioman was beside him. Barzcz had sent them down to assess our situation. His dulling eyes blinked up into the cold cloudless sky and he whispered, "Don't leave me here, Mercy."

I unconsciously projected those words of my own fear and which every soldier in Korea dreaded most to hear. "Don't worry, sir, we'll send somebody back for you." Instantly the soldier I'd left behind at Chinju sized my mind and I saw again his pleading face in the lieutenant's near tearful eyes: *I can't do that twice...Christ, why made me say that?* He anxiously gulped for air and I gripped his shoulder. "Don't worry, sir, I swear I won't leave you, or any wounded behind. I don't know why I said that, sir, I'm sorry. Some of my men will carry you out right now."

I wasn't overly surprised by my inner thoughts: *Carrying a wounded officer up a mountain to safety...under fire...and killing some Gooks in the process...could get you a CMH—but...you've got work to do here.*

Two sturdy ROKs and a guard for the lieutenant began their brutal climb to the summit. Nearby a grenade blew off a Fox Company soldier's hand, who I reminded to turn the tourniquet I applied every five minutes. As I moved to gather up my troops Richard leapt up from a nearby gully with trickles of blood beneath his eye.

"A Gook tossed a grenade, didn't even see the bastard!"

I swept up the last of our grenades and bandoliers and shouted to him and Robertson. "It's time to pull 'em back, I'll stay and cover you guys for as long as I can!"

Firing from behind a pile of rocks I scored two easy kills. Fifty yards away two more Chinese cleared the crest. They immediately knelt beside my ROK with the bullet between his eyes and I watched them through my sights. As they gently rolled him over and checked his wound they sneaked cautious glances up at the departed platoon, still far away from the summit.

They took no souvenirs, as I'd so often done: *Why don't you kill them...what are you feeling...compassion...or are you falling for some Chink psych-warfare ploy? Amazing what a little show of kindness can do...but they're not shooting at me or the platoon...so why tempt fate...just for another kill...I never thought I'd think this way.*

Behind me our platoon took heavy fire from the flanking draws as they struggled up the ridge: *Not much time left...they're trying to cut us off!* Twenty minutes later, as I passed 'Bug-out' Wassick's deserted positions, I caught sight of a fast moving enemy platoon just below me on the right, and raced towards the tracer-lashed peak vowing to kill Wassick if any of our platoon was lost because of his cowardice.

Then I heard the reassuring sound of Robertson's rapidly firing BAR and figured he must have been cleaning out a draw somewhere ahead. The 1st and 2nd Platoons stood dispersed just below the crest. Further on some ROKs fired down a flanking ridge. I spotted the weaponless Sergeant Wassick making a dash towards the far crest. I caught up with him and spread my gun hand wide across my holster "Where's your platoon?"

He stuttered through bloodless lips. "Gee, Mercy, when I saw your guys bugging out, I mean, pulling back ..."

As I un-flapped my holster, he stumbled backwards down the steep incline and never once looked back: *Was he always like this...in WWII...or did something happen there...and maybe here, too? His memories will be...crueler than anything I can do.*

The distinctive sound of an American LMG ripped through the air. I looked to where Toshi sat, a hundred yards away, with two bullets in his leg. The captured gun fired from somewhere down the draw and deliberately peppered the ground around Toshi with misses; making him bait to lure in would-be rescuers and his helpless expression seared my mind. I shouted for him not to move, figuring the gunner would soon shift his fire to more interesting targets. Then I spotted Han and the Ritz brother LMG gunner Lee coming out of the draw, and I ran to them. *"Antano kikenju o doko ka* [Where's your machine gun]?" Han took a defiant step forward with hands rested on his hips. "Is back there! Many, many Chinese come. We must go, no have time take gun." I quivered with rage, sensing it to be the gun that wounded Toshi and drew my pistol. They turned and ran! *Jesus Christ, I should just kill that son of a bitch, and do it now!" Why can't you do it? Why...?*

I thought my answer was in the 155mm artillery round that exploded twenty yards from me only minutes later. It left a jagged foot-long chunk of smoking steel protruding from an earthen mound, only inches from my body. *Damn...I wonder if that goddamned thing would have hit me...if I'd killed Han?*

Enemy artillery dusted off the now empty high ground. My brother had left and a medic carried Toshi away while Robertson reassembled the platoon on the road below. Last to leave the hill, I watched the Chinese swarm onto the smoky gray summit not eighty yards away. With targets galore I strangely lost my appetite to kill: *God damn this fucking war.*

CHAPTER 27

Twenty-Seven Days at Yongdang

I caught up with the platoon as it trailed behind the company's column. It followed our dispirited army that trudged below snow-laden clouds for the next two days. Most of the men hoped they'd soon find themselves in the warm awaiting arms of love-starved women back in the States. Some of them talked of warm clothes and hot food. None spoke of saving South Korea, or the battered honor of our routed army that left immeasurable quantities of weapons and ammunition casually abandoned without a second thought. Perhaps because their country's survival really wasn't at stake, death and mutilation was too high a price to pay for the barely understood and dubious political goal of 'communist containment.' Yet we three agreed that if the Chinese and NKs had only half of those abandoned supplies, they might conquer all of Asia—if we didn't use "The Bomb."

As we flanked Seoul, the rear echelon replayed their Pyongyang fiasco and unwittingly aided the local guerrillas by destroying more tons of ammunition, food and weapons. Rattled and undisciplined they shot at anything that moved, usually unarmed civilians, in the belief the Red army was only hours away. Many indulged in limited sprees of looting, murder and rape. They were quelled by some called in infantry units and an MP battalion that imposed strict nighttime curfews. Order and military discipline prevailed in nearby marine controlled Inchon while landing craft evacuated civilians and service troops. Army demolition teams and Navy frogmen worked together to destroy as many port installations as they could.

Out on the open sea, razor-edged sub-zero winds slashed at the crystal-encrusted hulls of the *Bataan* and the four other carriers that lumbered through churning white-capped swells. Their flight deck crews bulldozed and shoveled six-foot deep snow from the decks so they could launch their Panther jets. Cannonades from the fleet's cruisers and destroyers rained down an impenetrable wall of steel around the imperiled port city that denied safe use of the roads to the approaching enemy. Navy jets and eight-inch guns kept the vast encircling Chinese army at bay.

GHQ in Tokyo worried about the increasing losses of B-29 bombers to aggressive Russian-piloted MIG fighters over the Yalu River. They were also concerned about the seemingly inexhaustible columns of communist armies that moved south on the sleet-pelted roads. These caravans of artillery, tanks and self-propelled guns were occasionally "strafed" by the normally high-flying B-29 Superfortresses, a first in aeronautical history.

Below the 38th Parallel, the Chinese moved to destroy the important UN communications center at Wonju before pressing on to take the terror-stricken city of Pusan where U.S. engineers hastily constructed new fortifications along the old Naktong River defense line. General McClure's 2nd Division was to defend and hold Wonju, but he feared another high casualty encounter as at the Kunuri-Sunchon pass and opted against deploying his regiments on line. He counted on our massive artillery and air power to stop the Chinese advance. Lieutenant General Matthew B. Ridgeway knew better and ordered all regimental and battalion commanders to show themselves at the front to restore morale and strengthen the resolve of the dispirited troops. Those who didn't immediately comply were relieved of command—and any future career considerations.

Our trucks rumbled into the Yongdang 'rest area' and the ROKs deployed on the high ground. Our right flank locked into a denuded forest that sloped down into a gully. On the left a series of fingers stretched down from the ridge towards a quiet six-house hamlet. Between these points and some 200 yards below us were a small isolated hut and then a series of elevating hills. Our patrol found it and the village uninhabited.

Richard returned from the hospital at the close of an uneventful week and pitched a still-pinned grenade into my foxhole from the hillcrest. The shrapnel wound beneath his eye twitched as he spoke.

"I got combat fatigue from all the rear-echelon war stories, and decided to bug-out to someplace safe."

I laughed. "You found it—we haven't seen a Chink in weeks." He looked dejected as I continued. "But yesterday a lieutenant from battalion got knocked unconscious when the Korean he was questioning on the road whacked him with the carbine he had hidden under his jacket. Why his throat wasn't cut is the sixty-four dollar question."

Robertson exclaimed, "How did you made it back to the outfit?"

Butterball smiled. "With this," he said, raising up his Thompson-sub. "And a fellow hospital malcontent from Easy Company."

We found a Korean MP asleep in his Jeep and jettisoned him out along the road, then traveled nonstop. I thought Barszcz might have to pistol whip that scrounge Tubbs to keep him from painting 'G Co. 2nd Bn.' on the bumpers when we pulled in."

We laughed and lighted up the cigars he'd brought back. "The captain told me to get up on the hill and stay put. If MPs showed up he'd claim he didn't know anything about the Jeep."

We ran a 'celebration patrol' down into the deserted hamlet then returned to the hill and deployed almost a dozen cases of grenades and trip flares along the platoon's front. Their cords could be pulled from our foxholes for independent firing. By dusk the small hut below us and every other bush, rock and tree on our forward slope was tied into a web of trip-corded grenades. They were taut and near invisible. We had pulled all the pins halfway out, which made them sensitive to the slightest touch. I requested one of the newly arrived infrared night-scoped .30-caliber carbines that Sergeant Tubbs kept locked in his truck.

"Damn it, Mercy, I can't run the risk of losing one, they're expensive."

I tried sarcasm. "No way near a congressman's weekend fact-finding junket to Bermuda! And you might not have noticed, but most of our fighting takes place at night, which is what that weapon's designed for. Okay, how about a bow and arrow then, and maybe throw in a couple of spears?"

The next night peering through thick flurries of snow, I spoke into our WE-8 phone. "Captain, sir, I'm sure those grenades you heard exploding were set off by snow piled up on the trip-cords."

He snapped, "Go check it out anyway, Mercy, I don't want any surprises." Two more grenades went off.

"Roger that, Captain, over and out."

With a ROK at my side we cautiously moved through the blinding snow towards where another grenade had detonated. I hoped he couldn't sense my sudden unaccustomed fear. We paused and knelt in waist-deep snow before the ROK wordlessly moved out into the swirling pallor and I held fast until he returned

"*Yuki desu, Sahji* [Is snow, Sergeant]." I knew I'd have to make up for this failure.

The next day's blizzard and mercilessly harsh winds amputated limbs from ice-coated trees and pierced Robertson's quilted sleeping bag and mine as we lay shivering on the foxhole floor: *Maybe getting an overcoat...and long underwear...from supply wouldn't have been such a bad idea...despite the drawbacks.* Richard's teeth chattered in the 21° below zero temperature, as he 'bunny hopped' into our hole in his zipped up sleeping bag.

"Barszcz said battalion's expecting an attack and he wants everybody to turn in their sleeping bags, so we'll all be awake for the party when Joe Chink gets here."

Robertson moaned and sank deeper into his quilted sack. "Christ!"

We complied, but I wondered if the battalion staff and clerks had surrendered their cots, stoves and heated tents to remain alert. One G.I. in our company refused to comply and went unpunished while we wrestled each other throughout the long miserable night to ward off the snarling winds. We watched bleary-eyed at dawn as Our Man Friday lead the bearers back from the CP with our cherished sleeping bags. Richard came bunny hopping back that night with more news.

"The Chinks should have issued their men the same orders we got yesterday because a company-size patrol from the 2nd Division found over a hundred of them fast asleep in their comfy little captured bags near Wonju, and killed them all!"

I casually added, "Poor bastards, they wear sneakers and aren't issued gloves, socks or shoes; and never see hot food or even know what toilet paper is."

Richard nodded. "Yeah, I wonder what their reenlistment rate is."

We found no enemy on our morning patrol into the village, nor the parents of the dozen kids that followed behind me at the rear of the column as we headed back up the hill. The C-ration candies I gave them almost put a glint in their weary melancholy eyes. I was deeply touched when one forlorn little girl in a torn smock ignored the extended candy bar, but softly gripped my hand. The warmth that engendered in my heart had me turn to hide the surprising single tear she'd brought to one eye; then I ran to the crest and caught up with the platoon. Robertson half-jokingly sneered, "You're becoming a real poster soldier."

I felt strangely guilty. "They're just kids—"

He cut me short. "And they'll all be carrying burp guns in six years, Boy-san. I think you're going soft on these people. Don't forget what they've done to our G.I.s." He rose to his feet.

I felt no anger, but it seemed our friendship was at stake and I thought it the perfect time for a Gary Cooper impression. "I'm a hopin' we ain't gonna have to draw, Ringo."

After a pause Robertson's taut mouth broke into a reluctant grin. We laughed and mimed a very-slow-and-empty left hand draw.

Near dusk hot chow arrived along with the requested .50-caliber machine gun. I set it up on a tripod wondering if it took ten clicks of headspace for calibration, like the .30 caliber LMG. The third test fired round exploded in the chamber and peeled back its steel latch cover as though it was an over ripe banana. *Obviously that was the wrong headspace.* I staggered away with a dented helmet and awaited the arrival of an incensed Sgt. Tubbs waving his Statement of Charges.

Accumulated tensions from lack of combat found release in my sleepwalking. I saw the face of a child in the sputtering flare that Richard fired down to light my zombie-like walk through the darkness. A Korean voice intruded with the cry, *"Nugeyaaaaar, nugeyaaaaar* [Who's there, who's there]?"

From inside my dream I called back, *"Watakushi-wa Masan Gunsho desu* [I am the Masan Squad sergeant]!"

I awoke standing beyond the small yellow triangular sign that warned of mines where I was ringed around by trip-corded hand grenades; and feeling quite lucky, too, that the ROKs weren't trigger happy.

Weeks of relentless boredom prompted more cultural exchanges between ROK Richard and me. I showed him the 'girly magazine' Butterball had brought back from the hospital. His eyes literally popped out of his head! "Me never see before." Given his secretive and repressed culture I wasn't surprised. His mind struggled over the buxom blond pinup superimposed in front of the Plaza Hotel on New York's busy Fifth Avenue. She walked partially nude among disinterested strollers, save for her over-swelling bra, garter belt, black mesh nylons and spiked high heel shoes.

ROK Richard was astonished. "Ahhh! American men no care their women walk so?"

I reflectively sucked air in through my teeth. "Yes, care very much! No see this way all the time!"

He sighed sorrowfully. "Hmmmm, *ah so desu* [It is so]."

I nudged the ball into his court. "ROK Richard, why traditional dress of Korean women has one sleeve white and other red?"

He fired back with gusto. "Ah, *Sajhi-san*, long time ago, first time China come Korea, men take girlfriend white dress, hmmm, 'camouflage' to fool Chinese who think see women. Korean men kill enemy soldier, clean sword blood on dress sleeves. Color red."

Our Man Friday joined us and giggled over the picture. He pointed to the Plaza Hotel. *"Sahji,* you here live?" Saddened by my negative reply he mimed eating with chopsticks and extended an invitation I would always remember. "You, *Sahji*, my house come, please, war end?" I bowed my deep appreciation then his cherubic face altered slightly. He mimed raising a lighted match. "*Sahji* burn down Friday house-ou?"

I gave a reassuring grin that I wouldn't: *They think I'm a pyromaniac*!

Sometime later, Butterball read aloud from one of the unfailingly contrived human interest stories that the *Stars and Stripes* so excelled in. He quoted a 'friendly' young nineteen-year-old orphaned soldier from Pyongyang who'd been captured: "Me no want fight American G.I., really. Bad leader, my school come and make go. I look always to surrender, first G.I. see." The psych-war article concluded with an expressed wish from the nice POW. "When bad war over, I go back school. Maybe one day, come America."

Butterball smiled. "Heart rending."

Robertson repetitiously flicked his carbine's safety from on to off. "Maybe we ought to take up a collection for the son of a bitch's boat ticket!"

I smirked. "Imagine this yarn in the hands of a liberal Democrat."

Richard laughed. "I don't think my tear ducts could stand it. Look, here's something on the Red breakthrough at Uijongbu: 'Only light action along the entire front with insignificant casualties for our side.'"

Robertson snickered. "They must think we're all brain dead."

I spotted ROK Tom watching us from the sideline and manufactured a shocked reaction and cursed loudly in Japanese over the paper.

"*Doystano, Sahji-san* [What's the matter, Sergeant]?"

I hissed back, "*Nippon-no heita koko eirashai desu. Kenka Chinajin.*" [Japanese troops come Korea, fight Chinese].

Tom's brow knotted and his eyes narrowed. "*Gunsho-san, hunto desu ka* [Honorable Sergeant, is true]?" Assured that it was, he reappeared minutes later with the entire platoon. His raised index fingers 'fenced' in the idiomatic war gesture of clashing swords.

"*Sahji*, me for all soldier speak. We go Pusan, now! Japanee fight-ou! Kill come Korea!"

I'd ironically ignited a suppressed seething hatred, as MacArthur had the previous day when he suggested the use of Japanese troops to Syngman Rhee, who also promised a blood bath if they ever attempted to land. Knowing that I'd jolted the hornet's nest I solemnly bowed my head then horizontally held out my sheathed sword with both hands before slowly exposing but an inch of its polished steel hilt. The gesture symbolized that what I was about to swear to, on the uncovered blade which signifies the soul, was my honor. "*Sumi-masen, Tom-san, watakushi wa jodan-o warui suru desu*," [I'm sorry, Honorable Tom, I made a bad joke]. Tom searched my eyes, grunted his acceptance then left.

Days had passed when Richard, Robertson, myself and two other G.I.s sat in our partially zipped-up sleeping bags and bemoaned our not being up on the line with the 2nd Division at Wonju. That's where all the action was. For a moment I didn't believe my eyes when I suddenly glimpsed a Chinese soldier dart behind a leafless tree. It sent an electrical current through me. The others had their backs towards him. He stared maniacally at us over his raised Thompson-sub, not forty feet away! *Why isn't he shooting...he doesn't know I see him...he's trying to get closer...if I can just get the pistol out of my bag.* I whispered frantically to the others, "Don't move. Stay calm. There's a Chink on our right rear flank."

In a blink they turned with weapons raised in a minute of pensive silence until Richard laughed and the others looked back at me with questioning expressions. "Holy Christ, he's asleep again! It's absolutely amazing that he can do this with his eyes open! Who would know?" He was wrong, it was my first hallucination.

I panicked: *What's wrong with them? Can't they see that Chink? He's standing right there...in the open...why can't they see him? The son of a bitch is going to fire...he isn't going to get me.* I leapt up with the pistol half drawn inside my sleeping bag. Robertson quickly zipped it shut up to my chin. I shouted over their laughter, "Get down, he's aiming! GET DOWN!!"

Robertson cried, "Jesus Christ, look out!"

They all dropped as I spun around in a half crouch. Eight rapidly fired rounds spewed singed feathers and sparks through the front of my shredding comforter. As I wiggled free, I slapped a fresh clip in my piece and raced towards the fallen soldier, shouting, "I got him! I got him!"

Reaching the spot where I saw him fall, my body chilled—He'd evaporated! *I'm not asleep, and I'm not crazy! Where is he?* Robertson called out from behind. "Did you get him, Boy-san?"

My brother laughed, "He's more fuckin' dangerous asleep then awake!" I laughed nervously with them and lied through what I hoped was a convincing grin. "Hey, come on you guys, it was a joke. I made it all up."

Richard knew better and glanced from me to the unknown officer that was walking up to us. "Hi, I'm Lieutenant Turk; the captain wants you men to show me around."

Robertson toured the somewhat mystified Turk by the minefield and booby-trapped knolls. He requested that Turk requisition some barbed wire to wrap around the explosives to increase their shrapnel output. I spiced it up with a request for some napalm canisters to place on our forward slope. Later Butterball pointed to an insurance company ad in the frayed *Time* magazine he pulled from his jacket He suggested that the depicted young G.I. dug in on the front lawn of his home, with his brooding parents standing in the warm light spilling from the open doorway behind him, reminded him of Lieutenant Turk.

Richard read at his cynical best. "In order to protect them, he must be out there instead of inside his cozy home."

Robertson snickered. "Rear-echelon son of a bitch. Why would anybody want to be a civilian and live inside?"

Richard completed the thought, "When they can be out on a listening post with a fucking LMG?" We all gave a genuine cheer.

The next morning's patrol through the village netted us seven nervous young men dressed in white. I herded them into an open courtyard at bayonet point and handed Tom my .45, instructing him to shoot if they tried to escape. I made a quick check of the other houses then returned and found Tom standing alone. The prisoners were gone. I took the pistol from his hand and pointed it at his head and bellowed in Japanese.

"Where are prisoners?"

He calmly replied. "They no soldier, *Sahji*, only schoolboy. No good, give MP."

My skull throbbed. He was probably right, but he disobeyed an order. I didn't want to kill him. Tom stoically stared into the pistol's barrel as I pondered his fate: *I could surprise him...blow his head off...Can't let him get away with this...And yet...I didn't kill those others.* I was again entangled in that familiar web of mental struggle to break the bond I sensed between us and disregard his uncanny similarity to my uncle. The weapon lowered from his expressionless face: *I should have executed him...Yang, the legionnaire Markoff or any Jap, Russian or German officer wouldn't have hesitated...it's so easy to do—in the movies, but one day I might even surprise myself.* The surge of self-resentment that moment engendered drove me back to the deserted village, which I burned down for having harbored 'draft dodgers.' Back with the platoon Richard's news perked me up.

"We're pulling out for the line. The engineers will come up and remove the minefields."

I asked Robertson about the booby-trap grenades. He laughed. "The natives will figure it out, Boy-san, after somebody's class picnic gets fucked up."

The night's long march ended when we reached the LD (Line of Departure), and the company bedded down in a dozen deserted huts by the roadside. I plunged my bayonet into the clay floor and kept my pistol on the opposite side of my unzipped bag where Robertson was sound asleep. I don't know exactly when the ceiling slowly morphed into a Taejon hillside, where I strained through the night's thickening humidity trying to pinpoint the encroaching sound of something scraping. My heart pounded: *The Gooks...they're here! One's crawling towards me...he's inches away...use the pistol!* My hand moved as stealthily as a snake and coiled a finger around the pistol's triggers. When I slowly took up the slack it raised a question in my mind. "If it's a hot summer night, why is the handle of this weapon so cold? Why? Why?" The pistol was pointed at Robertson's back when reality broke through my dream and bolted me upward.

He rolled over, and asked me what was up. I shammed a yawn, wondering if he could hear my heart pounding. I answered, "I'll tell you about it in the morning, Ricardo." He went back to sleep, and I quietly removed the chambered round and magazine from the pistol. I marveled at how a logical process had worked its self into my dream: *Damn...that was close...just use the knife if a Gook shows up.*

CHAPTER 28

ROK One...KIA

Awakening with a sense of impending death, I joined Richard and Robertson by their small fire and we sipped boiled coffee from charred canteen cups. Richard reported on last night's patrols from battalion.

"They didn't spot a single Gook. Maybe the Chinks are pulling another disappearing act?"

I answered quietly. "My dreams tell me they're still here." Suddenly Han, ROK 'Slick' and four others were beside our fire.

Han spoke up. "We go sick call." Both he and ROK Slick were worthless in a firefight and wouldn't be missed, but their request indicated they knew something we didn't. My intended questions were cut short by Hungerford's shout from the road.

"George Company, saddle up! ROK Platoon, take point!"

We made our way up onto the first fog-shrouded crest, with the company stretched out in column behind us. I hesitantly spoke to my brother and Robertson.

"I don't want to be in the assault this time. I want to bring up the rear and work with the LMG, if that's okay with you guys?" They nodded unquestioningly. I went and scouted ahead then answered Barszcz's call on the walkie-talkie.

"Nothing yet, sir, the fog's pretty thick and it's hard to see."

He crackled back. "Stay awake, ROK-5 and keep your eyes peeled, over."

I unwittingly paraphrased a line from any number of class B Westerns on signing off. "There isn't a Gook within miles, sir, over and out." Incredibly an unexpected shot shattered the radio from my ear. I laughed while diving for cover: *No one will believe this...it only happens in the goddamned movies.*

ROK Tom's arrival with the squad drew rifle and machine gun fire while the company maneuvered a hundred yards below and set up its 60mm mortars. Richard and Robertson brought up their troops. I fired at four quilted figures that darted out of the veil of fog fifty yards ahead who must have thought we were a small patrol and easy to prey. One, barely alive rolled down to within my reach. I used his body to balance my rifle's next shot that mortally wounded another.

The well-camouflaged Chinese wounded a score of G.I.s and drove the ROK who'd accidentally shot Buckley into my foxhole as Tom dashed with the squad to the flank. I stared blankly at the soldier, with no thought of revenge until a particular scene from *Beau Geste* popped into my head. Then, like Sergeant Markoff in the film, I forced our ROK to look over the lip of the foxhole at gunpoint; and knew that I was being driven by a dark force beyond my conscious will that left me feeling more hollow than heroic. I wasn't surprised that he remained behind when I dashed forward towards the misty outline of a machinegun bunker that loomed up 120 yards ahead; and noted, too, the small elevation seventy yards to its left. It was a perfect position for the Chinks to cover the bunker: *That could be a problem later.* The MG in the dugout kept up sporadic fire as Robertson and my brother, on my left, readied the platoon for its assault on the abutment.

With the LMG I commandeered from the Ritz Brothers I took cover under a nearby isolated tree. Our 60mm mortars fell on the impervious enemy fortification, but managed to silence the rapid eruption of burp guns on its flank where the 1st Platoon's advance was held up. A general lull in firing followed and, with drawn sword, I peered over the crest and followed a compulsion to amuse my troops. That gave vent to a scene I remembered in a Toshiro Mifune *Samurai* film, so I hurled *Kabuki*-styled Japanese epithets and challenges at my well camouflaged Chinese audience.

"*Stori fudadi wa mendoda tabaninatte, kakata koe* [Whatever number of you wish to fight me, come forward]!"

The ROKs threw out their own Japanese accented taunts between fits of raucous laughter as they deployed along the abutment. Below them was the wide draw they would descend and the seventy yards of open terrain they'd have to cross to reach the sandbagged bunker. Robertson and Richard rose and shouted for the men to fix bayonets. Fifteen yards away ROK Tom lay at my side ready to feed the gun. I bellowed to my brother to hang onto his helmet! Robertson barked back reminding me not to let the MG fire get too close. With cries of *"Tatzuzeki!,"* Robertson and Richard ran forward—unknowingly alone—down into the bullet-riddled ravine. The frightened platoon was psychologically pinned down with fear and was deaf to my bellowed command of *"Mae-e* [Forward]!"

I swept the LMG up into the crook of my arm and shouted, *"Ugoku ato shinu* [Move or die]!"

A stream of rounds ricocheted and churned up dust in its slow incremental march towards the platoon I hoped to avoid decimating. They raced down the hill like sandpipers before a pursuing wave, and I stood ankle deep in a smoldering heap of ejected casings.

Tom hissed, "You, *Japanese-ou*, same-same."

I nodded a bow. *"Arigato."*

On our right a G.I. platoon held up on the ridge finger forty yards short of the bunker. Tom fed a fresh belt of ammo into the receiver and I shifted my focus in that direction. One squad of the 1st Platoon, against no opposition, had been unable to maneuver up the ridge; nor see the handful of Chinese that emerged from trapdoor spider holes just behind them. From eighty yards away they looked quite passive with their rifles slung, but couldn't fire without hitting our troops.

The Chinese moved up swiftly through the motionless G.I. skirmish line and swifter still until they were down unseen amid the thickets on the forward slope before anyone knew or could react. Even then the G.I.s weren't sure of what they'd just seen—or thought they imagined, as they peered down into the gully. I was filled with admiration for the discipline and bravery of the Chinese: *When we get to China...I've got to get some of those guys as replacements.* Inspired, I started short bursts of covering fire between troops, and over the heads of other startled G.I.s. Some turned and nervously stared towards me as uncomprehending Tom exclaimed, *"Sahji, Sahji,* is G.I., is G.I. *desu.!"*

I answered tersely. *"Wakata, wakata* [I know, I know]." He mumbled his usual refrain.

Lieutenant Walters arrived and pointed to three motionless ROKs in the field below. "I see you lost a couple of men."

I sent a dozen rounds perilously close to their conniving heads and they magically returned to life—and their squads. Walters, Tom and I went forward. The 2nd Platoon remained motionless along the adjoining finger. The executive officer, Lieutenant Tony Dannucci, screamed furiously into his radio handset.

"Why haven't you taken that bunker? Have you tried standing up and leading the charge yourself? Do you know what you're telling me, Lieutenant?"

I whispered to his radioman Johnny Murr, "Is he talking to Lieutenant Herbert?"

He laughed. "Nah, you'll never find him up this close! It's that young West Point kid, Turk. Poor bastard, he couldn't hit his ass if he had a bat in each hand."

Dannucci thrust his unsheathed bayonet skyward in Centurion fashion and led the screaming G.I.s up to the bunker's trench line. Robertson couldn't resist joining the charge. Their firing was intense. One frightened Chinese soldier in the trench yanked his jacket over his head, like a blindfold and a G.I.'s bayonet nailed his skull to the parapet wall as he pole-vaulted over.

Walters murmured through the din of bullets, grenades and screams, "I've never seen braver men." Then he nodded towards the elevation twenty yards to the left of the bunker. "Mercy, take your platoon and clear that ridge."

I came close to something resembling the position of attention without saluting, to avoid notice by any officer-hunting snipers. "Yes, sir."

Richard formed the platoon up in the smoky, body littered draw and I pointed to the objective. "*Tsuke ken* [Fix bayonets]. *Statzuzeki!*" Perhaps it was the sight of Dannucci's bayonet charge and the strewn about bodies that herded them into what resembled a pack of mindlessly reluctant wildebeests that stumbled and froze in place. They were immune to my shouts, threats and even the few rounds I fired ominously close to their feet and heads. Richard and I, widely separated, charged the hill alone and minutes later victoriously waved to each other from atop the deserted summit. We returned to the bowed heads of the glassy-eyed platoon that had collectively suffered a serious loss of 'face.'

I called them to attention, "*Kyotsuke!*" *Some Chinks should pop up from a spider-hole...and give them a burst of six...they're nothing but a pack of goddamned civilians.*

While I was berating the squads with every vile international curse I knew ROK Slick arrived and saluted.

"Me back from sick-call-ou, Sahji-san." An unrestrained punch to his jaw sent him reeling back down the slope of the hard-won hill.

For three days the regiment moved beneath skies smeared by columns of black smoke and rained down slivers of steel from the concentrated artillery fire that left the muddy pockmarked slopes littered with swatches of Chinese dead. Their thick quilt padded jackets made me wonder if a thrown bayonet could pierce them. I decided it would be better to find out now than when I was out alone on an OP, like in the film *Objective Burma*. Robertson and I both threw our bayonets at two bodies we'd

235

propped against a tree. The blades penetrated not only the jackets, but also the sensitivities of a new replacement that cried out from the high ground for us to stop it. Undaunted, we straightened out the slumped cadavers and had he raised his rifle I wasn't sure which of us would have shot him down first.

The ROKs regained their spirit, which allowed them to maneuver through the next day's heavy machine gun fire while Richard's binoculars studied the high ground.

"Must be NKs up there—they're piss-poor shots."

I smiled and said, "Maybe we'll get lucky and take some prisoners."

Robertson yawned. "Why break our record?"

Hours later, as I sat compulsively studying the eyes of the three Chinese dead that had been left behind, PFC Lauro arrived and delivered a message from Barszcz.

"A general is coming up and he wants you to impress him by having your troops do something like bayonet drill."

Richard and Ralph Lauro on an LMG (light machine gun).

My glance fell over Lauro's shoulder and onto the approaching distant figure of the officer in question. I quickly ordered the thoroughly confused ROKs to fix bayonets and string-out along the incline of the fissured crest; and had them shout as they made parries and thrusts "*EEEEEYAAAAA!*"

The general eventually called out across the chasm. "You're doing great work, Sergeant. Keep it up!"

ROK One.

My mind raced, deciding whether to tell him I was only a corporal. "Thank you, sir."

We had no supporting fire for our morning's assault against an escaping NK platoon on the high ground. Robertson emptied his full carbine clip into an NK. I put a tracer round in another's skull and added two of his gold-capped teeth to my collection. Just then, Tom stopped by my side.

"*Sahji, Sahji*, you come, you come!"

I joined the four others who were kneeling beside ROK One. Even with two burp gun slugs in the stomach and one in the chest he was exceedingly serene. With his hand in mine I told him in Japanese that I'd get him to the battalion aid station, and that he'd be all right. Blood pumped from his chest wound and we both knew better, though there was a million-to-one chance when a Bell "Dragonfly" helicopter suddenly appeared overhead and Johnny Murr, the CO's radioman, arrived.

"Get on your radio and tell that chopper to come down and pick up a seriously wounded man."

Radioman Eugene "Johnny" Murr (left).

He called then stared back at me over his hand held receiver "They refused. He's afraid of drawing enemy fire." The next thing I knew the air ambulance's wafer-thin fuselage was framed in my sights.

They'll court martial you for sure...goddamned Army...if ROK One was a commissioned officer...they'd be down here real quick. I put a blanket roll under ROK One's head and his dimming eyes slowly rolled away from the departing chopper. He wheezed out his last words. "Thank you, *Sahji-san*." All of those around him bowed deeply then we moved on.

Our night patrol led us into the nearby village of Sangpum-ni and the one hut we commandeered. While Robertson converted his .45 rounds into dum-dums, I sipped tea with the woman of the house. She said an enemy company left the previous night carrying forty wounded. They also shot a number of civilians and gave hand grenades to the local children as toys. She smiled and pointed out the window. "Is many, many more Chinee in close by village of Chuo."

"...tell that chopper to come down and pick up a seriously wounded man."

CHAPTER 29

Cemetery Ridge

I lost track of the number of gray, dank days the battalion spent searching the mountains for the Chinese MLR (main like of resistance). We drew fire from a machine gun outpost as our truck column reached a village road intersection. I crawled towards a hole in the nearby fence. From that vantage point, I could see, eighteen hundred yards away, the summit of the hill we'd come to know as 584. Excellent camouflage hid its widely scattered foxholes and the trenches connecting its well-constructed bunkers. These fighting trenches were also used to transport out the wounded and bring in supplies. It turned out that this was the linchpin in the Chinese defense perimeter on the southern banks of the Han River, just a few miles beyond.

An LMG burst flew overhead, which could have come from the farmhouse 100 yards past the intersection. I raced to a Jeep-mounted machine gun. The driver, face down in a drainage ditch, called out, "For Christ's sake, don't shoot! You'll draw more fire."

I burned off half the belt towards the unseen gunner. "You stupid bastard, that's what we're here for!" I thought of the Nam River farmer and the crying baby I'd driven out into the bitter cold of Sinuiju: *Innocent people could be in there...but where else can the gun be?* The firing stopped.

The platoon moved across the road and dug in atop a small hill fifty yards away. It sat right in the middle of a barren field. This mound, thirty feet high and seventy yards long, would be the link between the 1st and 2nd Battalions' rear areas although it was vulnerable to attacks from any direction. Its narrow summit had literally entrenched our platoon shoulder-to-shoulder. The battalion's WE-8 phone line was too short to reach the crest so Butterball and Robertson set the phone up in the OP, forty yards further down the ridge. After we'd booby-trapped the base of the hill with flares and grenades, Butterball gave us the latest news.

Cemetery Ridge Tactical Situation.

"When Barszcz caught two slugs in his leg a few days back Herbert took over. During his first commanders meeting at battalion he got carried away and volunteered George Company to lead one of last week's assaults."

I sighed. "To desert or not to desert, that is the question."

Richard continued, "Then, during the attack, as the story goes, an NCO found him hiding behind a pile of rocks some distance from the action. He brought him back to battalion HQ—at gunpoint. Kind of hard to believe, but that was the last I heard about it. Now Dannucci's been promoted to captain and has the company."

Sergeant Tubb's carrying party arrived at sunset with rations and ammo and he drawled out the latest orders.

"This comes straight from the Ol' Man. You guys ain't to leave this hill under no circumstance, and if it's overrun, we expect to find your dead bodies when we get back up here."

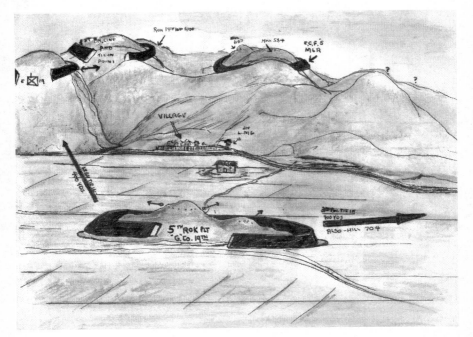

Cemetery Ridge.

Smiling cynically, Richard asked him, *"We*? When '*we*' get back up here?"

Robertson hissed through a strained smile. "If you're worried about us bugging out, why don't you unsling that Thompson and stay here to make sure we don't? You do know how to fire that thing, don't you Tubbs?"

Tubbs turned, left mumbling and headed back up the half-mile of eastbound road to the company CP. Determining that we were in an indefensible position Richard christened the hill "Cemetery Ridge."

Exploding shells and tracers careened through the following days and nights after a failed battalion attack by the 19th ROK Infantry Regiment was pushed back from the high ground on 584; and suffered more casualties when they were mistakenly bombed and strafed by Night Intruder B-26s.

Robertson glanced down towards the roadside village. "I bet there are Gooks closer than we think."

We ran a patrol and found nothing. The next morning Robertson shot an ancient long-bearded Korean dead on the roadway 100 yards ahead. I quickly scanned the eyes of the age-revering ROKs who were shocked and mesmerized by the lifeless body that could have been a grandfather to any of them. Richard sitting beside him asked why he fired. He said he didn't know and was oblivious to the seething potential of the platoon. With an air of nonchalance I reluctantly prepared myself and the LMG, to suppress any passions that could get out of hand.

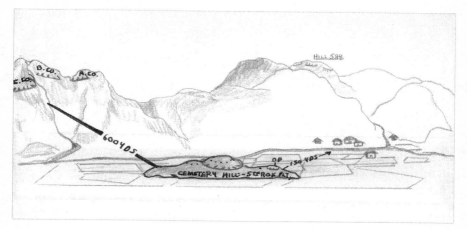

Cemetery Hill.

I tried to recall Robertson's personal history in search of some malevolent or demonic cause for his enigmatic nature. He had a tendency to brood in self-isolation, which could jeopardize our mission, yet I envied his killer instinct. He'd wake up feeling guilty, believing he hadn't fought hard enough and could have done more for his country. He had told us about the hired ranch hand who tried to kill him when he was twelve. He had run to the house for his .22 rifle, and would have killed the man had his father not suddenly arrived: *What will be his karma...if we are condemned to another life?* Clearly, we all somehow shared a fixation with death in the mythical grandeur of war and its adrenaline-driven sanction to kill.

A late-night wave of Chinese troops poured down from the heights of Hill 704 and, despite our heavy weapons and artillery, swept Easy and Fox Companies from their positions. Both companies suffered heavy casualties and were out of communication with the battalion's reserve, which was George Company who'd come under heavy mortar attack while ordered to recapture those hills. They lost nearly two platoons before How

Company's heavy weapons moved up and neutralized the Chinese counterattack. Battalion alerted Richard on the WE-8 phone line, letting us know that the Chinks had broken through in a few places and were being supported by horse-drawn artillery.

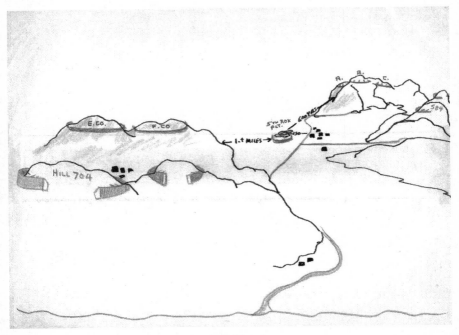

Hill 704.

ROK Tom called out from the edge of our tightly packed ridge. "*Shina-jin koko desu* [Chinese are here]!"

I echoed it down to Richard and Robertson. They vaguely heard the Chinese working their way up from the base of the hill under the staccato bursts from our LMG. Butterball murmured into his phone, trying to get hold of the 11th Field Artillery. When he did get through, he got a surprise after he identified himself.

"Hey, you one of them Mercy brothers?"

Richard's eyes rolled. "Yeah?"

The static-laced voice glowed, "Hey, how you doing, Mercy?" Courtesy is never out of place.

"Oh, I'm fine. How are you?"

'Private Cheery' audibly beamed, "Just great. What can we do for you?"

Richard quickly gave the fire command center the map coordinates for the nearing targets. Very soon, a voice crackled back that rounds were "on the way!" A distant shimmery light flared from behind a far off darkened ridgeline and heralded the whine of incoming 105mm shells that detonated into a blinding roar only fifteen yards forward of the OP.

Frantically Richard shouted into the phone, "Too close! *Too* close! lift your fire to Three Zero yards!"

An apologetic voice replied, "Sorry, Mercy, there's a lot more stuff coming your way right now."

The full battery barrage plummeted even closer to the nearly collapsed CP foxhole and rained down dirt, rocks and smoldering steel. Richard and Robertson mumbled dazedly in unison, "Goddamn!" Above, I ignorantly saluted their bravado for having called in such close fire: *Maybe I should put them in for a Bronze Star?*

I peered over the freshly shrapnel-splintered lip of my parapet wall and into the dust-raised stillness and faintly heard the sounds of snow being crunched. A figure was nearing the OP! I struggled against my inner voice that told me not to shoot, but use a rifle grenade instead of the LMG. I lost precious seconds arguing with myself. Finally, I ejected the clip from my M1, inserted the special crimped cartridge, and fired off a WP grenade.

It ignited into a sparkling blanket of white smoke not six yards behind the intended target that shouted and dove for cover, "You stupid fuck, it's me!"

My voice remained calm. "Sorry Richard!"

He laughed back from his foxhole. I then fired a burst of six from the LMG into the flanking darkness, from which the Chinese had mysteriously retreated: *Somewhere, somehow, somebody or something was clearly watching over us.*

At dawn I photographed Robertson thrusting his bayonet-fixed carbine into the back of one of the dozen enemy dead. Later I studiously searched the unrevealing eyes of all the dead. Richard commented on last night's rifle grenade incident. "You 'corporals' would do anything to create a permanent vacancy."

I got them both to pose for my camera. They stood a decapitated body up between them and sang the ever-popular *I Lost My Head over You*. I added a few more gold teeth to my collection. ROK Tom later covered us from the crest with the LMG when we headed to the village searching for any wounded Chinese.

I was touched by and couldn't help but return the compelling unguarded grin of the weather-faced middle-aged man who approached us. His mental affliction shone through vulnerable eyes that broadly smiled in our easy exchange in Japanese. Then he nervously misread something in my startled eyes and cringed back in fear. He couldn't see Robertson moving in behind him with a cocked pistol pointed to his head. I shouted, "Don't shoot!"

Robertson replied, "Look at him, he's crazy for Christ sake and not good for anything, so why not?" Both the unaware villager and the ROKs were equally baffled by our heated exchange of incomprehensible words.

"If you hurt him, I swear I'll see you stand a court martial and hang!"

He silently holstered his pistol and walked away. I wanted to tell him of my hapless mother's nervous breakdown and all the cruelties that incurred, but kept it a guarded secret. I soothed the Korean with a gentle smile, a pat on the back and some cigarettes. I was touched by his hopeless vulnerability as he bowed with each backward step he took into his war-torn village. Back on the ridge Robertson remained silently aloof on the OP with Richard. I wondered if the yawning gap between us could ever be bridged.

Johnny Murr dropped by and we watched our 1st Battalion's distant attack on Hill 584. Supporting mortar and artillery barrages rumbled in the background as Johnny spoke solemnly of the death of Captain Dannucci the previous night.

"We were counterattacking to recapture the positions Fox and Easy Companies lost. Screams and firing was going off all around us. I'll never forget him, with pistol in hand and out ahead of his troops. He looked back and yelled 'Okay George Company, follow me!' Just then two MG rounds caught him at the base of his skull. I lifted up his head and my hands felt like they were in a pan of warm glue. Maybe we should go see Dannucci's family, and Buckley's too, if and when we ever get back, okay, Mercy?" Hours later Charlie and Baker Companies fell back from Hill 584 with heavy casualties. Then shells fell on the hill throughout the night.

Perhaps it was the muffled drum-roll cadence of the distant shelling that had me strangely dream of a nearly forgotten scene from *Babes in Toyland*. I saw my face on the wooden soldier as I picked up the infant boy. He was Korean and smiled with each shot I fired from my bayonet-affixed rifle.

I awoke at dawn with an impression of impending death, for the dream seemed to say that my life had come around full circle. As my eyes turned up to the silent but cordite shrouded Hill 584, 'Big Stoop' Ken leaped into my foxhole wearing a serious expression.

"*Doy stano, Sahji-san* [What is the matter, Sergeant]?"

I was surprised by the unintentional melodramatic whispered reply. "I will die up there."

246

Robert with sword in front of Replacement Platoon. Most of the previous fifty-man platoon was killed on Hill 584. This shot was taken prior to Operation Ripper in March 1951. One-third of these men were either killed or wounded in that attack. It was the end of the 5th ROK Platoon.

Ken flashed his broadest gold-toothed grin. "Oh, never happen, *Sahji*!"

For unclear reasons and sensing no action would occur that day I let Ken talk me into leaving the hill. Guiltily, I followed him towards some undisclosed destination. We walked through the battalion HQ area and I returned the salutes of recognition from many of the unfamiliar ROKs who passed. I didn't know if it was the *Samurai* sword or their grapevine, but I felt a twinge of pride and a little bit like the immortal warlord Yang, even as Ken's oversized hand firmly gripped mine. He was oblivious of the incredulous stares we drew from the slack-jawed G.I.s who didn't know it was an Asian gesture of friendship between men.

An hour later Ken pointed to a cluster of dwellings five hundred yards away, and told me it was the village of Samhamni. He entered a hut, then came back out and signaled me to go in while he waited close by. Inside the empty impoverished room a fully dressed woman knelt on a sleeping mat. I felt suddenly honored by Ken's unsuspected and very un-Korean-like gesture: *They never offer up their women—particularly to foreigners.*

Her bowed head silently swayed to and fro, as if she was under a spell and I wondered if her wild unruly hair masked something less than a flawless face. A bottle of high-octane saké would have been nice right then. If I rejected her, Ken would feel hurt; he might even see it as an insult to Korean womanhood. I knelt beside her and my exploratory kiss pierced through her Voodooesque hairdo. Her young lips and firm body

247

had a surprisingly pleasant odor and I wasn't sure if she was just bashful, ashamed, or something worse. There were so many diseases out here and half of them didn't even have names. She giggled as her dress fell to the floor where I hoped for an Oscar performance, thinking about Marlene Dietrich's erotic legs in the film *Kismet*.

The sudden intrusion of her enraged father bursting through the door was stopped short when he found himself staring down into the barrel of my raised pistol. Catnapping Ken was suddenly behind him and pulled him away. Ken returned grinning from ear to ear.

"You die now, *Sahji*?"

I smiled in kind. "No, *Sahji* feel *jo-to,* okay! Will live forever!"

We were crossing a maze of low-lying hills west of the battalion CP when a passing lieutenant asked if I was one of the Mercy brothers. Smiling, I replied in the affirmative.

He raised one eyebrow. "Are you guys really ex-German *SS* paratroopers?" Where would an army be without rumors?

Torrential morning rains had grounded the usual flights of napalm-carrying planes, and pelted the sodden remains of the dead G.I.s left on the dark slopes of Hill 584. When the weather cleared, I leisurely snipped at a few Chinese who scurried for cover near a stopped troop truck on the road. Strangely, they didn't fire back. The driver, however, felt threatened by my carefully aimed rounds and took it as a personal challenge to his manhood. He vaulted up into the truck's ring mounted .50-caliber and shouted towards a cluster of unaware ROKs, seated some yards from me, who were huddled under their ponchos. "Cease fire, motherfucker, or I'll blow you apart!"

The crosshairs of my telescopic sight were between his magnified eyes. I watched them scan those of his bewildered cargo of troops for some acknowledgment of his spurious valor, which would be short-lived if he fired one round towards my blissfully unaware soldiers. I knew it could be an easy kill, and more importantly, justifiable: *One hundred and twenty yards and no wind drift...or aware witnesses to even guess the who, what and where the shot might have come from...and no one would care...he's one lucky dumb-ass rear-echelon son of a bitch.*

The next day Richard and Robertson's patrol brought back a 'civilian.' His regulation haircut and the way he braced on my shouted command of "*Charyott* [Attention]!" sealed his fate. His arrogant demeanor convinced us that S-2 wouldn't get anything from him before he was shot by a South Korean firing squad. Robertson prodded him off to a secluded place and sliced off one of his ears. With the threat of losing the other he admitted to being a spy and was made to haul ammunition up to our slope for the rest of the day. Richard, ever the MP, reminded Robertson that he'd violated the Articles of War by making a POW work.

Back row, left to right: Robert, Han, Loy (a former Japanese marine) and Richard. Robertson is kneeling with the sword. This photo was taken in a rest area village on 4 March 1951, before Operation Ripper. All of us except for Han were wounded three days later.

The captain's alert to an impending attack kept Tom and me awake until exhaustion overtook us near dawn. A brief time later we were startled to consciousness and exchanged blank stares on finding ourselves pressed against the foxhole's wall. My heart pounded on hearing the harsh Chinese singsong commands that rang up from somewhere just below us: *Did we get surrounded during the night? I hadn't heard anything...Am I dreaming?* We cautiously popped our heads up, and saw a psych-warfare truck parked on the nearby road, blaring out surrender instructions to the Chinks on Hill 584!

An enemy probe came that night. I ordered one ROK to scout out the base of the hill and he refused. For reasons known only to the deepest part of my inaccessible subconscious I didn't shoot him on the spot. I once believed killing a disobedient soldier would be as easy for me as it was for the cinematic officers and NCOs of foreign armies: *Is it religion, humanity or cowardice that keeps us from killing...when we seriously want to?*

Tubbs arrived in the morning and we loaded down the platoon with extra bandoleers and rifle grenades. Hungerford gave us a briefing.

249

"Regiment will feign a frontal attack and the 19th ROK Regiment will move in from the flank to take 584. By the way, Mercy, I know that you're carrying some undeveloped film. You wouldn't want that stuff to fall into enemy hands if you get killed or captured, would you?"

Instinct correctly told me that I'd never see those rolls again.

Objective #24.

Scorched earth.

CHAPTER 30

Take Hill 584

The platoon ambled off Cemetery Ridge past a young farmer swinging his hoe in the fields. Robertson, 'playfully' imagined it to be a *Samurai* sword and fired a burst from his hip held carbine. One round severed the farmer's thumb from the hoe. The man's cry was muted by the low zooming jets that skimmed by towards Hill 584.

Past the village and ahead up the ridge we saw the 19th ROK Infantry Regiment being driven off the summit and mistakenly attacked by U.S. planes. Near dusk Chinese artillery and heavy machine guns drove off our 1st battalion. We pressed on through the chilly night's aromatic scents of acrid gasoline, loam and sweet cordite. Robertson ignored my effort to make amends and dug in alone on the far flank.

The company attacked again at dawn and artillery fire caused heavy casualties on both sides. Moving two hundred yards closer to the objective, my squad stormed a bunker then made use of its firing port. Richard and Robertson had moved up on the flanks while I stood outside trying to get a better view of the terrain. An officer I didn't recognize approached and ordered that I stop my men's firing from the bunker; and cut me off when I started to protest.

Back inside I reluctantly relayed his vapid order to Tom and three others who stared at me as if I'd gone mad. Tom pointed through the bloodstained firing port to a seemingly unaware platoon-sized column of Chinese sixty yards below, with their weapons slung and moving towards 584. They were the closest and easiest targets I'd seen during the entire war and recognized we'd be able to kill more in those next few minutes than we had for months. I brought two down and had the third in my sights

251

when the stocky officer frantically bellowed again from outside. "Cease fire, goddamn it, that's an order!"

That little son of a bitch...he's afraid of drawing fire...and if he comes in here with a drawn pistol...shoot first! I defiantly emptied my clip then let common sense be vanquished anew by discipline. I cried to the ROKs, "*Utsi-ni, shoko no chumo suru* [No shoot, officer's orders]!" *I wonder how many G.I.s and Koreans will be killed by these Gooks because of that pig-headed officer?*

I dashed the squad forward to the company's strengthening line of fire eighty yards below the charred smoldering crest. Where amid the smoke lashed shards of bullet whittled trees, was an extended arm that protruded from a caved-in Chinese trench. Its limp hand gently swayed in the prevailing winds, reminiscent of dead Ahab's when he was enmeshed in tangled harpoon lines on the back of the breaching White Whale; beckoning me forth into a stark yet seemingly familiar perdition. I heard my unwitting whispered: "I've done this before."

Forward of our position bullet riddled bodies fell all around and a Chinese flamethrower drove back the lead G.I. squads; and drew fire in turn from every weapon on the hill. Lieutenant Walters slid up beside me.

"Would you, or any of your men, like to carry that flame thrower in the assault, Mercy?"

We watched as a G.I. picked it up, spewed out a stream of hissing flame then fell under a fusillade of enemy fire: *Just like the newsreel clips of the Marines on Okinawa...what an ugly weapon.* "No thank you, sir. I'll stick to my M1 and I can't ask any of my untrained ROKs to carry it either."

Richard, sixty yards below the summit, waved me forward. I formed up the platoon behind the blind side of a large abutment to pull a last minute closed-ranks inspection. I had them button their pockets and straighten out their helmets and cartridge belts. I buffed my boots on the back of trouser legs, thinking of the British troops in *Gunga Din* and *The Light That Failed*. I hoped to remind the ROKs of being disciplined soldiers and to be proud when we charged.

Richard and I fired off the platoon's supply of fifty rifle grenades at the enemy's positions and with each explosion the ROKs cheered. Robertson moved his *Chinju* squad left across the open napalm-blackened terrain, my squad took the center and Richard swung the Seoul and Teague squads on the right.

Three hundred yards beyond, in the wide gap between our objective and an adjoining hill, I spotted Chinese forces spilling down the forward slope of Hill 667. They pushed back Easy Company who relied on Navy

Corsairs to do the infantry work for them. Noting that they'd left their sleeping bags behind, I posted a guard to keep them from stealing ours while we were in the attack. Lieutenant Walters arrived as I centered myself in front of the platoon. He pointed to twenty riflemen he'd deployed behind us.

"I won't be going with you, Mercy, but will direct support fire from back there."

That surprised me almost as much as the unexpected appearance of the unarmed pair of combat photographers that were suddenly beside me. They'd volunteered to immortalize our charge.

"Do you guys know what you're doing," I asked. They smiled and nodded.

ROK Tom stood beside me on the abutment while an inexplicable compulsion caused me to tie the platoon's bloodstained flag *Samurai*-fashion around my head, signifying a willingness to die. Tom smiled.

"*Anatawa Hachimaki suru deska* [You pledge to the God of War]?"

I acknowledged with a determined grunt. He nodded and bowed as I shouted through the smoke laced wind. "*Juken suru* [Fix bayonets]!" The sharp swoosh of my drawn sword and rhythmical metallic clash of the bayonets locking onto rifle studs made my flesh tingle. With my pistol drawn, I looked into the pensive Mongoloid eyes of my troops and yelled "*Stat-zu-zeki!*" Then charged into a lifelong dream of withering fire, my pent-up cries echoed across the hillside: "*Banzai! Banzai! Banzai!*"

Richard's Thompson and Robertson's carbine on full automatic sprayed forward of their charging squads. On both sides, bullets ripped into bodies that stumbled and fell. I yelled, "*Tomeru nai. Tomeru nai* [Don't stop. Don't stop]!" A Chinese face popped up five yards ahead and caught two of my pistol slugs, as did another that charged towards me. I ignored the cries of my inner voice: *Use your rifle...sheath the sword*! I clung to the role I'd created, and charged forward into the fire. Two more of my squad died. Robertson let off a long burst that fragmented the head of the Chinese who'd killed three of his men. Richard lost Our Man Friday, ROK Slick and one of the Marx brothers. I fired close at the ROKs who had frozen in fear and even at the medic who bandaged the wounded. I slapped the butts of some others with the flat of my sword and shouted again "*Tomeru nai, tomeru nai* [Don't stop, don't stop]!"

Walters, behind us, kicked in the face of one supporting riflemen who'd been firing blindly with both eyes squeezed shut. Then further on I stood partially frozen, my sword halfheartedly raised over a mortally wounded Chinese soldier. I couldn't decapitate him, but ran him through instead: *So much for my having been Japanese.* I caught up to Richard firing an M1.

"What happened to the Thompson, Butterball?"

He frowned at me. "It was worthless. I emptied a full magazine at a LMG at forty yards and didn't even come close!" He glimpsed my sword and grinned. "You might want some more firepower yourself."

We simultaneously fired our rifles at a nearby LMG and three Chinese slumped over dead. Richard laughed. "That's better."

We moved closer and threw grenades over the bullet-splattered crest. Robertson had a smoking pistol in one hand and a carbine in the other when he brought his squad up on line. Butterball peeped over the crest. A string of machine gun rounds from the bunker some two hundred yards away on Hill 677 raked up swirls of dust from nearly every curve and notch on our ridge. Richard laughed loudly and blinked dust from his eyes when he held up the severely perforated helmet he'd raised over the crest with a stick. "I'd like to introduce that gunner to the *Stars and Stripes* reporter who said, 'Chinks are inferior to G.I.s in the field of modern weapons.'" As Walters arrived Richard dashed below the skyline and reached the far right flank. There he soon staggered and fell to one knee while bullets ricocheted all around him. Walters gasped, "He's hit!" My twin-sense told me he wasn't. "No sir, he's okay, he only slipped."

Our attention turned to the roaring guns of the blue Corsair that fishtailed in over a hundred yards behind us. Walters cried out, "Christ, he thinks we're the Gooks!"

Two of its wing-mounted rockets burned a fiery trail toward the center of our line. My mind raced: *Get flat...get flat... I can avoid the blast.* Walters, the ROKs and scores of G.I.s frantically jumped and dove back from the ridge in all directions. The projectiles were aimed at the Chinese bunker on the next hill and cleared our summit by inches. Seconds later the doomed bunker was swirled up into a smoky collage of timbers, weapons and dismembered bodies. The pilot did low lazy victory roll over the devastation and I shouted, "Fantastic shooting!"

As dusk began I went down the reverse slope and methodically dispensed the *coup de grace* to the half-dozen mangled Chinese that littered the field. A carrying party and some G.I.s motionlessly watched from the ridge: *If I were found...or any of my men...in this condition...I'd want the same.* I brought back in the posted guard who wisely hadn't resisted the anticipated theft of our sleeping bags by Easy Company's routed platoon. Walters briefed me.

"The Chinks are still hitting our left flank and Able Company's OP, and they're counterattacking Fox and Easy on the right from all sides. There's still a question whether we can hold on here for the night, even if we got the doubtful artillery support battalion promised."

The enemy's artillery fell haphazardly along the hill and their infantry was advancing. The ROKs covered G Company's withdrawal until Richard pulled them out. I stayed back and set booby-trap grenades around the ammo boxes and supplies. Walters called out with sage advice.

"Don't be fuckin' around with that stuff too long."

Tom and three other faithful ROKs silently waited behind to cover my retreat, just like Yang's personal guards. I harshly ordered them to leave and catch up with the platoon: *Why risk their lives...besides...it's easier to get out of here alone.*

I inched back below the dull umber skyline as dark silhouettes of Chinese soldiers appeared twenty yards away. They had to have heard the sounds our squads made filtering down the slope ahead, yet their weapons remained slung. I was in luck, they weren't looking for a fight and I made it down to where the company was dug in on Hill 392. Hours later Major Melicio Montesclaros of the battalion staff jumped into the foxhole Richard and I shared and shook our hands.

"Thanks, Sergeants, for taking 584." I was tempted to remind him I was only a lowly corporal and Robertson was still a PFC.

The regimental after-battle report showed that 1st Battalion sustained over one hundred casualties and Easy Company of the 2nd was reduced to one hundred men. We lost almost half of our platoon. The death estimate for the Chinese was fifty KIA and three hundred and fifty wounded. 584 would change hands again during the coming weeks.

CHAPTER 31

Let Me Talk to Them, Sir

The next morning, Tom and I sat together in a foxhole braced against the gusts of cold wind that frosted my sniper scope as I studied the unusually relaxed atmosphere on the Chinese forward slope of Hill 584. Unconcealed soldiers casually strolled along the crest between the exposed supply boxes I'd booby-trapped and that they in turn had decorated with draped laundry. No air or artillery strikes were called in on those inviting targets: *Maybe somebody declared a truce and forgot to tell us about it?* While I relaxed and contemplatively oiled my weapons and sharpened my sword an old Samurai film came to mind; and an idea of how I might get some of the Chinese on Hill 584 to surrender: *That should get me promoted if nothing else will.*

I called out as Walters happened by. "Sir, I would like your permission to try something."

He eyed me suspiciously. "Try what, Mercy?"

I drew a deep breath. "Well, sir, I would like to construct a *hatasashi* and—"

He cut me short. "You would like to do what?"

I got out three words. "Construct a *hatasashi* and…"

He leaned in closer, and asked, "and what in the hell is a hata… hatasassy?"

I stared at him blankly: *He's an officer, for Christ's sake. You'd think he'd know this stuff.* His eyebrow arched over as I slowly stressed each syllable. "*Ha-ta-sa-shi*, sir. It's a long pennant with written Japanese characters on it. Usually it's attached to a staff. Mounted *Samurai* strapped them to their backs so their foot troops knew whom to follow. Messages can be printed on them, sir."

He hummed condescendingly. "Hmmm, messages?"

My confidence grew. "Yes, sir, I'd get ROK Richard to write out a few words on this banner, in *Kanji*, sir—that's a form of Japanese script."

Walter's curiosity framed the hoped-for question. "Write out *what*, specifically, Mercy?"

I answered conspiratorially. "That I come in peace with an offer of surrender."

He blinked slowly. "You come in what? Peace? They are not stupid people up there, Sergeant—"

I interrupted. "Corporal, sir, I'm still only a corporal."

He overrode the interruption. "They invented gun powder, for Christ's sake, and probably the goddamned wheel for all I know, and you expect them to believe that *you* are coming up there in p-e-a-c-e?"

He had a point. "True, sir, but I think I could negotiate some sort of 'informal' surrender with them. As the lieutenant may know, sir, I have a way with Asians. It just might work." I spoke into Walter's vacant stare. "Fuck, sir, I'm sure they're tired of getting hit with air and artillery strikes every day. Who knows, they may just go along with it, even though I *am* only a corporal, which, of course, *they* would have no way of knowing, sir!" I sighed as he gave a meditative Humphrey Bogart style tug at his ear lobe. "Let me talk to 'em, sir." He gave a contemplative gaze. It fired my expectation: *I bet if I brought back a platoon... I'd get a battlefield commission.*

Butterball, Robertson, and I lay side-by-side during the cold frigid night and earnestly talked about our urgent need to find replacements, if we wanted to avoid the ugly spectre of separation and reassignments to G.I. platoons.

"Don't worry, Boy-san, a few days ago I sent Ken out on a 'special mission' to recruit some freelance rifles from the 19th ROK Infantry." Richard and I exchanged surreptitious stares as Robertson continued. "Yeah, and he actually got about eight of them to agree to a meeting." Richard and I asked in unison: "When?"

He replied, "Tonight."

The unusual serenity and the unofficially assumed 'truce' justified the risk of Robertson and me leaving the area. ROK Toshi knew our projected location and would be Richard's runner if we were needed back in a hurry. Richard deliberated.

"Okay, but stay alert. If the situation changes here I'll fire a red flare—then you guys hightail your asses back!" We nodded.

As we departed ROK Tom and 'Big Stoop' Ken dictated their terms of negotiation: Robertson and I were to just remain silent, listen and not speak.

Amazingly, we remained unseen and unchallenged by any trigger happy guards behind our lines and those of the South Koreans as we seeped through blind spots towards our destination. Two hours passed before we reached the rendezvous point and pulled ourselves up to the snow-covered crest. I posted Tom close to the seemingly abandoned Chinese bunker just ahead, in case of treachery or other surprises. Its firing ports were blocked with burlap sacks and the thick woolly hides that hung in the doorway concealed its smoky interior. We walked in and a miniscule fire eerily cast our shadows wide across the bullet-nicked timbers and reflected off the skin and inscrutable Mongoloid eyes of the six seated men who greeted us with perfunctory bows. They had the alertness of Doberman Pinschers and evaluated our every move. We bowed no lower than they had then sat cross-legged beside them around the warming fire. I placed my sword on the floor, with the handle out of reach to my right, the *Samurai* gesture of trust.

None wore a regulation uniform and their stained woolly yak parkas showed no rank or insignia. Two wore large Mongolian herdsmen-type hats and sported long stringy mustaches. Each had a curved dagger in his belt. Their weapons were Thompsons, burp guns and pistols. One had a nasty scar running from the corner of one droopy eye to his partially snarled lip. I inwardly smiled towards 'Big Stoop' Ken, who looked as defenseless as Shirley Temple seated among them: *MGM couldn't have cast this better, its right out of Fu Manchu. With a platoon of guys like these we could win the war in about a month.*

We intently listened through the play of flickering shadows when any one of the weathered Koreans spoke in their hushed guttural tones; and the light drumming of distant artillery added an indefinable conspiratorial flavor all its own. Twenty minutes had elapsed before Ken signaled it was time to leave—empty-handed. Outside he mimed the action of a firing squad and labored to translate our host's justified fear of being charged with desertion. They correctly surmised that we lacked the rank to alter that fate.

I joked as we grasped at sapling trees to slow our slippery slide down the snow impacted slope. "Maybe we should have asked to join their outfit?"

Robertson mumbled. "We had our chance, Robert, back in '49, when we could have used up our accrued furlough time and gone to China and helped Chiang Kai-shek."

Thinking back, I wished we had. A hundred dollar bribe to any

Shiogama smuggler ship would have gotten us there. I speculated that Chiang might have even made us captains and that we'd have lived the good life on Formosa; and hopefully been at the mercy of some of those great looking Chinese women.

He laughed. "Anyway, if we don't get some replacements soon I'm going to start taking prisoners…they might join us."

I laughed and asked if he knew about the Koreans who got captured in German uniforms during the battle for Normandy? He shook his head. "They'd been pressed into the Jap army to fight in China, like 'Big Stoop,' then when they got captured by the Russians in Manchuria, they made them fight the Germans, who in turn captured them and made them fight against the Americans."

Robertson laughed. "Now that's *karma*."

Lieutenant Walters greeted me the next morning. "Battalion has rejected your '*Hatasashi*' Peace Plan, Mercy, but you've been promoted to sergeant and Richard to sergeant first class."

Robertson, worth more than all the company NCOs combined, was upgraded to corporal. When I told him, he stoically smiled at the news. "If I have to ask for a promotion, then I don't want it."

I commiserated. "Yeah, and to think they made 'Bug-out' Wassick a master sergeant and all he does is carry ammo between the battalion supply and the company, which is a buck private's job."

The night of the Chinese attack on the flanking 19th ROK infantry brought Richard to my foxhole. "I think we've got a Gook patrol down below making a recon."

I read his mind. "And…" I asked.

He looked surprised. "And I want you to run a one-man patrol down the hill to see if they're behind us. If I send somebody else it will look like I'm playing favorites." Richard was always more of a "by the book" soldier than me, whereas I was liable to compromise and he wasn't. I smirked and returned at dawn with my report. "I ran into a Fox Company patrol. They were burning down several village houses with caches of rice and barley. None of us saw a Chink."

I shared Richard's binoculars and watched a 1st Battalion combat patrol being pushed back down from the division's nemesis, Hill 584.

He casually remarked, "I just heard that some nearby village came down with a bad case of smallpox."

The swaying head of 'Voodoo-woman' immediately jumped to mind. "Which village?"

He pointed on his map. "It's Somhamni… why?"

I lied. "No particular reason." *I wonder if that bitch had any red*

259

blotches under that hairdo. What did I do to earn this karma, to get killed in war by small pox? I wouldn't even get a Purple Heart and mostly because I didn't want to hurt somebody's feelings?

Richard talked about a nearby ROK headquarters that was overrun and nearly wiped out the previous night. "If I were at battalion during a raid like that I'd grab two clerks by their collars as shields and when I got out I'd put myself in for a Bronze or Silver Star, depending on how heavy they were." I laughed and he continued. "Speaking of grenades, you'd jump on one to save Lieutenant Herbert's life, wouldn't you?"

I laughed louder. "I've seen it done in the movies and it's a surefire ticket for a CMH, but…"

He cut me off. "But you wouldn't have a chance, because that son of a bitch would've pushed you on it before it went off!" His look turned instantly somber. "You can read all about this in that new field manual 'FM-368,' [the military code number for a mental discharge]: its entitled, Officers, Grenades, and You!"

For two hours Richard stayed on point as the platoon led the company across the silent moon-bathed terrain. Then he was racing towards me and looking backwards in his stampede through the underbrush before he breathlessly slid to my side. "Christ, he was over six feet tall!"

I peer over my front sights. "A Chink?"

He snapped back. "No, the goddamned snake that popped up in front of me! He looked me right in the eyes!" He laughed. "After we came face to face and scared the hell out of each other we simultaneously took off in different directions. The damn thing flashed up the hill with his head turned around looking at me, as I did with him!"

I did a quick impression of Sherlock Holmes. "Elementary, my dear Watson, his actions mean that he's not seen a human in the area."

At dawn the regiment closed in on the icy southern banks of the Han River. George Company stopped on a hillside near a patch of twenty Chinese who'd been killed in an earlier air strike. I compulsively explored their eyes for indications of what they saw and felt at death: *Hmmm… Fifty-calibers really do a mean job; those four seem to have more surprise than terror in their eyes. He looks like he's expecting something, but what? Was there much pain? Did they see God, or Buddha? Is that regret or sorrow I see in those eyes?*

The tip of my bayonet rolled the last body over, which was face-down at the tail of a two-squad column. His complete interior from head to toe was hollowed out like a child's thin-waxed mask, without a trace of blood, flesh, or bone: *Maybe a rocket cleaved him in half, or he was suctioned out by napalm. They're all in column, close together, looks like they never knew a jet was streaking in behind them.* I caught up with the platoon a mile ahead and Richard pointed to another batch of seventy dead and said, "When I saw their hair glistening in the sun I thought it was either axle-grease or that they were Italians. I threw a rock and a million shiny flies took off in all directions." He'd interrupted the insects' larvae laying process in the severed and blood-spattered Chinese skulls.

The next morning I glimpsed our new company commander as we closed in on the last ridge overlooking the Han River. He was an animated WWII retread, a Reserve captain named Doherty. Minutes later a few artillery rounds fell short and exploded on the nearby flank. I walked over and found Murr retching beside a G.I. whose near severed head had splattered gobs of gore onto his face and chest.

Murr was gagging on the phone to battalion. "God damn it, lift that fucking fire! For Christ's sake, lift it!"

I drove the dead soldier's bayonet-fixed rifle into the ground and rested his shredded helmet over the butt plate. I felt as though I was in a movie I'd seen a hundred times as I looked at the nearby mesmerized G.I.s, yet the gesture seemed strangely hollow. An hour later I was disappointedly told we were going into reserve.

The following morning ROK Richard approached with two aged and bowing civilians who nervously begged that our daylong artillery barrage of their distant village be lifted. I got a major at battalion on the phone.

"Sir, we're only inflicting causalities on old men, women and children. Let me run a patrol there and check it out."

His reply was cold. "Request denied."

I looked back into the men's tired anxious faces and for the first time felt a twinge of shame. I bowed my apologies and compliments for their bravery. Not an hour had passed before ROK Richard reported to me in mumbled Japanese. He was tongue-tied and near impossible to interpret as he pointed to a line of G.I.s beside a hut in the nearby village. Uncertain of what was said I shrugged and walked away; and only later learned that those soldiers were taking sexual turns with an unwilling girl of thirteen. Tormented over my missed translation, I wasn't sure if ROK Richard believed I'd actually misunderstood or was just being indifferent to the suffering of his people.

Had I known, I wouldn't have hesitated to give them what they deserved, and the Army would have no other political alternative than to support whatever force I used—maybe. I apologized for the crime and also my linguistic failures to ROK Richard who once said, "I thank great American Army who rid my country of Japanese." *What would General Yang do in my place? Commit hara-kiri perhaps for failure and loss of face?*

The next day, in the regimental rest area in the village of Wanchan, the platoon moved into a complex of three large huts. I had our CP room swept, mopped and again decorated the wall. I tried to wrench a seemingly prized brass decanter from the hands of our scowling host, thinking it would make a great coffee urn. This caused a moment of comic relief for the platoon.

ROK Richard bowed and whispered, "Sergeant-san, is chamber pot." *How American, we take over his house and leave him without a pot to piss in. Well, I really didn't want coffee anyway.*

Later that afternoon a radio's symphonic chords of *Clair De Lune* led me into a hut where a half-dozen homesick G.I.s sat teary-eyed and staring onto the floor. I heard Richard's laughter ring out from the next hut over, above the hoots and howls of his captive audience, who were old timers and some new replacements. They applauded his battle pantomime which included sound effects of weapons, rockets and planes—all depicting how he 'single-handedly' took Hill 584.

Richard (left) and a G.I. (right) whom Richard accidentally shot in the leg while at a rest area.

Richard had just snatched and twirled his pistol up from the floor, which then accidently fired the moment I stepped through the door. His face registered more shock and surprise than all the ten men that silently sat closely circled along the walls, except for the young corporal on his immediate right.

He turned ashen-white and softly moaned as his hands coursed his body. "I'm alright... I think..." All agreed that the spec of blood on his shinbone meant the slug had only nicked him. Miraculously, it missed everyone else in the tightly packed room. We all searched for the bullet as he spoke.

"I'll tell the medics I bumped my shin on a doorway. By the way, Mercy, I'm glad I wasn't in that Chink bunker!" The laughter stopped minutes later when Captain Doherty apprehensively stuck his head through the door. I thought it odd that he didn't smell the burnt cordite. "Did that shot come from in here?"

Richard answered. "No, sir." The others nodded.

An hour later the captain glared at him and waved the medic's report that showed the elusive slug had slid down beneath the skin of the soldier's shinbone and came to rest upright on the bridge of his foot. "Don't you ever, ever, lie to me again!"

Richard was humbled. "Sir, I had taken the clip out of the piece and placed them both on the floor to my left, which I usually do when I'm socializing. Whoever was sitting there reinserted it, without my knowledge."

The captain was even more vexed the next morning on seeing 'Big Stoop' Ken between the two MPs who apprehended him on a visit to a woman in a distant village. I thought the odds were a thousand to one against Ken being stopped and questioned by MPs. So I wasn't worried about the bogus pass I'd given him with the captain's rank and signature. I escaped a court martial because the captain would soon need the cooperation of his unfailing assault platoon, yet I was warned to never try anything like that again.

Boredom and inactivity initiated a new eating binge among the ROKs. Each day they gulped down great quantities of *kimche* and rice between our three regular hot meals. The pathology proved contagious to all but one of the thirty new replacements that battalion had just sent down. His name was Kim and Han had personally brought into the compound. He said he'd served with the Japanese Imperial Marines and wanted to fight the Chinese again. I was suspicious: *He looks like he might have seen some combat but I'll keep an eye on him.*

The platoon's added poundage showed in Richard's ire during an open ranks inspection.

"If these guys get any more inflated we'll have to tie strings around their necks and float them up to the line like balloons."

We drew sporadic jeers from the ever-slovenly E and F Company troops on our morning two-hour runs and staged assaults on the nearby slopes.

"Hey, Mercy, what are you going to do when this war's over?"

I paused. "Wait for the next one! Unlike you people, this is the only platoon in the whole regiment that has never, ever bugged out!"

One afternoon we had the platoon up on a hillock for target practice and had laid out staggered lines of empty five-gallon cans. These stretched across three hundred yards of open rice paddies, but not once, in the hundred rounds fired did we see a single splash.

Richard moaned as we stood in speechless disbelief. "Maybe they're aiming for something in Sumatra?"

After another thousand rounds were fired and no improvement noted we returned to the CP. That night Richard expressed our collective sentiment. "Take my word for it, the Commies can't win, because now there is absolutely no doubt about it. God is on our fucking side!"

The next morning we posted the platoon around the frozen paddies of a flanking village where C-47s would drop supplies of rations and ammunitions. We were to guard against theft by villagers and keep the parachutes out of the hands of G.I.s who'd been cutting them up for decorative scarves and other improper uses that caused a serious shortage of cargo chutes in Korea. Robertson deployed the troops and Richard, ROK Tom, Han and I drove towards the people gathered in the village square. The setting humorously reminded me of a scene from the film *The Moon is Down* where a Nazi officer threatened a Norwegian town with executions if they protested his orders. An irresistible urge compelled me up onto the hood of our halted Jeep.

"*Hostages vill be taken unt shot at zee first zign of disorder or attempted zeft of* Wehrmacht *zupplies*. Is this clear?" Han stared as blankly as the uncomprehending villagers who shuffled, kowtowed and bobbed back with apprehensive smiles.

Richard grinned. "If the Italians drove the Germans nuts imagine what these guys could have done to them."

The drone of C-47s overhead drowned out my next monologue. We tossed out green smoke grenades so the planes could judge the gusting winds that scattered the dropped cargo far and wide. A thin young man snatched a bundle far afield and ignored my shout and warning shots. The next carbine round brought him down near the door of his hut. The fifteen-year-old boy sat quietly with the C-ration case on his lap while his tearful mother stood behind him clapping her hands in Buddhist prayer. The bullet missed the intended fatal mark by an inch. The boy's frightened eyes were filled with fear of death and mine with deep regret.

"*Naza irasshai masen tomeru ka* [Why didn't you stop]?" Han dared not complain when he arrived and then summoned an ambulance. I returned to the DZ.

Lieutenant Walters, promoted to executive officer, joined us over a chicken dinner in our CP. "Men, will you give me the same commitment, loyalty and dedication that you gave to Buckley, Barszcz and Dannucci?"

I responded rashly. "Yes, sir! If there's a tough job and you need somebody to make *Banzai*, you can count on us." I was surprised how empty my words sounded.

Walters left with a smile that wasn't reflected in the face of my brother and Robertson who then asked, "Why should we always be leading the attacks? Let the G.I. platoons take their turn at it for a while."

I filled our cups with the remaining saké. "Why not volunteer? They'll order us up front anyway, right?" We shifted the conversation to whether we should extend our duty tours for another year and what might happen to the ROKs if we didn't. We agreed that the foremost patriots were ROK Richard, Tom and Ken. The others were savvy enough to survive under any regime—other than Japanese. Our thirty-odd new replacements were less trained and enthusiastic than our original lot, and we couldn't be sure what they'd do against determined Chinese resistance. Robertson offered a plan.

"If the next Chinese offensive pushes us off the peninsula we'll form them up into a guerrilla band. This isn't a great war, but it's the only one we got, so whatever you guys want to do is okay with me."

The two weeks spent in reserves could have been less boring had we known about the nightly movies shown somewhere in the regimental area and of the available hot showers and new fatigues. During that time twelve general courts martial were held for the crime of desertion, a practice so pathetically commonplace that many NCOs didn't even bother to report it to their company commanders. They in turn could no longer immediately confine a guilty soldier unless charge sheets had been signed and approved by the regimental commander. In some cases, men convicted by special court martial were given a second chance, in lieu of a light six month sentence, if they promised not to desert again. So a good liar got his first desertion free.

Only the most flagrant violators were ever tried. A case in point was that of a Lieutenant Leon Gilbert, a black platoon leader in the 1st Battalion of the 24th Regiment, 25th Division. When ordered to attack an enemy position in the vicinity of Masan he refused on the indefensible grounds that it endangered his and the lives of his men. His court martial death sentence was later commuted to twenty years, then to seventeen, but eventually he served only five years before being released with a Dishonorable Discharge. Political pressure from various coalitions had intervened.

Things were a little different in WWII where there was only one known summary execution of an American soldier for desertion and that was the case of Pvt. Eddie Donald Slovik. General Eisenhower's firing squad put him to death for his blatant desertions and his written refusal to return to the line even if given another chance, which he was. His execution drastically cut down the growing desertion rate in the ETO [European Theater of Operations].

Despite the specifications of the Uniform Code of Military Justice the ultimate penalty was never applied during the Korean War. This and the Officer Corps' failure to enforce a stricter code of discipline contributed greatly to the American Army's overall poor performance, which did not bode well for the future.

I called together 'Big Stoop' Ken, Tom and ROK Richard and told them we three decided to stay in Korea for another year of war. Surprisingly all nodded in agreement as ROK Richard spoke. "Maybe is better if *Sahji* go home." Slighted, I repeated the story to my brother and Robertson later that night. We half joked about joining the French Foreign Legion to fight in North Africa or Vietnam. That night I had disturbingly lucid dreams and shared them with the same three ROKs in the morning.

"Tomorrow I will be hit by a grenade."

ROK Richard asked, "You die, *Sahji-san*?" Their eyes searched mine.

"No, only wounded." I paused: *Strange. Like Sergeant Jackson at the Naktong River, I'm not frightened and have no desire to escape. It's inevitable.* That night, as Richard and Robertson slept, I polished my 'last round' and sharpened my sword by candlelight: *What will tomorrow bring?*

After breakfast the platoon was ready to move out on General Ridgway's new battle order, codenamed "Operation Ripper." Three new replacements were missing, having deserted during the night. Not even Robertson's murderous eyes could coerce Ken into confessing whatever he knew and my sixth sense proved elusive as to what direction they might have gone. There was no time to launch a patrol to find and then execute them before the assembled platoon as an object lesson.

Hungerford bellowed from the road. "George Company, saddle up!" My mind scrambled. *We might find them yet.*

CHAPTER 32

You'll Remember This Night

We marched first then rode until 1800 hrs. As we leapt from our truck the driver shouted, "Give 'em Hell!"

Ahead, Superfortresses hit strategic targets, while B-26s and Navy night fighters struck CCF front line positions north of the Han River where heavy enemy tank traffic was noted on the Kumhua-Chunchon road. Somewhere ahead were twelve fresh Chinese divisions with cavalry along with some reconstructed NK infantry formations. The objective of the division's three-prong attack was to kill as many NKs and Chinese as possible, secure an area known as the Chunchon and seize intact the dam at the Chongpyong Reservoir. This would put UN Forces just ten air miles from the 38th Parallel.

The regimental column moved down the straight narrow road between tall flanking hills that thundered and shook under our artillery's incessant barrages. Their showering sparks of burning iron made crimson the darkened skies and smoke shells masked to enemy eyes our approach to the LD. Near 2300 hours Lt. Walters pointed to his map.

"Take your platoon up to Ockchon-ni and reconnoiter the village, which will be the jump off point for the attack. The regiment will hold here along the road and whatever size Chinese unit you run into, take them on! We'll be up as quick as we can."

We drew some ineffectual mortar fire during the predawn hours but found nothing significant before we'd returned to the regimental column then led it back to the intersecting roads at Ockchon-ni. Soon spearheading Patton tanks with painted tiger faces on their bows were all around. They lurched over paddy walls and spewed out 90mm rounds at enemy bunkers on near and distant hills. Heavy mortars and artillery rained down in support of our battalion's attack. Troops moved through the smoke-shrouded fields and fought with rifles and bayonets against the Chinese rear-guard battalions. I screamed just to see if I could hear my own voice through the melding din and clamor of clanking armor, diving bombers, shells exploding and machinegun and rifle fire—I couldn't.

I looked up from a roadside ditch and there, a few yards away, was General Matthew Ridgway wearing his iconic grenades and pistol. Flanked by a phalanx of staff officers two rows deep and a retinue of Thompson-carrying MP guards as he watched his infantry swarm over the hills; a soldier's soldier at home in his element: *He's right in the middle of it, and those itchy trigger finger MPs should be looking to the flanks, and not our own troop.*

Our platoon stood congested in the narrow alleyway where I led them, between swatches of shanty houses that seemed to give some cover while I awaited word from Richard to move. Minutes later a powerful premonition compelled me to shout out. *"Hashiru, eki masho, hashiru* [Run, let's go, run]!" Only seconds later after most of us turned into a passageway did a Chinese 120mm mortar exploded in the very center of where we'd stood shoulder to shoulder; and left behind between the blood-smeared walls the smoldering legless torsos of the three soldiers who hadn't rapidly complied. I pondered the origins of my inner voice not knowing which deity to thank: *That would have taken out the whole platoon! I wonder where that FO is.*

We reached the far side of the village where Robertson and Richard stood looking down into a trench at a fear-maddened Fox Company G.I. He hid out after his company come under mortar attack and dug into the ground with his bare hands. He tearfully screamed. "I can't...I won't do it...I won't!"

Richard smirked. "He probably knows what we're having for lunch." Then he ordered me to scout out a farmhouse on our flank where I crashed through a plywood-covered septic tank filled hip deep with putrid human waste. Helmets full of nearby ditch water couldn't eliminate the stench: *The Chinks will smell me coming for miles.* My nervousness amused Robertson who forcefully brushed the sleeve of his jacket and produced the distinctive *swooshing* sound of an incoming mortar round. I hesitated to dive in any direction.

I soon passed some Fox Company mortar men that stared blankly at an unconscious boyish Chinese soldier. Their NCO kicked aside his cap and weapon then barked, "Either kill the bastard or bandage him up." Doing neither they followed the sergeant back to their 60mm tube emplacements.

I knew, standing alone beside him, that I wouldn't follow my first faintly felt subliminal inclination to bayonet his bare chest that showed no wounds beneath his open quilted jacket—I lacked the hatred to do it. My next incongruous thought surprised me even more: *No. He looks about fifteen—and helpless. If I knew a little bit about medicine maybe I could...Strange, maybe that last dream is making you feel this way, knowing you might die... or... or what?*

My mind, divided, was still clouded as I caught up with Richard and Robertson in the growing tempo of fire where a G.I. approached guarding two POWs. I immediately interrogated the frightened duo in Japanese as I clutched my sheathed sword and overrode their guard's objections— thinking that my attitude and pose might ignite some bad memories from the Japanese occupation. It only drew blank stares.

Bilingual ROK Richard did better. "*Sahji-san*, they say, know very little." My mind reeled through half a dozen films and found the one it needed. I lead the eldest of the pair behind a boulder and slid a finger across my throat to signal silence. He nodded. I fired a single shot and emerged with the smoking pistol. The young shocked soldier shook like a leaf and the G.I. guard and my squad all stared in silence. ROK Richard questioned him again.

"He say four heavy machineguns ahead. Order hold up American company, get much ammo this morning."

Richard nudged me from the side. "Ask him if he's got any fortune cookies."

Returned from the boulder with the 'dead prisoner,' undisguised tears of joy streamed from his young friend's eyes and both were deeply moved; as were the ROKs when they were led away alive, which confirmed for me what I've always known: there was no fun in inflicting that kind of sickening fear...but had they been the murderous NKs...?

On Richard's orders I scouted ahead with my squad while he took the platoon on a wide sweep around the left flank. A hundred yards on I saw seven Chinese pile caps barely clearing the lip of the low silhouetted bunker's firing pit where they were sitting: *Why didn't they see me? Don't use grenades, might be more of them in the bunker then you'd never get close, surprise them.* I made a lightning dash forward with my M1 raised as laughter trickled from my lips. My sights swept across a masterpiece of demented battle humor. Some earlier passing G.I.s had sculpted a hilarious poker game of five-card draw in which each player held cards that seemed to justify whatever expression death had written upon their faces.

One's unlit cigarette rakishly dangled from his lips as he painfully squinted at a pair of deuces. On his shoulder the head of his partner rested in a frozen scream that could be read as uncontrollable laughter. He'd drawn a full house. The one with an ace-high straight lay spread-eagled, as though shocked into a dead faint. Next a smirking face with a bullet between its crossed eyes had an ace of spades sticking half out of his quilted sleeve. Another quizzically gazed at a worthless hand and the last two scoffed and winced over what the others had drawn: *Christ, and me without my camera!*

I turned towards a barrage of mortar rounds that fell a hundred yards away and emptied a clip into the raised clouds of dust used by the Chinese as an escape shield. Ricochets zinged up around my feet then at the next crest long blasts from a bunker-emplaced machine gun greeted our arrival. We kept the gunner busy while Walters, Richard, and Robertson closed in on both his flanks while his harmless rounds lashed overhead and pressed our frightened replacements face down into the ground.

The half belt of LMG ammo I'd burned into the bunker's firing port momentarily silenced the gun. I deliberately ignored the shouts from Walters and Richard to come forward and that momentary disobedience felt good. I fired off the remaining rounds then moved to within forty yards of the bunker's trench line, and their gun suddenly came to life. It killed three soldiers and shattered the legs of one nearby who screamed and rolled in pain as dusk melded into darkness. When the rest of the company arrived Captain Doherty's voice rang out. "Take the high ground!"

Robertson and Richard tried to flank the momentarily silent bunker as a number of staff officers arrived behind my squad. Amazingly they stood perched shoulder to shoulder on a boulder, in obvious compliance with General Ridgway's order to show courage at the front: *I'd be more impressed if they drew their pistols and joined the assault. Standing bunched up like that could draw in Chink battery fire and get everybody killed.*

I whispered, "Psst, sir! That bunker up there hasn't been cleared."

One officer stoically grunted, "Keep moving, soldier."

A split second later we all leaped for cover to escape the three blue-edged swords of light that wildly slashed mile-long gashes across the murky night sky. The ROKs froze in place and G.I.s dove and shouted "Turn those goddamned things off! Turn them off!"

I turned to Walters, "Why the lights, sir?"

He mumbled. "It's a wartime first. Psych-warfare thinks the Gooks are undernourished and suffer from night blindness, and looking into this glare will blind them further."

I grunted. "And what about our troops?"

He exhaled deeply. "Everybody knows we don't like to fight at night.

This might make it easier."

I smirked. "Yes, providing you don't mind being brightly silhouetted when you get up to move."

Determined Chinese salvos tried to squelch the battalion's lights and drew counter battery fire as we rose up in the welcomed darkness and found all the officers had gone. The platoon stormed the deserted trench and bunker, from where I pointed up thirty yards to the misty crest and whispered to each ROK that passed. "Stay awake, they're still up there."

No one told us that we had no flanking tie-ins and were to be the OP for the company that had quietly pulled back two hundred yards to the higher ground behind us.

Inside the bunker, Robertson looked through the blood-spattered firing port at the ground we'd crossed.

"We'd be dead meat, Boy-san, if the Gooks hadn't pulled out with their KIA and wounded."

The thirty-eight hours we had all gone without food or rest made staying awake difficult in the anesthesia of our cordite-scented chamber. I lay flat clutching my rifle to my chest by the gunnysack-curtained entrance, as did Robertson beside me and also Richard next in line. Reminiscent, I thought, of the reclining granite statues of crusading kings who clutched their swords in a death-like sleep. Later, in the stillest hour, an animal instinct roused me from total oblivion and I heard myself bark, "They're here," as I sprang out and knelt into the firing pit.

I was about to fix my bayonet when the blinding orange blast of a concussion grenade hurled me upward. I didn't know, in my descending somersault to the ground that the scream I'd heard was my own: *The Gooks will be in the trench any minute. Where's my rifle!* Dizzily, I spied Robertson exit the bunker as a soup can size concussion grenade exploded at the level of his chest. It swept him over the parapet wall: *No, he can't be dead!* A heartbeat later the grenade that exploded at Richard's feet launched him, too, over the side, but instinctually I knew he wasn't dead. I marveled at how I miraculously escaped the shrapnel at such close range, as my hands fearfully inched down my thighs: *God! My legs are still there. The Chink must only be a few feet away lying in the dark...why hasn't he shot me? Can't stand up... Where's my goddamned rifle?!*

Silvery flashes from M1 fire pierced the trench's misty darkness where nearby 'Big Stoop' Ken leapt up with a fixed bayonet. A Thompson-sub stitched half a dozen rounds across his chest. Others bodies moaned and fell before the stealthy shadows that had then silently closed in: *The platoon was... too quiet. They might all be dead.* With the strength of desperation I pulled myself over the sandbagged wall and crawled twenty yards down to prop myself up against a severed tree trunk.

I plunged my bayonet into the ground beside me and set out two clips of ammo across my numbing thighs. With pistol in hand I waited and heard the whispers of the Chinese in the trench.

Dinner with the Chinaman.

Without my rifle the unthinkable ran across my mind: *Maybe they'll take prisoners.* I heard my boyhood voice the day that cop chased us across the Idyllwild dunes, "Never surrender!" I suddenly recalled the dream when I was fourteen of the three soldiers under the boxcar, the exploding grenade and the awaited *banzai* charge. Everything was clear: *This is my prophesied destiny. I was meant to die right here where I've always imagined I would. They'll be coming soon, moving on to attack the company. Maybe Richard, Robertson and the whole platoon are already dead? I've got twenty-two rounds for the pistol, I wonder how many I'll get before I'm bayoneted, like Robert Taylor in the film Bataan?*

Unseeing, Robertson staggered blindly down the slope. He finally determined why the darkness was so impenetrable when the finger of his fractured arm probed into the empty blood-caked hollow of one eye He slowly drew his pistol while his fingers pensively probed with dreaded expectation the other splattered socket from where only darkness reigned; and knew what he would do should it prove empty. He had no deity to thank after rubbing clear the coated blood from his one remaining eye. What had saved him from total blindness was the angle at which he held his rifle at High Port; and that the kapok fibers of his shredded jacket had adhered to his many wounds, which kept him from bleeding to death. He staggered and stumbled for two more hours before he reached the battalion aid station. Hard-warring Robertson, as merciless on himself as the enemy, wordlessly remained at the end of a sick call line filled with nicks, sprains and 'duty escapees' until he finally shuffled up to a corporal's reception desk. Johnston, our medic, looked up over the spectral light of his Ronson lamp into the blood dripping empty socket of Robertson's eye and the *one hundred and forty-two* other shrapnel perforations that left his uniform and entire body aglow from head to toe in purple iridescence—then promptly fainted.

I sat transfixed breathing in the sweet scent of wafting cordite, wishing I had an LMG, or at least more pistol ammo; and heard again, too, the melodic voice of Ronald Coleman in *The Light That Failed*: "*Ah, perfume of the queen of battle.*" Then my mind flooded with every recalled cinematic bayoneting scene that ranged between *All Quiet on the Western Front* and *The Sands of Iwo Jima*. I found strength to face the inevitable in a repeated heartfelt mantra: "*You're a soldier... you're a soldier... you're a soldier... die like one!*"

That anxiety was momentarily altered on hearing the faint whisperings from the G.I.s that were advancing up the hill behind me: *Christ, if the Chinks start shooting I'll be caught in between, and even if they don't the G.I.s will fire at anything that moves!*

I felt the throb of twin-ship watching Richard limp on a broken ankle fifty yards off on the flank. With a fixed bayonet he led the skirmish line of G.I.s who followed seventy yards behind. He drew no fire from the bunker where he hoped to find Robertson and me alive before the nervous troops arrived. Fear of 'friendly fire' kept me silent until I heard Johnny Murr's whisper.

"Robert! Robert, where are you?"

I clutched his hand: *God, I never thought I would see him or anybody else again. I wonder, when I do have to die, will all this make it easier?* Johnny moved towards the trench and an NCO's prophetic warning came to mind as two G.I.s put me on their stretcher: "If you get hit, give whatever you have of value to your buddies because you won't have it for long back in the field hospital." I reluctantly surrendered my pistol and brass-knuckled bayonet, but not the Mauser pistol in my jacket pocket. Johnny returned with ten ROKs who survived by having played dead. They carried me two hundred yards down the trail and stopped above a murky ravine, from where the murmurs of Asian voices rose. The ROKs, whispered among themselves and slowly lowered me to the ground before they cautiously inched back up towards the high ground. I was overwhelmed with disillusionment and felt defenseless without my .45 and rifle.

I began repeating my earlier mantra, pointing my .32 Mauser down the draw when I glimpsed our medic Kumasuri step behind the mostly new men with his rifle meaningfully raised. I shouted, "Kumasuri-san, let them run if they want, but leave me rifle." After their brief hoarsely whispered heated exchange they returned and all circled in around me.

"Is OK, *Sahji*, soldier now stay."

Through the near impenetrable darkness of the winding valley rose the sounds of rippling winds that had me imagining the flowing Yangtze River. I whispered: *My troop's faithful, they die with me.* Tense minutes passed before G Company's carrying party emerged through the gloom to stare into the muzzles of our raised weapons. We all sighed with relief.

An hour further on, I bellowed over my aimed pistol at the fifty shadows that darted around the base of the hill. "Halt! Who's there?"

They silently scurried into nearby huts between the pulsating moments of light and darkness that was thrown from fizzling out parachute flares and the shells that exploded along the crest of the encircling hills. They were emblematic of the rumored nightly G.I. desertions—which you'll never see in any movie.

"You're deserters, cowards and traitors! How can you live with yourselves? Soldiers are up there fighting and dying! You'll remember my voice and this night for the rest of your miserable lives!" I'd have given anything for an LMG.

My nervous ROKs tried silencing me for fear of what might occur as we headed for the thin sliver of light escaping from the Aid Station tent. Inside they put me down and grunted a simple farewell then melded back into the night.

The dimly lit interior was packed with harried medics and moaning men and I exchanged a glassy-eyed stare with Kim, our former Imperial Marine replacement. He sat three stretchers away, his right arm severed at the shoulder. Nearby a Korean from another unit sobbed over his lost foot. A burly medic arrogantly struck him hard across the face and shouted, "No cry! You no see G.I. cry!" I gripped the pistol in my pocket: *Should I kill him where he stands?*

I was rattled back to consciousness in the upper litter rack of the ambulance that headed for the field hospital. Below me and across the aisle was a wounded Chinese soldier. Suddenly, in my semi-delirium, I found the Mauser pistol in my hand and an urge in my mind to shoot before sinking into unconsciousness.

The MASH stretcher team carried the Chinese and me to adjacent cots at the far end of field hospital tent and later we silently studied each other with neither enmity nor anger. In the passing hours we wondered whether to smile at each other or not: *Christ...and I wanted to kill him an hour ago.*

My turbulent sleep put me back on the line and I seized the wrist of the hand that was lightly moving across my chest. The nurse's hand dropped the money pouch she'd lifted from my shirt pocket and hurried down the aisle yelling diverting assertions from left to right: "You goddamn phony, looking for sympathy, I've got more important work to do than wait on a moaning fraud like you! There are real wounded men here!"

Too dumbstruck to warn the other semi-conscious soldiers I struggled over whether to wound or kill her with the pistol. The Army, of course, "for the sake of discipline and order," would not forgive the shooting of an officer by an enlisted man—for any reason: *These rear-echelon bastards would general court martial me for sure. Is there not one of these bastards who won't steal, even at Aid Stations and Grave Registration?*

I glimpsed the look of compassion on the Chinese soldier's face. He saw it all and I felt embarrassed for my country and uniform. In his poor but disciplined army she'd be shot. I didn't have the Mandarin words to say "we're not all like her."

Or are we?

The doctors were gone when I came to consciousness in the OR and I drowsily looked up into the hate filled eyes of Nurse 'Deep-pockets.' Her poisonous stare peered over her appropriately worn mask as she busily dressed my wounds. I thought of vulnerable Veronica Lake attending the wounded in *So Proudly We Hail;* and the axiom of a bygone era—"*why can't life be more like the movies?*" My legs felt like shattered glass during the bouncy ambulance ride back to the Pusan Army Hospital the next morning.

The only change I noticed in the main receiving room since last August was the addition of the two fatigue-clad Red Cross Gray-Ladies that joylessly handed out one envelope, one short two-inch pencil and one miniscule sheet of paper to each new arrival. Requests for more were coldly ignored. Undaunted, I foolishly asked for a fresh pack of cigarettes, as mine were crumbled and soggy wet from sweat. Her acidic smile and reply gave credence to all those sordid Red Cross tales the soldiers talked about in WWII. "There are some men here who don't have any, so you'll just have to wait I'm afraid."

The only comfort I felt was the Mauser pistol in my shirt pocket: *They sure are different from the cheery girls in those fund-raising films that pull in countless millions.* I was cursing them and the thieving nurse at MASH when they rolled me into the OR where a doctor greeted with...

"So how'd you get hit soldier?"

I shrugged, "Grenade, sir."

He pulled off my blanket and swore. "God damn it, who treated this wound?"

I answered casually. "The field hospital, sir. Why?"

He huffed, "Because somebody sutured it by running adhesive tape inside and around the open wound. Now lay back, Sergeant, here's where we separate the men from the boys."

I clenched my teeth as he tore off a ten-inch strip of tape dripping blood, flesh and ligaments: *Fucking rear-echelon thieving slut officer! If this were a real goddamned army, a bitch like that would be shot in ten seconds flat.*

I was put aboard the gleaming white hospital ship that sailed for Japan some hours later. I wondered about Richard and Robertson and if there were enough ROKs left to form a platoon when I got back.

CHAPTER 33

Sir, Send Me Back To The Line—Please!

I enjoyed the rays of sun that glimmered through the glass panel slots of the ambulance as our medical convoy tacked through the streets towards Kobe's general hospital. Once inside, a gurney ride down a third floor corridor put me into to the last bed at the far end on the ward, where I secured my automatic in the pillowcase.

It was difficult to get comfortable in the unaccustomed softness of the bed, and I passed the tedious hours hoping the female visitors on the ward would leave. I was determined not to mar my debut back into mixed company by calling for a bedpan and borrowed a crutch from an adjacent bunk then limped towards the latrine. Halfway down the hall I fell then crawled past rows of visiting viewers that either looked askew or cheered me on to my destination. For the first two nights, after 'lights out,' I slept on the more appealing floor. But objecting orderlies ended that Spartan practice.

The doctors' fear of patient addiction limited their use of pain medication, and filled my sweat-drenched nights with chaotic dreams. In one, I'd managed what was impossible do to while awake when seeing myself back in the field. I knelt upon one knee atop my bed and watched the parachute flare that drifted through the illuminated night sky. Then an explosion of orange flame and pain hurled me backwards on the mattress; my eyes followed the hypnotic oscillating swing of the medic's flashlight from beside my bed.

"Wake up," he said. "you're dreaming."

After the next morning's operation they wheeled me back to bed, with the memorabilia shrapnel they'd extracted taped to my chest. I patted the pillow-hidden Mauser then called for my beautiful nurse Kuniko, who quickly brought the food I needed. I rewarded her with a hissed out impression of the sinister villain of Asian films Mr. Richard Loo. "*Domo arigato, Ojosan. Hmmm... Anata-no utsukuski kalada-o imoto imasu* [Thank you, Miss. Hmmmm...You have a very pretty body]."

Her giggles made me laugh. I realized how slight my wounds were as I looked around the ward at the fifteen other G.I.s and wondered how seriously Richard and Robertson had been hit, along with the platoon.

Next morning I greeted the face of an Asian G.I. in the adjacent bed, but he couldn't, or wouldn't, respond. The three LMG rounds he caught in the back left him with half a stomach. I thought he was Japanese, given his profound self-consciousness. Later, a civilian laborer walked in and held his nose to indicate the room needed ventilation. He immediately took this as a comment on his personal hygiene and flushed an angry violent red, all the while ignoring the humorous railings from 'Reb' in the next bed. Reb constantly threw defiant barbs at the medical staff for prognosticating his impending death.

"By God, I tell ya, I ain't gonna die and I ain't lettin' no damn carpet-bagging Yankee gummint cheat me outta ma combat pay!" At fifty extra tax-free dollars a month the sum came to $350.00. A week later he was yelling more defiantly and twice as loud when the nurses wheeled him out to the infamous "Blue Room" sanctuary the hospital reserved for those at the brink of imminent death. "God damn it I ain't gonna die! This here gummint ain't gonna rob me!" We laughed and applauded our support, then fell silent when the nurses returned and wordlessly stripped his bunk of pillows and sheets. *How can he be dying and have all that energy?* Five days later we applauded again when against all medical odds he, limped back into his old bed. "Goddamn, didn't I tell you'll I weren't gonna die! Now they gotta gimme ma combat pay! Alleluia! Do I have a witness?" He damned near made a believer out of me.

I turned down the alcohol the walking wounded smuggled in nightly, after the doctor gave me the results of my blood test: Yellow jaundice; Malaria; hookworms and a tapeworm.

I made the mistake of telling Joe, in the bed directly across the aisle about the rat I saw climb up the draw-cords of our shared Venetian blinds the night before. To calm his provoked fears I flashed my pistol with a promise to keep watch and kill it should it return. The good deed didn't go unpunished. I was on quasi-guard duty until near dawn and told the doctor on his morning rounds about the rat being as large as a cat. He smiled and said that I'd just dreamed it

As he left, the prettier of his two American nurses remained and I rolled over for my birdbath. She nodded at my pajama drawstrings. "Is that thing loaded?" I arched an eyebrow and she pointed to the Mauser. My ego was deflated. I put the weapon in the pillowcase and waited with lascivious expectation for her massage. "Don't worry, there's nothing in the chamber."

Her warm fingers and soothing voice convinced me to surrender the pistol into her safekeeping, even though my trust in officers had diminished and I felt uncomfortable by being totally disarmed for the first time in years.

The next day a visiting Red Cross lady oddly asked to hear any 'unusual experiences' I might have had in Korea. I overrode my instincts and naively told her the innocent tale of the three girls who hid from our Happy Valley guerrilla patrol last winter. Her cold suspicious eyes beneath pencil thin brows grew more accusingly severe before she loudly hissed out her own creation of the story's ending: "Then you raped them, didn't you?" The piercing charge turned the heads of a few nearby men and catapulted her onto an illusionary moral high ground. "You're all alike! *We* know what you *men* have been doing out there, and don't you think we don't!"

The voice of a soldier pierced the long silence. "Hey, Sarge, I think the bitch wants you to fuck her!"

Another yelled, "She's a goddamned liberal who's shacked up with some commie Gook slime."

Someone else threw in a medical evaluation. "The sick bitch looks like a walking dose of clap to me!"

Her face became a kaleidoscope of burning rage when she screamed, "H-h-h-o-o-o-w-w d-a-a-a-r-e y-o-o-u-u-u!" before hoots and jeers drove her from the room.

Another Gray-Lady probed the ward the next day jangling her collection jar, reminiscent of the dowdy Red Cross women, or their impersonators, who nightly preyed on the easy-going servicemen along wartime Broadway. A nearby soldier struggled to reach the billfold on his night table while her hand grandly fluttered toward the few beds where Monopoly boards, cards and old magazines were strewn. "These things cost money, you know."

Joe, across from me, wished his thrown pinochle deck that splintered across her back was a grenade. The checkerboard I hurled zoomed at her as though it were a knife. A victory shout rang out after a dozen more thrown articles had ignominiously driven her off the ward. Minutes later a flushed-face nurse steamed in with her fists clenched to her hips.

"I demand an explanation!" We stared in blank silence while she

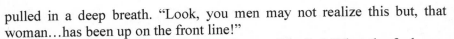

pulled in a deep breath. "Look, you men may not realize this but, that woman...has been up on the front line!"

The least dumbfounded of us spoke up. "Really? What the fuck was she carrying, a BAR?"

The nurse huffed into an about-face and marched out.

Next morning I anxiously watched as the doctor cupped the heel of my foot in his palm and nodded reassuringly as he slid the inflexible leg towards the edge of the bed. He winked at his cortege and dropped the leg to uncongeal the ligaments, then quickly wheeled off to the next patient. I groaned. "G-o-d-d-a-m-n it, s-i-r-r-r!"

Later, Kuniko warmly whispered into my ear. "Is *breakfas-tu*, Bobbie-san."

Gorgeous Kuniko, most favored in the pantheon of Japanese nurses, tactfully avoided my lovesick stare. I professed vows of eternal love over the food tray, and tried to innocently pull her into bed. The tray dropped and she fled in seeming shock. Minutes passed and she returned with an angry American nurse captain and her staff by her side.

"Don't you *ever* dare try anything like that again with any of my nurses in this hospital. Is that clear?"

Seditious hormones overwhelmed my hapless eyes and logic, too, while they scanned the captain's attractive body from head to toe. I quickly gambled that a humorous impersonation of Cary Grant might lessen my chances of being court martialed for gross insubordination. She flicked her eyebrow and sailed out of the room.

I walked without a cane by month's end and found myself on the hospital's isolated roof looking down at the evening crowds that flooded the streets. Then I reminiscently struck endless books of matches, recalling the adrenal rush that came with the enemy fire that would normally have followed. I was 'homesick' for war, without which life seemed so empty and meaningless: *What will I do when it ends? And if I leave the Army, where will I go, and what will I do? Maybe become a cop...or a soldier of fortune?*

In the morning I sat near the roped-off officers section in the hospital cafeteria and heard the snickers of a gangly young second lieutenant a few feet away. As he spoke, a doctor got up and left the table. "God damn, you should have seen that damn EM jump when I popped out from behind the door and he saw I was an officer. He damn near shit! I stood him at attention with his face to the wall for a half-hour for failing to salute me!" His laughing spasm blinded him to the two other embarrassed doctors that silently departed an adjoining table. The self-possessed lieutenant turned to leave and looked down at the enlisted men's tables with an upper-classmen's sneer. His message was clear. "You can never be one of us."

I gestured to a nearby NCO. "Who is that jerk?"

He moaned. "He's the goddamn hospital's security officer, some punk ROTC college kid."

I followed a G,I.'s direction to find the PX and walked through the hospital's main door without a second thought about my institutional-styled pajamas, seedy knee-length bathrobe and cloth slippers until I found myself out on the main thoroughfare. The steely-eyed Japanese security guard I surprised was decked out in his former Imperial army cap and forcefully shoved my chest. "No... You G.I., go back!" Four years of occupational duty put a disbelieving glare in my eyes and a challenge in his as he drew and raised his club as though it were a sword.

MacArthur's 1945 edict blared in my ears. A Judo throw sent him onto the hood of a parked car under a rain of profanity that drove him back into the building; while I fantasized how many rounds I'd have pumped into him as an MP, were it only one year back in time. Nearby two bespectacled clerks at the curb shook their disapproving heads. Times had changed, but not my growing contempt for the rear echelon.

The security officer's orderly woke me from my noontime nap and I reported, as ordered, to the contemptuous lieutenant who sneered, "Stand at attention in the presence of an officer!"

I attempted logic. "Sir, I'm doing the best I can, my legs are still too swollen. I just came out of surgery."

He screamed, "ATTENTION! Why did you attack my guard?"

My explanation amplified his rage and he incredulously proclaimed with conviction, "The Japanese are not a warlike race and its people like you who make them hate us!"

I chose my words carefully. "Perhaps if the lieutenant had a map, sir, he would allow me to point out a few spots he might not have heard of: Manchuria, Nanking, Hong Kong, Borneo, Pearl Harbor; Bataan, Corregidor, Guadalcanal, Guam, Saipan, Okinawa and Iwo Jima?"

He turned an apoplectic purple. "I'm going to court martial you for insubordination! Get back to your ward and consider yourself under arrest!"

Later, a captain wearing a Combat Infantry Badge and two rows of South Pacific ribbons stood beside my bunk and asked what happened.

"Sir, has everybody forgotten the death marches, the bayoneting, the beheadings, the people buried alive? That guard was one of *them*."

He nodded knowingly. "I feel the same way. I fought the bastards in the Philippines and I know who and what they are. Instead of a court martial would you accept a one day restriction to bed?"

I felt betrayed by the Army and continued. "I could make a big issue of this, sir, contact the press or a congressman. Imagine the newspaper headlines, with a file photo of me marching with my twin back into Taejon where so many atrocities had taken place. It would make great reading, sir. I can just see it now: *'Lieutenant forced wounded G.I. to stand at attention while shrapnel wounds bleed following assault by a former Jap soldier.'* The civilians and congress would really love that, sir. Maybe this could get as big as the Patton incident."

The captain lowered his eyes to half-mast. "That's all true, Sergeant, but it would only hurt the Army and I'd bet my Combat Infantry Badge that you wouldn't want to give those bastards that kind of ammo, would you?"

I was touched. "Ok, sir, as a favor to you, I accept the bed restriction."

Days later my brother walked onto the ward and I smiled. "Richard, what a surprise to see you here; and in a class A uniform, too."

He laughed. "Yeah, they're shipping me back to the States."

I paused. "How bad were you hit that night?"

He grinned. "Fortunately, the Gooks were throwing concussion grenades and I only got a broken ankle. If they'd been using ours we wouldn't be here. They sent me to the hospital in Osaka and my malaria broke out again. I got into a little trouble there too. I saw some overstuffed medic slap a G.I. who'd asked for some medication and I called him on it. He turned around and slapped me. I knocked the bastard senseless and in the morning I had to report to a captain who was wearing one lonely Meritorious Service Ribbon. He said, 'Not everyone can be a combat soldier.' I looked at his shirt and said 'I see that, sir.' Then the *shmuck* gave me the big threat: 'I'm sending you back to the line.' I laughed and thanked him and told the *putz* that's just where I wanted to be. He was dumbfounded."

I asked what happened next. "I wasn't back in the company a week before they gave me my orders and I thought I'd stop off to visit Robertson up in Tokyo. He looked like something right out of *The Mummy's Curse*, all bandaged up from head to toe, except for the mouth and his one good eye. So I took him out on the town, glucose bottle, wheelchair and all. We went club jumping along the *Ginza* and got blind drunk. We even got into a verbal fight with some Japs and a couple of MPs. Robertson was feeling no pain by the time I got him back to the hospital area. That's when he says, 'this calls for a final *banzai* charge, just like the old days.' So I wheeled him out of the dark at 20 knots and he threw the empty saké and beer bottles he had in his lap as grenades against the hospital wall; as we closed in screaming, *Mansai! Mansai! Mansai!* Then, as planned, I left him to be 'captured' by the team of security guards and irate medics that came running out."

As Richard and I spoke, neither of us knew that the gods were not yet quite through with Robertson. Much of his body cast showed the cracks and strain of their night on the *Ginza*, so the medics fitted him with a new coat of plaster. His freewheeling Japanese gurney attendant, like the one that came running from the opposite direction at equally high speeds, crashed head-on in the corridor. Thrown to the floor his wet cast shattered and had to be replaced again. The doctors figured he was a liability and got him aboard the next four-engine Super Constellation that was headed for the States. Thirty other seriously wounded, mostly amputees and their four nurse staff were on board. The plane came in too low on its approach to the short runway on Midway Island and struck an embankment. The ship skidded in on its belly in a shower of sparks and flames. All the traction-suspended patients flew into a jumbled heap against the forward bulkhead before the smoldering plane skidded to a stop at the far end of the field.

Emergency crews, fearful of combustion quickly carried the traumatized and immobile wounded to safety. Robertson could do nothing when one gliding seagull from a circling flock of hundreds nested on his forehead; where it remained for the long hours he lay roasting in the merciless tropical sun. He eventually got to San Francisco.

Richard told me another story. "I was in ranks with the battalion for a decoration ceremony and surprised when the Adjutant called out 'Sergeant Robert Mercy, front and center.' I just automatically stepped out and took your place."

I paused. "What for?"

He smiled. "For the Silver Star you earned at Uijongbu." That came as news to me. Richard continued. "It was for crawling up to the Chink's main line and stopping them with grenades from building up a line of fire; then voluntarily staying behind for almost an hour to cover the platoon's escape; and knocking off some Gooks in the process. It was a lot to write up, so we shortened the process and just said that you charged a Chink MG with grenades." I laughed and he went on.

"When we were dismissed one of those fuckin' old time company NCOs sneered 'nobody believes you did that shit, Mercy,' so I laughed and said that's what I expected to hear from a rear-echelon non-combatant, loudmouthed, son of a bitch like him."

I asked Richard about the platoon. "The ROKs have been disbanded and those left after Operation Ripper are laborers in the G.I. platoons; and they're not a very happy lot."

Richard left and I was depressed over the missed citation ceremony, another lifelong fantasy gone anti-climatic.

The next morning the doctor called me to his office and I met two CID agents that wanted help in an investigation. *Maybe they want me to uncover some corruption or black marketing here in the hospital. Or maybe it's the pistol I gave to that nurse?* "How can I assist?"

They exchanged successful smiles. "We want you to keep an eye on a guy in your ward. He's in the bed directly across from you, Joe?"

I stared at them blankly. "Why, what has he done?"

They sidestepped the question. "We need the name, rank and description of all the people who'd visited him since you got here."

I repeated my question.

"He's been dealing in drugs."

So they think I'll spy for them. Maybe if I didn't know the guy. There was a long pause. "I'm sorry, that's not my cup of tea. I'm a rifleman."

Later I was surprised to learn from the doctor that black market drugs had become a major problem for the Army. I was torn between what's good for the service, and betraying a wounded soldier: *But if he's guilty?*

Over the next few days I was aware of being followed: *There's that medic, who always seems to be around wherever I am, but why?*

The heavyset and bespectacled twenty-year-old medic tailed me down a semi-darkened and isolated corridor where I waited in the shadows. I leapt out and grabbed his throat. "What are you up to, and who told you to follow me?"

He was frightened. "Nothing personal, honest, I was just following orders."

I cocked back my fist. "*Whose* orders?"

He snapped a reply. "Okay, okay... Our security officer told me to get anything I could on you, you know, clipping food from the mess hall; stealing, gambling, anything that could get you a court martial!"

I wasn't surprised. I compromised with the medic. "Let's leave it at this, you don't tell him about our conversation and I don't catch you following me again, okay?" We shook hands and went our separate ways: *Now, do I get even with that lieutenant?*

The next evening at midnight I smoked by an open third floor window and by chance spotted the approach of my nemesis officer in the deserted alleyway below. I remembered a certain crime film when I spotted the handles of the heavy trashcan at my side and thought about reaching for its handles with my pocket handkerchiefs. I was stunned by the momentary criminality of my thoughts and banished the provocation from my mind; but couldn't expunge the emptiness of soul I still felt in having killed that farmer at the Nam River.

In the morning I pleaded with my doctor. "Sir, send me back to the line, please. I'll only get into serious trouble if I stay around here."

He studied me in a thoughtful silence: "Okay then, Sergeant, if that's what you want. Good luck in Korea."

I bade farewell to the trusted nurse who returned my Mauser and the guys on the ward; then privately stole a delicious kiss from Kuniko. The ship I boarded that afternoon slipped into Pusan Harbor on the next morning's tide.

CHAPTER 34

The Last Reel

The city crowds had grown and escaped the spectre of being overrun by the Chinese who'd reportedly lost over a million men. This news would have been much more welcome had they been North Koreans who, nevertheless, agreed to attend peace negotiations in the city of Kaesong. The American Army suffered more casualties, too, from the increasingly more accurate Chinese artillery. General MacArthur was being relieved of duty for, I suspect, trying to win the war. And the new draftee soldiers seemed far less promising than the undertrained volunteer army that arrived the year before. The impending ceasefire would lessen their inclinations to take chances. I knew I had also changed as I looked at passing formations of lackluster troops and tanks: *Without Richard and Robertson... all of this isn't quite the same... but maybe when I get closer to the line....*

As our northbound truck halted by a hamlet miles from the front we all got a painful glimpse at the difficult start General Walker's Army integration policy was having; and also the unfathomable depths of our nation's racial tensions. By the roadside, a black soldier acted out his sexual prowess on the willing lips of a shantytown lady while his open rage-filled eyes challenged the troops onboard.

He insolently shouted, "How about that, white boy?"

Someone fired back, "That Gook slut is about the closest thing you'll ever get to anything white, Sambo."

Though the air suddenly thickened with emerging racial enmities neither blacks nor whites unslung their rifles. Another resonant voiced snarled out, "Welcome to the line, white mother-fuckers!"

I reassured the dismayed recruit at my side. "You'll find the Chinese are better mannered."

286

The truck pulled into the 24th Division's repo-depot and two nearby G.I.s feigned drunkenness with raised half-empty bottles and cried, "Y-o-u-'l-l b-e s-o-r-r-y!" It was the perpetual need of the rear to appear battle weary. I reached the 19th Regiment's 2nd Battalion Headquarters and made a request to the S-1 officer, which was more obligatory than heartfelt. "I want to get back into the line, sir."

He smiled. "I'm sorry, Mercy, but you're up for rotation so line duty is out. Besides, after you boys got hit the battalion gave up on the idea of using ROK combat platoons. So, how about you take over our Korean labor battalion? They've got an 80% sick call rate every morning because the NCO who runs the show doesn't really know how to handle them. We could use you, Mercy."

Those carrying parties do get ambushed from time to time, and I'll be able to roam around near the line, so there's a chance for at least one more good firefight.

I drew a Thompson from supply and went to the tent I'd share with two G.I.s and the Korean interpreter who was a clone of the devious Han. At morning roll call I inspected my collection of undernourished and underpaid laborers. Had it been in my power to follow moral correctness I would have had a hospital tent constructed over the entire formation and confined them all to bed. They suffered from the same multiple diseases as the general population, but even those with brass-coated tongues, yellow eyes, and puffed livers carried supplies or constructed bunkers. A week later when sick call was down by 20 percent it gave me no satisfaction, no pleasure in subjecting them to more hardship than they already knew.

I drove my Jeep through the battalion sector late in the day and saw a ROK guard, not one of my former platoon, about ten miles south of the post and knew he'd deserted; and surprisingly felt no impulse to either shoot or pistol whip him for his dereliction of duty. Despite what I knew to be my unalterable military mindset I became aware of some subtle changes in my thinking about the war.

Yet "the line" still held its perpetual allure; and each night I lay on my cot in the darkened tent, cradling my Thompson-sub and enthralled to the hypnotic call of heavy distant fire: *It sounds like the Chinks are making a probe... Platoon size... Go on, get up there, and get into a good firefight. Why don't I go? I never thought I'd end up in the goddamned rear echelon!*

It was the start of another boring day when I spotted a forlorn but familiar face on the roadside and excitedly called out, *"Oye, Tom-san, watakushi wa die go shotie gunsho desu* [Hey, Tom, it's me, 5th ROK Platoon sergeant]!"

287

He stiffly turned wearing a weary expression. "Oh, *Sahji*-san, is you-ga?" Combat and concerns had etched their mark on his time altered face as he listed the ROK who'd been killed or wounded: 'Big Stoop' Ken, ROK Richard, Our Man Friday, Lee the machine gunner, Slick, "Bad Ass."

Others died later or were demeaned with assignments as laborers throughout the battalion. My spirits nevertheless soared with momentary hope that he'd rejoin me in the labor battalion to recreate some semblance of what had been. He spoke emotionally in the familiar half English and Japanese jargon, but with a frozen sadness in his eyes. "You *Sahji*, mountain many-many, you boom-boom, many-many. Now, go home. Is okay. Me, Tom, what? Stay? Die?"

After a life of endless war he wanted to go home and I felt his past loyalty should be rewarded. He awaited my return from the battalion tent. I gave him the three bogus passes that I drafted and signed as 1st Lieutenant R. Mercy, Labor Bn., 19th Regt, and 24th Div. I drilled and he repeated which pocket held the specific pass for the next three months and he learned quickly. Then we stared wordlessly at each other. His unfocused eyes seemed to look right through me when he grunted his farewell devoid of emotion, salute or bow. I felt a nameless emptiness as I watched him, the twin embodiment of Asian wars and the long venerated spirit of Yang, dissolve into the voluminous dappled clouds of truck raised dust, as though in a dream: *Good luck, Tom, hope you can make it past the MPs. I'm going back up to the line.*

Once there I hovered like a disembodied spirit on the forward slope and wistfully recalled all our battles and skirmishes between Taejon and the Yalu River. The nearby troops were readying to move out when I proudly saluted the burly officer who approached. I soon recognized the new George Company commander as the former lieutenant who'd commanded Fox Company when it was overrun at Uijongbu. He looked me up and down. "You're one of the Mercy brothers, right?"

I snapped, "Yes, sir."

He puffed out his chest and withdrew from his scabbard a familiar looking brass-knuckled bayonet and tauntingly twisted it to and fro before my eyes. "I've got your bayonet, Mercy."

Captain Edward L. Shea enjoyed his reputation of battalion bully and barroom brawler and his sneered pugnacious tone suggested that I should try to take it from him. My pistol hand flinched: *You lowlife filthy thieving dog. If he goes for his gun, and I draw mine, it's a capital offense when done "in the face of the enemy." Could get death or twenty years, or gunned down by any of these other new guys who don't know me, or what's really going on and who might think I've gone crazy.*

I saw the irony of being robbed in the company I had faithfully served, honored and willingly would have died for. I left filled with disgust for him and what he represented: A failed Army Officer Corps, greed and the petty criminality that debase the human spirit.

My dream of war was over.

★ **THE END** ★

EPILOGUE

"The fearless hero in defying death can utilize those elemental forces within himself to derive mankind's eternal values, yet in so doing he himself becomes the victim of his own heroic enterprise since the experiencing of these irrational forces must prove disastrous in one way or another."

—Otto Rank

Robertson was discharged from the Arizona Army post at Fort Huachuca in 1953, and was ceremoniously awarded a much-deserved Silver Star for his deadly work with a BAR during the battle at Uijonbu. His marriage the following year produced a girl, and a boy who later died in a childhood gun accident. Still driven by adventure, one of his many "sports" was to water-ski over the chummed up waters of the Pacific and harpoon the hungry sharks he had drawn in, a difficult act to follow. He moved to Singapore where he worked for a shipping and salvaging company and despite his missing eye, earned his captain's papers. He became internationally famous for his daring rescues of distressed ships in the northern Pacific.

He answered his country's call again near the end of the Vietnam War. He was 'unofficially' asked to help stem the tide of high-sea crimes against Vietnamese boat people. They had suffered countless beatings, robberies, rapes and murders at the hands of the bloodthirsty buccaneers of Thailand, Cambodia and Vietnam. He collected a mercenary crew of cutthroats and soldiers of fortune and cleared the Gulf of Siam. They left an impressive body count, over nine hundred men dead and countless crafts and sampans destroyed. More importantly, thousands of hapless refugees were saved.

My brother **Richard** married his childhood sweetheart Joan. They had five children and then adopted a beautiful Vietnamese baby named Kim. He earned a college degree while serving on the New York City Police Department and achieved the rank of lieutenant. He went on to operate his own private detective agency and works for some of the top-gun lawyers on the Eastern seaboard. He also retired from the National Guard as a major and like Robertson, he too lost a son, but to spinal meningitis; and then two more over the passage of time to the present date.

General William Dean was released from a North Korean POW camp in 1953, and awarded the Congressional Medal of Honor for the actions he personally took in the defense of Taejon. The two "friendly" Korean guides that turned him over to the NKs as he slept during his lonely escape from the overrun city—for the sum of twenty dollars—were eventually captured and received a firing squad.

General Paik Sun-yup, who was the commander of the 1st ROK Division that kept the U.S. Eighth Army retreat route open during the initial Chinese offensive, became the first ever five star general in Korean history. After his retirement he still served as an advisor to the government on military matters, became active in veteran's affairs and wrote an autobiographical book entitled *From Pusan to Panmunjon*.

Colonel Ned C. Moore, who had taken over as post commander from Colonel Bottomly at Camp Schimmelpfenning after my court martial, went on to command the 19th Regiment at Taejon. He retired as a general to gracious living in Virginia. General Moore donated the flag I had liberated at Sinuiju to the war museum at Newport News, Virginia. It has never been put on display.

Major Melecio J. Montesclarous, our battalion S-3 (Operations Officer), who had congratulated Richard and me on the taking of Hill 584, never responded to my one letter.

Captain Barszcz went on to serve with distinction in Vietnam as a battalion commander and retired as a full colonel. He died of a heart condition in the late nineties. I wrote him one letter, which he never answered.

Lieutenant Robert Herbert remained in the service and retired as a lieutenant colonel. He later purchased two 7-11 stores close to Ft. Lewis in Washington State, where fate caught up with him. He was shot and killed by a bandit team of two men and a woman during a holdup. To his credit he killed one with his concealed .45 automatic.

Lieutenant Frederick Walters, who occasionally led the 5th ROK Platoon following the death of Lieutenant Bill Buckley, died in the crossfire between a Chinese heavy machine gun and two American Quad-.50s some months after we left the company.

Lieutenant William Buckley's parents did not receive the Army's customary condolence telegram, but found out about his death when Captain Barszcz's brief note from Korea arrived with his personal effects: "He was a good soldier and we'll miss him..."

Master Sergeant Victor Hungerford returned to the States late in 1951 and was reinstated to his former WWII rank of major. Bizarre behavior and severe headaches followed and he stood before a court martial for having written large bogus checks at the Officers Club. He was dishonorably discharged, literally drummed off the post then marched into prison.

Two years later he was released from confinement and exonerated of all crimes. The doctors found a lemon-sized tumor at the base of his skull. This was the result of the tank shell fragment that had lodged into his brain during the battle of Taejon, for which he had then refused medical attention. Ironically he also won a Silver Star there for conspicuous courage. He died in a veteran's hospital, circa 1996, from a heart attack at the age of eighty-two after thirty years of Army service. He left behind his German war-bride who died two years later. Her former husband was a *Waffen-SS* tank commander who had won the Knight's Cross with Oak Leaves on the Russian front.

Sergeant Tubbs, our supply sergeant who later went on to become George Company's first sergeant, was last seen driving a cab in San Diego to supplement his NCO pension.

Corporal Richard Rundell, the company cook, became a police officer in Peekskill, New York, and was credited with talking a bank robber into surrendering without even drawing his gun. A good thing, too, as he didn't even have it with him at the time!

Corporal Johnny Murr, our radioman, took a furlough from his 2nd Armored Division unit in 1952 and came to New York to join Richard and me on a visit to the families of Captain Dannucci and Lieutenant 'Buck' Buckley. Both were appreciative of the stories we told. Murr called me once in NYC in the late sixties then totally disappeared.

As for **Cass** and **BB**...I never heard from either.

Corporal Frank Korbell, the 'poor man's Glenn Ford,' who Richard and I met aboard the troopship *General Brewster,* visited me in NYC with his wife in 1970. He died unexpectedly four years later of cancer at the age of forty-four.

The two 'sharp medics' referred to in the chapter *The Post* both died months apart in 2003. Rocky was beaten by cancer and Frenchy took the soldier's way out, after long and interminable suffering from a painful medical condition.

Richard and I with three of Captain Anthony Dannucci's children when Johnny Murr and we visited the family home in New York City in 1951.

Han, our devious interpreter, continued to work for the U.S. military along the DMZ right on through the 1960s. According to an NCO friend who'd met him there while on assignment, Han had nothing but glowing things to say about the ROK platoon and its three NCOs. I am still not sure why I never shot him. No contact was ever made again with any members of that most memorable 5th ROK Platoon.

Kwong Taek, the NK major who'd ordered the execution of fifty captured G.I.s on the Naktong River line before his own capture, and who I 'met' in the POW camp in Pusan, never did face a summary court martial and execution. He was quietly repatriated home at the conclusion of the war in order to avoid any 'complications' in the exchange of prisoners between America and North Korea. Hopefully his appropriate *karma* has been collected in full.

Richard and I were discharged at Fort Benning, Georgia, in 1955. There was no formal "thank you" formation for any of the departing soldiers, only a verbal notice that all discharge papers could be found in a cardboard box in the mess hall after noontime chow. Perhaps not surprising, Richard and I shed tears listening to the amplified bugle sounding *Retreat* before we left the post for the final time after eight years of service.

Richard (left) and I (right) acting as Army advisors for the 42nd "Rainbow" Division National Guard at Camp Smith in Peekskill, New York. This was shortly after I had volunteered to serve as an advisor during the battle of Dien Bien Phu in Viet Nam.

Marilyn, whose letter I read after the *Run to Chinju*, was then developing a truly unique beauty that launched her theatrical career with a start in *Earl Carroll's Review* then into the world famous Hollywood Moulin Rouge as a featured showgirl. She eventually married the man of her dreams, an oil and land tycoon whom she and all their friends said was "more like Jesus than anyone they ever knew."

The path from military to civilian life seemed more like the road to Damascus, upon which fate saw fit to strike me with a bolt out of the blue. I found myself in show business and was offered a small role in a *Playhouse 90* TV episode as an English soldier in the infamous Black and Tan Regiment during the Irish 'Troubles.' Many other roles in films, TV and stage productions followed. I also got back in uniform again, this time as a German *SS* officer in the TV series *Combat!* I am now a sometime drama coach, who occasionally acts and directs. For more career details

294

and displays of my art work, go to: http://www.robertwinstonmercy.com

That's me on the right in one of my many roles as an SS officer on the popular 1960s television series Combat! It's hard to break old habits!

Last but not least I salute the "chroniclers of the times," the movies! It was in the paradise of film that I had taken the first metaphorical bite from the forbidden fruit of knowledge that led me onto a military path in search of idealism and glory. Films have directed and influenced my life beyond all measure and inspired this story. The bugle's last mournful note sounds in the call of *Taps*, for all the remembered dead of George Company, whose casualties ran into the hundreds: Captain Dannucci, Lieutenant Buckley and Walters, Sergeant Jackson, ROK One, Ken, My Man Friday, Slick, Toshi; and thirty other ROKs including Smiley, who died in my place at Uijumbu; and the millions of others who fell...in my very own private movie.

Robert on the set of Combat!, visibly thinking, "Damn, wish I could see one more good firefight."

Robert wearing his own citations on the uniform he borrowed from his brother Richard—then a National Guard Special Forces major, mouthing, "That's the third inspection your men failed, Captain.

Robert on the set of Combat!

Robert on the set of Combat!

WESTERN UNION

1201

W. P. MARSHALL, PRESIDENT

CLASS OF SERVICE
This is a full-rate Telegram or Cablegram unless its deferred character is indicated by a suitable symbol above or preceding the address.

SYMBOLS
DL=Day Letter
NL=Night Letter
LC=Deferred Cable
NLT=Cable Night Letter
Ship Radiogram

The filing time shown in the date line on telegrams and day letters is STANDARD TIME at point of origin. Time of receipt is STANDARD TIME at point of destination

1950 AUG 21 PM 3 20

SYA286

SY.WA172 XV GOVT PD=WUX WASHINGTON DC 21 253P=

MRS MARGARGET HANOLD, REPORT DELIVERY=

8281 166 ST JAMAICA NY=

THE SECRETARY OF THE ARMY HAS ASKED ME TO EXPRESS HIS
DEEP REGRET THAT YOUR NEPHEW CPL MERCY RICHARD J WAS
SLIGHTLY WOUNDED IN ACTION IN KOREA 16 JUL 50 ADDRESS
MAIL QUOTE RANK NAME SERVICE NUMBER HOSPITAL DIRECTORY
SECTION APO 503 C/O POSTMASTER SAN FRANCISCO CALIFORNIA
UNQUOTE=

EDWARD F WITSELL   MAJOR GENERAL USA
THE ADJUTANT GENERAL   OF THE ARMY=

THE COMPANY WILL APPRECIATE SUGGESTIONS FROM ITS PATRONS CONCERNING ITS SERVICE

WESTERN UNION

1201

(09)

W. P. MARSHALL, PRESIDENT

CLASS OF SERVICE
This is a full-rate Telegram or Cablegram unless its deferred character is indicated by a suitable symbol above or preceding the address.

SYMBOLS
DL=Day Letter
NL=Night Letter
LC=Deferred Cable
NLT=Cable Night Letter
Ship Radiogram

The filing time shown in the date line on telegrams and day letters is STANDARD TIME at point of origin. Time of receipt is STANDARD TIME at point of destination

SYA387 RA583

R.WA603 RX GOVT PD=WUX WASHINGTON DC 28 803P=

MRS RGARET HANOLD=   1950 SEP 28 PM 8 38

8281 166TH ST JAMAICA NY=

THE SECRETARY OF THE ARMY HAS ASKED ME TO EXPRESS HIS
DEEP REGRET THAT YOUR NEPHEW CPL MERCY RICHARD J WAS
SLIGHTLY WOUNDED IN ACTION IN KOREA 14 AUG 50 HE WAS
RETURNED TO DUTY FROM PREVIOUSLY REPORTED INJIRIES 2 AUG
50 PD ADDRESS MAIL QUOTE RANK NAME SERVICE NUMBER HOSPITAL
DIRECTORY SECTION APO 503 C/O POSTMASTER SAN FRANCISCO
CALIFORNIA UNQUOTE=

EDWARD F WITSELL MAJOR GENERA=
USA THE ADJUTANT GENERAL OF THE ARMY=

WESTERN UNION

W. P. MARSHALL, PRESIDENT

CLASS OF SERVICE
This is a full-rate Telegram or Cablegram unless its deferred character is indicated by a suitable symbol above or preceding the address.

SYMBOLS
DL=Day Letter
NL=Night Letter
LT=Int'l Letter Telegram
VLT=Int'l Victory Ltr.

The filing time shown in STANDARD TIME at point of origin. Time of receipt is STANDARD TIME at point of destination.

SYA404 PB667

P.WA815 RX GOVT PD =WASHINGTON DC 24 712P=

MRS MARGARET HANOLD, REPORT DELIVERY=
=8281-166 ST JAMAICALONSISLAND NY=

THE SECRETARY OF THE ARMY HAS ASKED ME TO EXPRESS HIS DEEP
REGRET THAT YOUR NEPHEW SGT MERCY RICHARD J WAS SLIGHTLY
WOUNDED IN ACTION IN KOREA 5 JAN 51 DATE RETURNED TO DUTY
FROM PREVIOUS WOUNDS UNREPORTED PD ADDRESS MAIL QUOTE RANK
NAME SERVICE NUMBER HOSPITAL DIRECTORY SECTION APO 503 C/O
POSTMASTER SAN FRANCISCO CALIFORNIA UNQUOTE=
    EDWARD F WITSELL MAJOR GENERAL USA THE
    ADJUTANT GENERAL OF THE ARMY

THE COMPANY WILL APPRECIATE SUGGESTIONS FROM ITS PATRONS CONCERNING ITS SERVICE

WESTERN UNION

W. P. MARSHALL, PRESIDENT

CLASS OF SERVICE
This is a full-rate Telegram or Cablegram unless its deferred character is indicated by a suitable symbol above or preceding the address.

SYMBOLS
DL=Day Letter
NL=Night Letter
LT=Int'l Letter Telegram
VLT=Int'l Victory Ltr.

The filing time shown in the date line on telegrams and day letters is STANDARD TIME at point of origin. Time of receipt is STANDARD TIME at point of destination.

SYA233

SY.WA117 LONG GOVT PD=FAX WASHINGTON DC 22 102P=

MRS MARGARET HANOLD=
    8281 166 ST JAMAICA NY=

THE SECRETARY OF THE ARMY HAS ASKED ME TO EXPRESS HIS DEEP
REGRET THAT YOUR NEPHEW SGT MERCY, ROBERT W WAS SLIGHTLY
WOUNDED IN ACTION IN KOREA 7 MAR 51 ADDRESS MAIL QUOTE RANK
NAME SERVICE NUMBER HOSPITAL DIRECTORY SECTION APO 503 &
POSTMASTER SAN FRANCISCO CALIFORNIA UNQUOTE ACTION IS BEING
TAKEN TO NOTIFY CORPORAL RICHARD MERCY BROTHER WHO IS
RESIDING IN THE COMMAND=
    EDWARD F WITSELL MAJOR GENERAL USA THE ADJUTANT
    GENERAL OF THE ARMY=

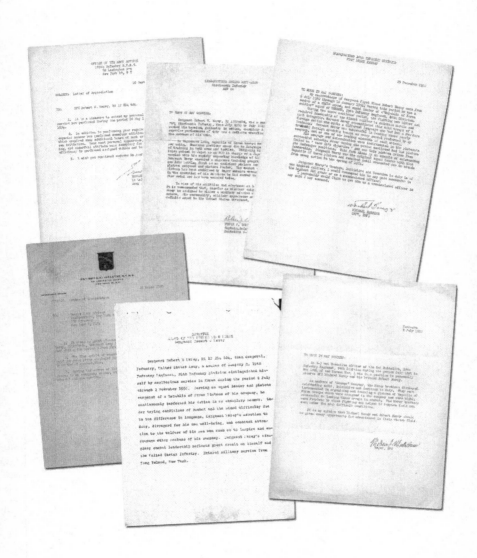

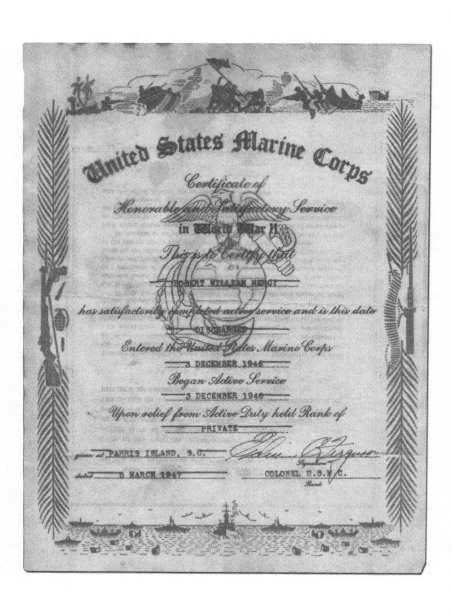

NA NOT APPLICABLE

CHARACTER OF SEPARATION	REPORT OF SEPARATION FROM THE ARMED FORCES OF THE UNITED STATES	DEPARTMENT
HONORABLE		ARMY

SEPARATION DATA

1. LAST NAME – FIRST NAME – MIDDLE NAME	2. SERVICE NUMBER	3. GRADE–RATE–RANK AND DATE OF APPOINTMENT	4. COMPONENT AND BRANCH OR CLASS
Mercy, Robert William	RA12 294 624	Sfc(T) 30Oct51	RA

5. QUALIFICATIONS		6. EFFECTIVE DATE OF SEPARATION	7. TYPE OF SEPARATION
		DAY Nov 55	Discharge

SPECIALTY NUMBER OR SYMBOL	RELATED CIVILIAN OCCUPATION AND D.O.T. NUMBER	
111.70(see 38)	NA	

8. REASON AND AUTHORITY FOR SEPARATION	9. PLACE OF SEPARATION
AR 615-360 SPN 38	Hq Special Troops Command, Ft Benning, Ga

10. DATE OF BIRTH	11. PLACE OF BIRTH (City and State)	12.					
13 Oct 30	Brooklyn, N.Y.	DESCRIPTION	SEX Male	RACE Cau	COLOR HAIR Brown	COLOR EYES Brown	HEIGHT 5'11" WEIGHT 158

13. REGISTERED	SELECTIVE SERVICE NUMBER	14. SELECTIVE SERVICE LOCAL BOARD NO. (City, County, State)	15. INDUCTED
YES NO	NA	NA	DAY MONTH YEAR

SELECTIVE SERVICE DATA

16. ENLISTED IN OR TRANSFERRED TO A RESERVE COMPONENT	COGNIZANT DISTRICT OR AREA COMMAND
YES NO NA	NA

17. MEANS OF ENTRY ... Vol Ext 1 yr 70ct53; Vol Ext 1 yr 1Nov54	18. GRADE–RATE OR RANK AT TIME OF ENTRY INTO ACTIVE SERVICE
ENLISTED ☐ REENLISTED 3 yrs ☐ COMMISSIONED ☐ CALLED FROM INACTIVE DUTY	Pvt

19. DATE AND PLACE OF ENTRY INTO ACTIVE SERVICE		20. HOME ADDRESS AT TIME OF ENTRY INTO ACTIVE SERVICE (St., R.F.D., City, County and State)
DAY 18 MONTH Nov YEAR 49 PLACE (City and State) Brooklyn, N.Y.		8281 166th St, Jamaica Long Island (Queens) NY

SERVICE DATA

21. NET	NA	I SERVICE COMPLETED FOR PAY PURPOSES EXCLUDING THIS PERIOD	A. YEARS	B. MONTHS	C. DAYS	23. ENLISTMENT ALLOWANCE PAID ON EXTENSION OF ENLISTMENT, IF ANY
			NA			DAY MONTH YEAR AMOUNT
22. NET SERVICE COMPLETED FOR PAY PURPOSES THIS PERIOD			6	0	0	NA
23. OTHER SERVICE (Act of 16 June 1942 as amended) COMPLETED FOR PAY PURPOSES			2	3	27	28. FOREIGN AND/OR SEA SERVICE YEARS 1 MONTHS 6 DAYS 6
24. TOTAL NET SERVICE COMPLETED FOR PAY PURPOSES			8	3	27	

25. DECORATIONS, MEDALS, BADGES, COMMENDATIONS, CITATIONS AND CAMPAIGN RIBBONS AWARDED OR AUTHORIZED
United Nations Service Medal-National Defense Service Medal-Army of Occupation Medal (Japan)-Combat Infantryman Badge-Korean Service Medal w/6 Bronze Service Stars-Silver Star GO#40 Hq 8th Sta Hosp dtd 23Feb51-Purple Heart GO#222 Hq 24th Inf dtd 7Mar51-Bronze Star (see 38)

26. MOST SIGNIFICANT DUTY ASSIGNMENT	27. WOUNDS RECEIVED AS A RESULT OF ACTION WITH ENEMY FORCES (Place and date, if known)
Platoon Sergeant, Det 2 1242d ASU 270 Broadway N.Y., N.Y.	Shell Fragment, Right Leg & Left Knee, Korea dtd 7 Mar 51

29. SERVICE SCHOOLS OR COLLEGES, COLLEGE TRAINING COURSES AND/OR POST-GRAD. COURSES SUCCESSFULLY COMPLETED	DATES (From-To)	MAJOR COURSES	31. SERVICE TRAINING COURSES SUCCESSFULLY COMPLETED
None	NA	NA	GED High School Dtry Compl May 52 Series 10 Compl Sep 55 (Infantry)

INSURANCE AND PAY DATA

GOVERNMENT INSURANCE INFORMATION: (A) Permanent plan premium must conform to be paid when due, or within 31 days thereafter, or insurance will lapse. (B) Term insurance not under waiver same as (A) above. (C) Term insurance under waiver — premium payment must be resumed within 120 days after separation. Forward premiums on NSLI to Veterans Administration District office having jurisdiction over the area shown in item 47. Forward premiums on USGLI to Veterans Administration, Washington 25, D.C. (See VA Pamphlet 9-3). When paying premiums give full name, address, Service Number, Policy Number(s), Branch of Service, date of separation. Contact nearest VA office for information concerning Government Life Insurance.

32A. KIND & AMT. OF INSURANCE & MTHLY. PREMIUM	32B. ACTIVE SERVICE PRIOR TO 26 APRIL 1951	33. MONTH ALLOTMENT DISCONTINUED	34. MONTH NEXT PREMIUM DUE
$10,000 ($6.40) NSLI	☒ YES ☐ NO ☐ UNKNOWN	None Waiver	Mar 56

35. TOTAL PAYMENT UPON SEPARATION	36. TRAVEL OR MILEAGE ALLOWANCE INCLUDED IN TOTAL PAYMENT	37. DISBURSING OFFICER'S NAME AND SYMBOL NUMBER
NA	NA	NA

AUTHENTICATION

38. REMARKS (Continue on reverse)	39. SIGNATURE OF OFFICER AUTHORIZED TO SIGN
Item 3-Pfc(P) 23Mar50 Item 5-Light Weapons Infantryman, Blood Group "A" Item 27-GO#408 19th Inf APO 24 dtd 27May51-Distinguished Unit Emblem DAGO#45 dtd 22Dec50-Good Conduct Medal Clasp w/2 Loops GO#34 Hq NTMD dtd 3Jun53-Republic of Korea Presidential Unit Citation Co"G" 24th Inf dtd 26Dec50. No days lost under Sec 6(a) App 2b MCM 1951.	*(signature)* A. O. Hensley CWO USA Asst Personnel Officer

40. V.A. BENEFITS PREVIOUSLY APPLIED FOR (Specify type)	CLAIM NUMBER
COMPENSATION, PENSION, INSURANCE BENEFITS, ETC. None	NA

PERSONAL DATA

41. DATES OF LAST CIVILIAN EMPLOYMENT	42. MAIN CIVILIAN OCCUPATION	43. NAME AND ADDRESS OF LAST CIVILIAN EMPLOYER
FROM 1945 TO 1946	Lumberjack 6-30.160	City of Miami Construction Inc, Miami, Fla.

44. UNITED STATES CITIZEN	45. MARITAL STATUS	46. NON-SERVICE EDUCATION (Years successfully completed)				MAJOR COURSE OR FIELD
☒ YES ☐ NO	Single	GRAM. SCHOOL 8	HIGH SCHOOL 4	COL. LEGE 0	DEGREE(S) None	GED

47. PERMANENT ADDRESS FOR MAILING PURPOSES AFTER SEPARATION (St., R.F.D., City, County and State)	48. SIGNATURE OF PERSON BEING SEPARATED
7304 North Atlantic, Portland (Multnomah) Oregon	*(signature)* Robert W. Mercy

DD FORM 214 EDITION OF 1 JAN 50 IS OBSOLETE	INDIVIDUAL'S COPY (TO BE DELIVERED TO THE INDIVIDUAL BEING SEPARATED)	1

HEADQUARTERS 24TH INFANTRY DIVISION
APO 24

GENERAL ORDERS
NUMBER   222

23 February 1951

AWARD OF THE SILVER STAR

By direction of the President under the provisions of the Act
of Congress approved 9 July 1918 (WD Bul, 43, 1918) and pursuant to
authority in AR 600-45, the Silver Star for gallantry in action
against the enemy in Korea is awarded to the following named enlisted
men:

*   *   *   *   *   *   *   *

Sergeant Robert W. Mercy, RA12294624, Infantry, United States
Army, a member of Company G, 19th Infantry Regiment, 24th Infantry
Division distinguished himself by courageous action near Uijombu,
Korea on 3 January 1951. His squad was occupying a position on the
left flank of the company when the numerically superior enemy launched a strong attack. The squad soon came under heavy automatic weapons
fire from a position where the enemy was attempting to build a firing
line. Realizing the grave threat that this action posed he determined
to eliminate this source of the enemy's strength. Completely un-
mindful of personal safety he left his position and armed with hand
grenades crossed approximately 75 yards of open ground, in the face
of intense fire, to a position near an enemy machine gun. Courageously
exposing himself to the full fury of the enemy's fire he hurled grenades into the position, destroying the gun and crew and breaking the
enemy attempt to flank his company's position. Sergeant Mercy's
courageous action and complete devotion to duty reflect the greatest
credit on himself and the United States Infantry. Entered military
service from New York, New York.

BY COMMAND OF MAJOR GENERAL BRYAN:

OFFICIAL:

OLIVER G KINNEY
Lt Col   GSC
Acting Chief of Staff

/s/ E. R. Ekblad
/t/ E. R. EKBLAD
    Major   AGC
    Actg Adj Gen

A TRUE EXTRACT COPY:

WILLIAM G. FRITZ
Lt Col, Artillery

DISTRIBUTION: "C" and "G" plus
    4-TAG Wash 25 DC Attn: AGAO-I
    3-TAG Wash 25 DC Attn: AG-PD
    2-CINCFE APO 500 Attn: AG-PD
    2-CINCFE APO 500 Attn: AG-PA (DandA)
    2-CG EUSAK APO 301 Attn: KAGM
    2-CG EUSAK APO 301
    1-PIO H24D

Richard (left) and I (right), getting ready for civilian life in New York.

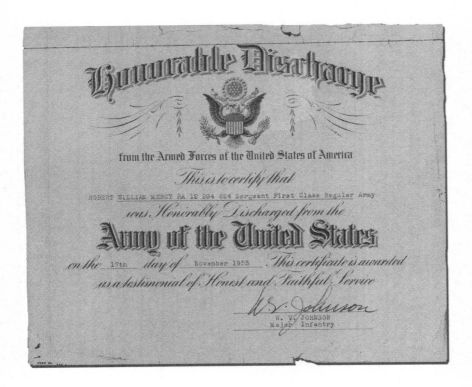

GLOSSARY

120mm	—	A very large Russian mortar shell
.30 caliber Ball ammo	—	Standard issue for rifle & machine guns
.30 caliber AP ammo	—	Steel-tipped armor piercing round
.30 caliber tracer ammo	—	Red-tipped incendiary round
.30 carbines	—	Full & semi-automatic light weight weapons
.50 caliber	—	Heavy machinegun ammo, ball, AP & tracer rounds
BAR	—	Browning Automatic Rifle
Barrzcz	—	Surname of our company commander, pronounced "Bars"
Chinju	—	City in South Korea
CID	—	Criminal Investigation Division
CMH	—	Congressional Medal of Honor, highest U.S. military honor
CP	—	Command post
Dog Robber	—	Negative term for one who steals for an officer
EM	—	Enlisted man

G-2A	—	Divisional-level Intelligence unit
GHQ	—	General Headquarters
Infantry Company	—	A unit of (usually) four platoons
KP	—	Kitchen Police
LD	—	Line of Departure (jump-off position for attack)
LMG	—	Light machinegun
M1	—	Standard issue .30 caliber gas operated rifle (weight 9 lbs.)
M16	—	An open half-track vehicle with four .50 caliber machine guns mounted on a single rotating open turret
MASH	—	A field hospital, usually found well behind the front line
MG	—	Machinegun
MR	—	Morning report
MLR	—	Main Line of Resistance
NCO	—	Non-commissioned officer
OP	—	Outpost
OR	—	Operating Room
Platoon	—	A unit of fifty men
Point	—	Usually one or two men out in front of a lead unit
S-1	—	Administration
S-2	—	Intelligence at battalion or regimental level
S-3	—	Plans, training, and operations.

Silver Star	—	Third highest U.S. military honor
Squad	—	A unit of (usually) twelve men
T-34	—	Russian-designed medium tank.
Thompson	—	A .45 caliber sub-machinegun with magazine or drum attachment

ABOUT THE AUTHOR

Robert W. Mercy was raised in New York City and traveled extensively with his family during his formative years. He served in the New York National Guard starting at age thirteen, then the USMC and eventually the 11th Airborne Division before war broke out in Korea. He served with a rifle company and led an all-Asian assault platoon, earning a Silver Star, a Bronze Star, a Purple Heart and a Presidential Unit Citation for one of the many bayonet assaults his unit led during the eight campaigns in which he participated. After he left the military, his long-standing film interest projected him into a theatrical career in which he played leading and support roles in several major television shows and films. While doing off-Broadway shows and commercials, he pursued a lifelong interest in psychology, particularly dream analysis, and earned a

Bachelor of Arts Degree at Norwich University. He then continued his Masters studies at NYU.

Robert has lectured at medical schools and appeared on numerous radio talk shows discussing his independent study work on *Dermatoglyphics* and the profiling of personality. He successfully combined and applied all of those modalities in The Manhattan Actors Lab, a group therapy/acting workshop that he founded. He has also enjoyed a tremendous success bringing out the inner lives of his students. Literature, psychology and helping others develop their acting skills have remained his primary interests, and he recently taught a community theater program at Humboldt State University in Northern California.

He's a successful artist working in oils, practices Buddhism and has toured his one man Shakespearian show in many northern California communities. He's presently up for a major supporting role in an independent film and is preparing to present his newly written one man show—An Evening with James Mason; and the impersonating skills that got him into theater in the first place. Robert is also currently singing with the Mountain Mojo Blues band in Northern California.